Philosophy Outside-In

A Critique of Academic Reason

Christopher Norris

EDINBURGH
University Press

© Christopher Norris, 2013

Edinburgh University Press Ltd
22 George Square, Edinburgh EH8 9LF

www.euppublishing.com

Typeset in 11/13 Sabon
by Servis Filmsetting Ltd, Stockport, Cheshire, and
printed and bound in Great Britain by
CPI Group (UK) Ltd, Croydon CR0 4YY

A CIP record for this book is available from the British Library

ISBN 978 0 7486 8455 7 (hardback)
ISBN 978 0 7486 8456 4 (webready PDF)
ISBN 978 0 7486 8457 1 (epub)

The right of Christopher Norris
to be identified as author of this work
has been asserted in accordance with
the Copyright, Designs and Patents Act 1988.

Contents

For Shelley Campbell

Introduction

I

This book is aimed squarely against the kinds of ultra-specialist interest or ultra-professionalised narrowing of focus that have been such a prominent and – to my mind – such a damaging feature of much recent philosophical work. It seems to have come about largely through the idea that philosophy could best lay claim to academic respectability by pushing as far as possible in its emulation of the physical sciences, or determining to tackle only those well-defined technical problems that were sure to have some likewise well-defined technical answer. Such was Thomas Kuhn's description of how 'normal science' typically carried on during those periods of relative calm between great 'revolutionary' shake-ups when it was business as normal for most working scientists since any paradigm-threatening obstacle – any discrepant data or empirical anomaly – could always be put down to some observational error, imperfection in the measuring apparatus or questionable choice of auxiliary hypotheses. I don't at all wish to go along with the popular misreading of Kuhn which ignores his stress on the comparative rarity of full-scale scientific revolutions and finds little or nothing of interest in the notion of science as making progress through a placidly constructive engagement with manageable problems. Still I would venture to say that the discourse of present-day academic philosophy, at least in the analytic mainstream, is 'normal' to the point of intellectual stagnation and that this has chiefly to do with the effect of an overly specialised professional culture and an over-concentration on issues that lend themselves to quasi-scientific formulation.

So one central aim is to recommend a more Aristotelian approach to philosophy, or the idea that philosophers shouldn't be so keen to advertise themselves as philosophers *of* or experts *in* some closely specified subject domain. It may be replied, and justifiably enough, that we nowadays know a lot more than Aristotle knew about all those multifarious topics (the natural sciences included) that he took as falling within his investigative purview. Philosophers had much better pick their specialism with an eye to current trends and should definitely not – on pain of ignorance or amateurism – lay claim to anything remotely like an Aristotelian breadth of interests. On this view philosophy started out as a universal discourse of (purported) knowledge and truth but was thereafter subject to a long history of rifts, separations or independence-movements whereby its erstwhile component disciplines achieved intellectual maturity and, along with it, a new-found sense of autonomy. Probably the last one to go was psychology, at least to the extent that empirically minded psychologists increasingly defined their discipline so as to exclude all reference to epistemology or philosophy of mind, while philosophers were just as keen to reciprocate by disavowing any taint of vulgar 'psychologism'.[1] At any rate there is general agreement that the exponential growth of human knowledge across so many fields of enquiry has produced a situation in which, for better or worse, it is no longer possible for anyone to claim expertise – or even a decent level of competence – in more than one such specialist corner of one such specialist field. This applies all the more in the case of philosophy since here, so the argument goes, there is a standing temptation for some practitioners (in particular philosophers of science) to issue large claims on the basis of a knowledge that is often simply not up to the mark in terms of the latest research. After all, if scientists themselves have learned to respect these disciplinary markers – even as regards areas of closely convergent interest such as molecular biology, organic chemistry and genetics – then surely philosophers will be best advised not to tread on such specialist turf. Or again, they should have the proper modesty to do so only under expert guidance and without any thought – heaven forefend! – of helping scientists to a better understanding of conceptual problems on their own turf.

As I have said, my book sets out to challenge that view of things and put the case for thinking of philosophy as a discipline of thought that can and should have useful things to say across a great range of topics by way of addressing and (on occasion) resolving just such problems. This connects with my second purpose which is basically to offer a sequence of essays in philosophy that are also essays on diverse topics which, for various mainly non-professional reasons, have come to exert a special interest or fascination. In fact the two purposes are really one and the same since it is a part of my argument here that the problem of over-specialisation, or the cult of misplaced expertise, has typically gone along with a depersonalised approach to philosophy where assured command of 'the literature' associated with some given topic has taken the place of anything resembling a personal and deeply felt involvement with it. This is everywhere apparent in the choices of topic (narrowly prescribed), the tone of address (briskly efficient), the presumed readership or audience (a small peer-group of like-minded specialists) and above all the manifest aim (to move things forward by just so much as to make one's distinctive mark but not so much as to run the risk of offending one's colleagues or the academic community at large). That tendency is reinforced by the periodic scourge of a research assessment exercise that encourages savvy types to focus their efforts on short-term, 'manageable' projects of a suitably conformist, professionally sanctioned and often intellectually unambitious kind. Moreover, it maintains an incentive structure whereby those who have most thoroughly internalised such habits of thought are then strongly placed, as subject panellists, to ensure its effective passing on to the rising generation.

This is, to the say the least, a depressing scene and one that belies the constant stress on 'research' in an academic culture where any genuinely innovative work – any that raises a significant challenge to communal norms of belief, not to mention established reputations – amounts to the equivalent of letting the side down (in this case one's departmental colleagues) in a crucial qualifying match. Meanwhile the philosopher-specialists are apt to play themselves off the field, as did the logical positivists and logical empiricists before them, by imitating science in a different field of endeavour and thus inevitably lagging behind by any measure of substantive (as distinct from merely notional or intra-peer-group) contribution to knowledge. This is nowhere plainer to see than in the current exchange of hostilities – my topic in Chapter 3 – between 'experimental philosophers' who want to put things on a third-person empirical or observational basis and thus eschew all appeals to apodictic or first-person epistemic warrant and their opponents, the unreformed thought experimentalists, who cleave to precisely those traditional (and, they would say, philosophically indispensable) modes of enquiry. It also takes the form of that perceived imperative, among philosophers of an analytic bent, to hitch their professional-academic wagons to the star of what counts (again in their own specialist community) as a properly scientific method. Just as the positivists mortgaged their enterprise to the formal sciences on the one hand and the physical sciences on the other – through their programmatic refusal to recognise as truth-apt any statements other than logical tautologies or empirical observations – so philosophers in the present-day 'core' disciplines strive to come up with results that would invoke either rational self-evidence or else some kind of natural-scientific warrant. Hence the unfortunate impression often given by exercises in, for example, philosophy of mind or philosophy of perception that these are somehow hoping to bootstrap their way by sheer analytical acuity to discoveries of the sort more typically (and aptly) claimed by disciplines like neurophysiology or cognitive science. Hence also, more disturbingly, the tendency among analytic philosophers in various specialist fields to adopt a pseudo- or (somewhat less unkindly) a quasi-scientific rhetoric in order to dismiss any line of argument that fails or on principle refuses to comply with currently prevailing philosophical modes of thought.

This practice has been the stock-in-trade of analytic philosophers since the heyday of logical positivism when its exponents delighted in facile demolition-jobs on sundry 'continental' (i.e. typecast wild-and-woolly-minded) philosophers and when standards for this kind of knock-down rejoinder were, if anything, even less demanding than today. Still there is a need to muster some resistance when received ideas – or existing institutional mechanisms for preserving them – are so heavily weighted toward the maintenance of a professional (rather than critical-philosophical) status quo that effectively excludes or massively discounts anything too much out of kilter with its own in-house norms of reputable discourse. The effect of this is to render philosophy peculiarly impotent or tongue-tied against the imputation of those, like Stephen Hawking in a recent polemic, who proclaim its demise or chronic obsolescence in the face of giddying scientific (or techno-scientific) progress. Hawking fluttered the academic dovecotes by writing – and repeating to an eager company of interviewers and journalists – his opinion that philosophy as practised nowadays was a waste of time and philosophers a waste of space.[2] More precisely, he wrote that philosophy was 'dead' since it hadn't kept up with the latest developments in science, especially theoretical physics. In earlier times – Hawking conceded – philosophers not only tried to keep up but sometimes made real scientific contributions of their own. However, they were now, in so far as they had any influence at all, just an obstacle to progress through their endless going on about the same old issues of truth, knowledge, inductive warrant and so forth. Had they just paid a bit more attention to the scientific literature they would have gathered that these were no longer live issues for anyone remotely au fait with the latest thinking. Then their options would be either to shut up shop and cease the charade called 'philosophy of science' or else carry on and invite further ridicule for their head-in-sand attitude.

Predictably enough, the journalists went off to find themselves a media-friendly philosopher – not hard to do nowadays – who would argue the opposite case in a suitably vigorous way. On the whole the responses, or those that I came across, seemed overly anxious to strike a conciliatory note, or to grant Hawking's thesis some measure of truth as judged by the standards of the natural-scientific community while tactfully dissenting with regard to philosophy and the human sciences. I think the case needs stating more firmly and, perhaps, less tactfully since otherwise it looks like a forced retreat to cover internal disarray. Besides, there is good reason to mount a much sturdier defence on principled grounds. These have to do with the scientists' need to philosophise and their proneness to philosophise badly or commit certain avoidable errors if they don't take at least some passing interest in what philosophers have to say. Hawking had probably been talking to the wrong philosophers, or picked up some wrong ideas about the kinds of discussion that currently go on in philosophy of science. His lofty dismissal of that whole enterprise as a useless, scientifically irrelevant pseudo-discipline fails to reckon with several important facts about the way that science has typically been practised since its early-modern (seventeenth-century) point of departure and, even more, in the wake of post-1900 developments such as quantum mechanics and space-time relativity.

First is the fact that it has always included a large philosophical component, whether at the level of basic presuppositions concerning evidence, causality, theory-construction, valid inference, hypothesis-testing and so forth, or at the speculative stage where scientists ignore the guidance offered by well-informed philosophers only at risk of falling into various beguiling fallacies or fictions. Such were those 'idols of the theatre' that Bacon warned against in his *New Organon* of 1620, and such – albeit in a very different philosophic guise – those delusive ideas that, according to Kant, were apt to lead us astray from the path of secure investigation or truth-seeking enquiry. This was sure to happen, he warned, if the exercise of pure (speculative) reason concerning questions outside and beyond the empirical domain were mistakenly supposed to deliver the kind of knowledge that could be achieved only by bringing sensuous intuitions under adequate or answering concepts. While in no way wishing to lumber science with the baggage of Kantian metaphysics I would suggest that this diagnosis, or something like it, applies to a great many of the speculative notions nowadays advanced by theoretical physicists including proponents of string theory (Hawking among them) and some of the more way-out quantum conjectures. These thinkers appear unworried – blithely unfazed, one is tempted to say – by the fact that their theories are incapable of proof or confirmation, or indeed of decisive falsification as required by Karl Popper and his followers. After all, it is the peculiar feature of such theories that they posit the existence of that which at present, and perhaps forever, eludes any form of empirical warrant or inference to the best, most rational as well as evidentially sound explanation.

No doubt it is the case that science has often achieved its most notable advances precisely by venturing beyond the furthest limits of proof or ascertainment. It has typically broken new ground by following out some speculative line of thought or putting forward theories, conjectures and hypotheses that involve a readiness, at least for the time being, to make do without the props and securities of 'good' scientific method. Indeed, this reliance on theoretical commitments that exceed the utmost scope of empirical testing is something that many philosophers would attribute even to basic physical laws or items of widely taken-for-granted scientific truth. On their view there is no such thing as plain empirical self-evidence since observation-sentences and the perceptual content that they serve to convey are always in some degree theoretically informed. By the same token, scientific theories are always 'underdetermined' by the best evidence to hand and therefore open to other, equally rational interpretations given some adjustment to this or that 'auxiliary hypothesis' or negotiable element of background belief. All the same I don't want to push too far with that line of argument because it has now become – among some philosophers of science – an article of faith or a dogma maintained just as fixedly as any precept of the 'old', unreconstructed positivist creed. Moreover, it has given rise to a range of relativist or 'strong'-sociological approaches that take the theory-ladenness and underdetermination theses to warrant their programme of suspending the distinction between true and false theories, valid and invalid hypotheses, or science and pseudo-science.

II

Very likely it is notions of this kind – ideas with their home ground in sociology, cultural studies or on the wilder shores of philosophy of science – that provoked Hawking to issue his pronouncement. However, they are in no way germane to my point about the speculative element involved in many episodes of major scientific advance and how philosophy has played its jointly enabling and regulative part in that process. By this I mean its role as a source of new ideas or creative hypotheses and also as a source of guiding precepts with respect to such matters as empirical evidence, logical validity, inductive warrant, corroboration, falsification, hypothesis-testing, causal reasoning, probability-weighting and so forth. These serve to keep science securely on track and prevent it from taking the seductive turn toward pure, evidentially unanchored speculation or sheer science-fiction fantasy. That scientists can mostly do this for themselves is no doubt true enough although, I should add, it is very largely the long-term result of their having gone to school with philosophers – or their own philosophically minded colleagues – and thereby acquired an adequate sense of the relevant distinctions. Ever since Aristotle there has existed a close though historically fluctuating relationship between the natural sciences and those branches of philosophy that took it as a main part of their task to provide science with a clearer grasp of its own theoretical and methodological bearings. Moreover, it has sometimes been primarily a shift of philosophical perspective or worldview that has brought about some epochal episode of paradigm change such as those whereby, in the insouciant phrase of W. V. Quine, 'Kepler superseded Ptolemy, or Einstein Newton, or Darwin Aristotle'.[3]

I have no quarrel with Hawking's animadversions on philosophy of science in so far as they may have been provoked in some measure by the strain of wholesale paradigm-relativism that Quine is here seeking to promote. On his account we should think of scientific theory-change as involving so radical a shift of conceptual schemes as would, in effect, render the history of science rationally unaccountable and philosophy of science a poor (since entirely dependent) relation of sociology and behavioural psychology. If that were the sole position available to present-day philosophers owing to some large-scale failure of intellectual nerve then Hawking would be fully justified in launching his anti-philosophy salvo. However, this ignores the strongly marked turn toward a realist and causal-explanatory approach that has been the single most conspicuous feature of philosophy of science during the past two decades. In place of that earlier relativist drift these thinkers advocate a robustly specified conception of natural kinds along with their essential (kind-constitutive) structures, properties, causal dispositions, etc. Their approach also makes adequate allowance for the range of interactive relations between mind and world, subject and object, or human techno-scientific practice and those aspects or attributes of physical reality upon which such practices depend. Beyond that – crucially in the present context – it offers a critical purchase on the issue as to what properly counts as scientific enquiry and what should more aptly be assigned to the realms of metaphysical conjecture or (at the limit) fictive invention.[4]

Thus philosophy of science now looks set to reoccupy its native ground by getting back in touch with natural-scientific modes of enquiry. This is not just a relatively trivial semantic point about the physical sciences having been described as so many branches of 'natural philosophy' until quite recently. Rather it is the point that scientific theories – especially theories of the ultra-speculative kind that preoccupy theoretical physicists like Hawking – involve a great deal of covert philosophising which may or may not turn out to have promoted the interests of knowledge and truth. This had better be recognised if we are not to be taken in by a false appeal to the authority of science as if it possessed the kind of sheer self-evidence or indubitable warrant that could rightfully claim to evict 'philosophy' as merely a relic from our pre-scientific past. Least of all should philosophers carry their attitude of justified respect for science and its manifold impressive achievements to the point of ceding all authority over issues that lie squarely within their own sphere of competence. Thus it is counterproductive for everyone concerned, philosophers and physicists alike, when Quine and others suggest that we should change or abandon (what were once considered) the ground-rules of logic so as more readily to find room for certain otherwise puzzling, anomalous or downright baffling empirical results. Perhaps the seeming quantum paradox of wave/particle dualism can have its sting temporarily removed by lifting the classical rules of bivalence or excluded middle, i.e. those that would require that we accept *either* the statement 'light propagates as waves' *or* the statement 'light is a stream of particles' but surely not both on pain of logical contradiction. However, the revisionist 'solution' gives rise to yet more intractable problems since it leaves science and philosophy stuck with a huge normative deficit. After all, if Quine's proposal were accepted then they would lack the most basic conceptual resources when it came to assessing statements, theories or hypotheses according to standards of internal consistency or even, on a more pragmatic view, the extent to which they hung together properly with other items of scientific lore.

Here again philosophers would do much better to stick to their guns, reject this particular line of least resistance, and hold out for the indispensability (on empirical as well as 'purely' rational grounds) of a due respect for the classical rule of bivalent truth/falsehood. Not that it could ever achieve what Hawking seems to envisage in his final paragraph when he marvels at the thought of how 'abstract logic' could have thrown up the sheer wondrous profusion of present-day scientific knowledge. Here the point needs making – one to which his book bears ample witness – that the knowledge in question has resulted from a disciplined yet often highly inventive project of enquiry wherein 'abstract' reasoning plays a crucial though far from all-encompassing or self-sufficiently productive role. This project combines the basic procedures of logical, e.g. hypothetico-deductive thought and inductive reasoning on the evidence with a whole range of ancillary resources such as analogy, thought experiments, rational conjecture and – subsuming all these – inference to the best, most adequate explanation. Hawking offers numerous examples of each in the course of his book, along with other cases where their joint operation is the only hypothesis that could possibly explain how science has been able to achieve some particular stage of advance. All the same he is compelled by the 'abstract logic' of his own doctrinaire science-first approach to push that evidence temporarily out of sight when declaring the total irrelevance of philosophy for anyone possessed of an adequate (scientifically informed) world-view. Thus it may be good for philosophers occasionally to remind scientists how their most productive thinking very often involves a complex churning of empirical data, theories, working hypotheses, testable conjectures and (sometimes) speculative fictions. Likewise absent from Hawking's account is philosophy's gatekeeper role in spotting those instances where science strays over without due acknowledgement from one to another mode, or – as frequently happens nowadays – where certain evidential constraints are lifted and empirically informed rational conjecture gives way to pure fabulation.

Besides, there is the case of supposedly cutting-edge theories which yet turn out, on closer inspection, unwittingly to replicate bygone notions from the history of thinking about science that philosophers have been among the first to criticise and eventually lay to rest. Hawking's book puts forward two such theories. One is his linchpin 'M-theory' having to do with the multiple dimensions – eleven at the latest count – that are taken to constitute the ultimate reality beyond appearances despite our being limited, in naive (i.e. non-scientific) sensory-perceptual terms, to the three-plus-one of our familiar spatio-temporal world. On this account there cannot be a single, comprehensive 'theory of everything' of the kind favoured by sanguine types like Steven Weinberg but we can hope to get a whole range of specially tailored, region-specific theories which between them point toward the nature and structure of ultimate reality. The other, closely related to that, is Hawking's idea of 'model-dependent realism' as an approach that makes allowance (as per orthodox quantum mechanics) for effect of observation on item observed or theoretical schema on item theorised but which none the less retains an adequate respect for the objectivity of scientific truth.

Here Hawking's argument shows all the signs of a rudderless drifting between various positions adopted by philosophers from Kant to the present. Thus he spends a lot of time on what seems to be a largely unwitting rehash of episodes in the history of idealist or crypto-idealist thought which has cast a long shadow over post-Kantian philosophy of science. And indeed that shadow still lies heavy on Hawking's two central ideas of M-theory and model-dependent realism. They both look set to re-open the old Kantian split between a 'noumenal' reality forever beyond human knowledge and a realm of 'phenomenal' appearances to which we are confined by the fact of our creaturely cognitive limits. So if Hawking is right to charge some philosophers with a culpable ignorance of science then there is room for a polite but firm *tu quoque*, whether phrased in terms of pots calling kettles black or boots on other feet. For it is equally the case that an outlook of fixed hostility or indifference toward philosophy can sometimes lead scientists, especially those with a strong speculative bent, not only to reinvent the wheel but to produce wheels that don't track straight and consequently tend to upset the vehicle. With Hawking one feels that a firmer grasp of these issues as discussed by philosophers during the past few decades might have helped both to moderate his scorn and also to sharpen his critical focus on certain aspects of current theoretical physics. My point is not so much that a strong dose of philosophical realism might have clipped those speculative wings but rather that philosophers are well practised in steering a course through such choppy waters or in managing to navigate despite all the swirls induced by a confluence of science, metaphysics and far-out conjecture. After all, physics has increasingly come to rely on just the kinds of disciplined speculative thinking that philosophers have typically invented, developed and then criticised when they overstepped the limits of rationally accountable conjecture. Such are those 'armchair' thought experiments (discussed in my Chapter 3) that claim to establish some substantive, i.e. non-trivial, thesis concerning the nature, structure or properties of the physical world by means of a rigorous thinking-through that establishes the truth – or, just as often, the demonstrable falsehood – of any statement affirming or denying it.

No doubt there is room – philosophical room – to debate whether these are really (and remarkably) instances of scientific discovery achieved through an exercise of a priori reasoning or whether they amount, as sceptics would have it, to a species of disguised tautology. However there are just too many impressive examples in the history of science – from Galileo's marvellous thought experimental demonstration that Aristotle must have been wrong about falling bodies to a number of crucial quantum-related results – for anyone to argue convincingly that results thus obtained in the 'laboratory of the mind' are such as can only impress philosophers keen to defend their patch. Indeed, there is a basic sense in which the scientific enterprise stands or falls on the validity of counterfactual-conditional reasoning, that is to say, reasoning from what necessarily *would or would not* be the case should certain conditions obtain/not obtain or certain hypotheses hold/fail to hold. In its negative guise, this kind of thinking is deeply bound up with any causal explanation that involves reasoning to what *would have been* the outcome if certain causally or materially relevant factors *had not* been operative in some given instance. Hawking constantly relies on such principles – and on a range of others with likewise philosophically substantive and debatable import – in order to present and justify his claims with regard to the current and likely future course of developments in physical science. Of course he is very welcome to avail himself of them but he might do better to acknowledge their source in ways of thinking and protocols of valid argumentation that involve distinctly philosophical as well as scientific justificatory grounds.

III

This brings us back to the point that is apt to provoke most resistance from Hawking and the majority of scientists, or those among them – chiefly theoretical physicists – who have most to lose (on the Hawking view) from any assertion of philosophy's claim to a hearing in such matters. It is the point at which scientists tend to go astray when they start to speculate on issues that exceed not only the limits of current-best observational evidence but even the scope of what is presently conceivable as a matter of probative (empirically testable or rationally decidable) warrant. To speak plainly: one useful job for the philosopher of science is to sort out the errors and confusions that scientists – especially theoretical physicists – sometimes fall into when they give free rein to this speculative turn of mind. My book *Quantum Physics and the Flight from Realism* found numerous cases to illustrate the point in the statements of quantum theorists all the way from Niels Bohr – a pioneering figure but a leading source of metaphysical mystification – to the current advocates of a many-worlds or 'multiverse' theory.[5] To adapt the economist Keynes's famous saying: those scientists who claim to have no use for philosophy are most likely in the grip of a bad old philosophy or an insufficiently thought-out new one that they don't fully acknowledge.

There is a large supply of present-day (quasi-)scientific thinking at the more – let us say – creative or imaginative end of the scale that falls into just this hybrid category of high-flown metaphysical conjecture tenuously linked to certain puzzling, contested or at any rate far from decisive empirical results. Nor is it mere hubris for philosophers to claim a special competence in judging when thought has crossed that line from the realm of scientifically informed and rational though at this stage empirically underdetermined conjecture to the realm of unanchored speculation or, in extreme cases, outright sci-fi fantasy. Nowhere is this more evident than in the past hundred years of debate on and around the seemingly paradoxical implications of quantum mechanics, starting out with Max Planck's famously baffled response to his own inaugural (1901) discovery that energy was emitted in discrete quanta to the various excursions into speculative wonderland that enliven the pages of our popular-science magazines. Those paradoxes include wave/particle dualism, the so-called 'collapse of the wave-packet', the observer's role in causing or inducing said collapse and – above all since it appears the only way of reconciling these phenomena within anything like a coherent ontology – superluminal (faster-than-light) interaction between widely space-time separated particles. I shall here risk the charge of shameless self-advertisement and suggest that readers take a look at my above-mentioned book for a statement of the case that these are in truth pseudo-dilemmas brought about by a mixture of shaky evidence, dubious reasoning on it, fanciful extrapolation and a flat refusal to entertain alternative theories (such as that of the physicist David Bohm) which considerably lighten the burden of unresolved paradox. At any rate we are better off trusting to the kinds of advice supplied by scientifically informed philosophers with a well-developed sense of how speculative thinking can sometimes go off the rails than the kinds of advice – including the advice 'let's put a stop to philosophy' – issued by philosophically under-informed scientists.

Among other things philosophers are pretty good at spotting where claimants to knowledge have put their name to some piece of quasi-scientific speculation beyond the furthest bounds of rational, let alone verifiable (or falsifiable) conjecture. That role can scarcely be deemed redundant at a time when the distinction between theoretical physics and speculative metaphysics is often exceedingly hard to draw and when the latter just as often leans over into something very much like science fiction. One has only to pick up a copy of *New Scientist* or *Scientific American* to see how much of the latest thinking inhabits that shadowy border-zone where the three intermingle in ways that a suitably trained philosopher would be best equipped to point out. No doubt there is a fair amount of ill-informed, obtuse or ideologically angled philosophy that either refuses or tries and fails to engage the concerns of present-day science. One can understand Hawking's impatience – or downright exasperation – with some of the half-baked notions put around by refuseniks and would-be engageniks alike. All the same he would do well to consider the historically attested and nowadays more than ever vital role of philosophy as a critical discipline. At best it continues to offer the sorts of argument that science requires in order to dispel not only the illusions of naive sense-certainty or intuitive self-evidence but also the confusions that speculative thought runs into when decoupled from any restraining appeal to regulative principles such as that of inference to the best explanation. To quote Kant in a different though related context: philosophy of science without scientific input is empty, while science without philosophical guidance is blind. At any rate it becomes perilously apt to mistake the seductions of unrestrained fancy or pure hypothetical invention for the business of formulating rationally warranted, metaphysically coherent, and – at any rate in the long run – empirically testable conjectures.

What I therefore want to do in this book, if it doesn't sound too pompous, is recall philosophy to a sense of its proper vocation as a discipline which can and should address itself to issues of wider concern, whether in the physical sciences or elsewhere. I also, and conjointly, seek to make the case for approaches that don't so much trade on their own (quasi-)scientific credentials but which rather seek to bring an informed and intelligent awareness to bear on claims and conjectures that might otherwise receive too little in the way of such critical evaluation. Where analytic philosophers tend to go wrong is of course not in striving for conceptual precision or explanatory power such as typifies the physical sciences at best, nor in taking scientific methods and procedures as objects of study. Rather it is in the wholesale adoption of a (notionally) science-led 'research' culture where Kuhnian normalcy or piecemeal problem-solving is the order of the day and there is little or no room for the kind of nonconformist speculative thought that has been a regular hallmark of major advances in philosophy as well in the physical sciences. By surrendering that crucial margin of autonomy – the space for independent critical reflection on whatever engages its interest – philosophy in effect aligns itself not so much with science in some vaguely encompassing sense of the term but with a markedly conformist, workaday or paradigm-conserving type of scientific activity. For that reason it fails to make creative or self-renewing contact with just those developments – whether in the physical sciences or other regions of enquiry – that might yield a high rate of mutual benefit from philosophy's approaching them on independent and equitable terms.

The book is therefore meant as a practical advertisement for a conception of philosophy, or an idea of what philosophers can best, most usefully do, which goes clean against the self-image routinely endorsed by the majority of those in the academic trade. Each chapter advances the claim, whether overtly or by example, that philosophy is the place – the institutional locus but also, in a larger sense, the natural home-ground – for just the kind of free-ranging yet intellectually disciplined enquiry that can and should question received ideas concerning the proper, academically sanctioned division of specialist labour. Thus I agree with Jürgen Habermas that philosophy is often called upon to mediate between those various expert or technical discourses – from mathematics and physics via law, economics and the social sciences to certain challenging or avant-garde practices in the contemporary arts – with which it is able to engage at an adequate level of informed understanding while none the less having enough in common with the currency of everyday thought and language to communicate effectively across and between those otherwise separate spheres.[6] Yet I would also want to emphasise, again like Habermas, that if it is to perform this intermediary role in an effective way then it will need to hold onto that particular range of critical-reflective resources and conceptual-analytic skills that constitute not only philosophy's professional stock-in-trade but also, more importantly, its prime vocation as a discipline of thought. Thus the last thing needed is the sort of advice issued by a neo-pragmatist or 'post-philosophical' thinker such as Richard Rorty for whom 'the tradition' – the mainstream Western discourse of philosophy from Plato, Descartes and Kant right down to his own analytically minded ex-colleagues – has finally run out of intellectual steam and should henceforth give up its deluded claims to any form of specialist expertise.[7] Rorty sees this as a consummation devoutly to be wished since it will enable philosophers at last to find a voice in the 'cultural conversation' most vigorously carried on by poets, novelists and literary critics of a strong-revisionist persuasion. For Habermas, conversely, it is vital that philosophers should hold out against any such move to (in his phrase) 'level the genre-distinction' between philosophy and literature. It is only by preserving certain distinctive, i.e. discipline-specific and truth-oriented, standards such as those of logical rigour, conceptual precision and a constant readiness to justify its claims in the court of critical reason that philosophy is able to sustain its go-between role.

If anything I would press farther than Habermas in urging that a due regard for those standards can perfectly well coexist with an increased readiness, on the part of philosophers, to engage a great variety of topics encountered not only in the seminar-room but across the whole range of their 'outside' interests and concerns. Thus the chapters of this book will strike most analytic philosophers as addressing an oddly assorted range of topics and hence as pretty much unclassifiable by any (analytically) received conception of what constitutes a branch or constituent discipline of philosophy, properly so called. However they are related – convincingly so, I trust – by the twin criteria of (1) involving a distinctly philosophical, i.e. reflective and critical, treatment of certain albeit diverse topics, and (2) none the less reflecting a special interest in – and hence personal commitment to – these in particular rather than other, perhaps by common estimate more 'central' or 'core' areas. Of course there are those, Rorty included, who would say that all philosophy is in some way autobiographical, even where (as with much analytic work) this aspect comes across in a highly oblique, displaced or subliminal form. However, Rorty's urgings to this effect are a part of his general campaign to wean philosophy off its delusions of intellectual grandeur and coax it back into the wider cultural swim of things. Moreover, his argument suffers from the same self-stymying upshot, namely the fact that if philosophy did take this route – one also recommended by other jaded 'post-philosophical' types such as the later Wittgenstein or a multitude of postmodernist gurus – then it would rapidly find itself with nothing of interest to say, or nothing that could possibly rise above the babble of other contributory voices.

So my case is, first, that one can and should philosophise about any topic that justifies the effort by presenting philosophically pertinent issues, and second, that any specialist knowledge then deployed had much better (contra Rorty) be on the philosophical side rather than a matter of vainly striving to catch up with the latest stage of advance in this or that extra-philosophical domain. Of course – to take one salient example – it requires a good deal of well-directed reading around in neurophysiology, cognitive science, optics, kinaesthetics and so forth, if a philosopher of perception is to make any valid or worthwhile contribution to the subject. Still she will be spending her time more wisely – as I remarked in connection with the philosophy of quantum physics – if she focuses more on conceptual problems as these arise in the discourse of practising scientists rather than issues at the cutting edge of current research. What tends to happen when philosophers adopt the latter approach is that their own discourse soon becomes subject to the same law of sharply diminishing returns that dogged the logical positivists. That is to say, it falls into the same pattern of chronic alternation between, on the one hand, empirical or empirical-sounding claims that inevitably lag behind the science they emulate and, on the other, claims of a more 'philosophical', i.e. conceptual or analytic sort which have only a notional scientific import and which contribute little to philosophy save a heightened sense of intellectual and cultural isolation. This applies even to developments, like the present-day revival of causal realism, that would seem to hold out the promise of a genuine and decisive break with that whole bad legacy of vexing dualisms from Kant to Carnap and beyond. As I have said, this marks a welcome advance in so far as it offers to reconnect philosophy with a world of scientific or everyday realia that earlier thinkers – whether toilers in the wake of logical positivism or adepts of the linguistic turn – had seemed to count a world well lost for the sake of their own pet theories. However, all too often it takes the form of a second-order, drily formal, at times almost neo-scholastic disquisition on the various terms and concepts that characterise causal-realist talk or that are presupposed by the kinds of truth-claim typically advanced in its name.

To this extent Rorty and Hawking are right in their differently angled though otherwise strikingly convergent diagnoses. If philosophy – or the academic discipline that currently bears that name – is ever to break out of this corner then it will need to recover a sense of its own relative autonomy vis-à-vis the sciences and other topic-domains. 'Relative', that is, in so far as it depends upon them for its subject matter and critical orientation but 'autonomy' in so far as it cannot long thrive in a Lockean under-labourer role that denies philosophy the right to any exercise of critical reflection beyond whatever is currently enjoined by the arbiters of reputable doctrine and method. Moreover, it will need to regain the courage of those speculative powers that Kant hived off into a quarantine zone of pure reason where they could be kept safe from science and science kept safe from them, thus leaving it for later, more zealous boundary patrollers such as the logical positivists to declare that zone itself off-limits or merely non-existent. If one thing has become clear through all the travails of analytic philosophy since that inauspicious beginning it is the fact that any discipline whose vocation it is – or should be – to think creatively and critically as well as carefully and consistently is not well served by such doctrinaire restraints on its freedom to speculate in ways that don't conform to existing ideas of best or acceptable practice. The result, as I argue here in various contexts, has been not only to sap philosophy of much of its primary motivating force but also to create a dominant ethos wherein certain kinds of intellectual creativity become well-nigh unthinkable because the thinkable is fenced around with such a range of professional caveats. So when a 'continental' thinker like Gilles Deleuze puts the case – and seeks to show by example – that philosophy should properly be in the business of *creating* rather than merely or exclusively *analysing* concepts this idea is apt to strike most analytic philosophers either as wilful provocation or else as a downright category-mistake.[8]

However, there is nothing in common between the kind of conceptual creativity that Deleuze has in mind – a range of critical-exploratory procedures as demanding as they are inventive – and the kind that Rorty recommends with his notion of philosophy as a sub-branch of literature or literary criticism. What Deleuze seeks to do through his various terminological and other innovations is open the space for a speculative (and in that sense creative) approach that invents new ways of thinking in the absence of ready-made solutions to problems that happen not to fit with current modes of institution-ally accredited thought. Or again, he operates on the premise that any putative 'solution' to them by currently accepted communal or discipline-specific norms will be one that simply conjures away those problems – along with whatever further complications might come up – by a wave of the standard, analytically approved, all-purpose conceptual wand. Hence also the extraordinary cachet presently enjoyed by the late-Wittgensteinian idea of philosophy as a therapeu-tic exercise in self-abnegation, such that its sole legitimate business is to talk itself down, through a schooling in everyday 'language games' or 'forms of life', to a wise acceptance of its own imminent demise. That this idea has lately come to exert a powerful influence even on thinkers in the 'other', *echt*-analytic line of descent from Frege and Russell is perhaps the most striking evidence that there is – and always was – something peculiarly terminal or self-exhausting about that notion of philosophy as solely or purely a matter of conceptual analysis. The problem was pinpointed early on by G. E. Moore, another founding figure, who remarked on the 'paradox' – perhaps more of a classic *reductio* – that a strict enforcement of that cardinal precept would quickly reduce philosophical utterance to a string of vacuous tautologies.[9] That is to say, if one adhered to the rule that every statement should meet the requirement of logical self-evidence or a priori truth – the latter understood in a strictly analytic, i.e. non-Kantian or non-synthetic, way – then this would exclude any pos-sibility of those statements having any factual, empirical, informative or communicative content.

IV

So there is something awry with the analytic enterprise in so far as it has remained at least residually in hock to that early logicist ideal even in its later, more liberal phases when hard-line logical positivism had collapsed under the strain of various well-known problems, not least that of being unable to meet its own criteria for valid or mean-ingful utterance. Of course there is still a great deal of interesting and valuable work being done under the broad description 'analytic philosophy', including some that ventures into regions of speculative thought that the logical positivists would surely have banished to the realm of 'empty metaphysics'. However, to that extent it is no longer 'analytic' in any sense that would set it clearly apart from the kind of thinking that more conservative or unreconstructed analytic types would describe as 'continental', most likely with no very flattering intent. My point is that these terms have for a good while now been defined only by contrast or opposition, with proponents of each attacking the other more through a sense of vaguely focused suspicion or blanket hostility than through any substantive issue between them, or any that philosophers on either side could formulate in a coherent and convincing way. Now at last the situation is changing so that younger philosophers – some of them – can quite respectably combine an 'analytic' (in the broad sense) approach with an interest in continental thinkers such as Sartre, Foucault, Derrida or Deleuze. As a result those thinkers are themselves undergoing a marked new phase in their reception-history whereby they have not so much been made safe for analytical consumption as made available for readings of a different, in some ways more rigorous or exacting character than typified their earlier fortunes at the hands of (for the most part) literary and cultural theorists.

Still the lesson to be drawn has more to do with that breaking down of the old analytic/continental dichotomy than with any claim to superior credentials on either side. Just as (for instance) Derrida comes out of such analytically informed readings as a thinker of far greater analytic power and acuity than his erstwhile detractors acknowledged so likewise those philosophers of an analytic bent who have read him attentively are also among those, usually of the middling or younger generation, who have responded to the challenge of his work by taking a fresh and innovative approach to the texts of their own formative tradition.[10] Moreover – the claim that I hope to vindicate in the following chapters – that element of 'continental' influence is helping to change the culture of misplaced specialism or misdirected expertise that has characterised so much analytic debate. Thus it tends to release just the kinds of speculative or creative-exploratory thinking that were hitherto very largely held in check by various doctrinal or methodological sanctions. By the same token it works to encourage what suffered a relative eclipse during the period of *echt*-analytic hegemony, namely the practice of philosophy as a mode of intensely reflective, self-critical discourse that finds two of its chief (albeit in other ways highly dissimilar) exemplars in Derrida and Adorno. The shared point of origin for both these thinkers – although again one that they contested and transformed in highly dissimilar ways – was Husserlian transcendental phenomenology, a movement of thought which for a time exerted a certain appeal for some analytic philosophers but which they finally rejected (taking a lead from Frege's critique of Husserl) on grounds of its supposed 'psychologism' or subjective, i.e. logically opaque, mode of expression.[11] However, that critique was misconceived both in its failure to take the point of Husserl's transcendental reduction and in its commitment to a narrowly (uncritically) logicist approach that effectively repeated the self-stultifying error of logical positivism. At any rate one beneficial effect of the growing 'continental' influence has been to open a space for reflection – reflection in a critical and sometimes dialectical mode – that had been closed off within the analytic mainstream almost as a founding precept or article of faith.

Rorty is right when he says that philosophers should give up thinking of themselves as experts in this or that technical sub-branch of the discipline – especially epistemology – since that claim most often comes down to no more than a misguided attempt to deck out their enterprise in the borrowed fineries of science. However, he is wrong to conclude from this that philosophy, rather than a certain distorted or artificially narrowed conception of philosophy, has outlived its cultural-intellectual moment and should therefore now yield to a different, post-philosophical phase in the ongoing conversation. On the one hand he errs in supposing the mainstream analytic paradigm to constitute the well-nigh inevitable upshot or, as he likes to put it, the end of the road that philosophy has been travelling ever since Descartes took the fateful turn toward epistemology as its putative foundation. On the other he mistakes the lack of self-reflective or critical capacity that typifies a good deal of analytic work for a sign that philosophy had better cultivate the kind of literary creativity – the free-wheeling openness to new turns of metaphor, modes of self-description, narrative invention and so forth – which he sees as requiring a decisive break not only with the analytic paradigm but also with the entire previous history of thought to which, in many ways, that paradigm stood firmly opposed. Yet despite coming out very publicly as one who had first espoused and then foresworn the analytic enterprise Rorty in fact continued to endorse at least one of its main suppositions, namely that concerning its own privileged status as – in both senses of that double-edged phrase – the *ne plus ultra* of philosophy to date. Had he not bought into this parochial self-estimate – had he recognised instead how it ran into various intellectual dead-ends through having closed off some promising ways forward from a history of far from moribund ideas – then he might have come up with some better alternative to that trademark Rortian endgame scenario. At least he might not have been led to frame so drastic and patently rigged a choice as that between 'philosophy' as the last redoubt of fusty academicism and 'literature' (albeit in his greatly expanded sense of the term) as synonymous with all the creativity or hermeneutic flair that 'philosophy' has managed to expel from its own discourse.

There is plentiful evidence, past and present, that this is indeed a false choice and one that numerous philosophers – among them, for reasons cited above, Derrida and Deleuze – have not for one moment felt themselves obliged or inclined to make. Thus seeing where Rorty's diagnosis goes wrong is also, and for just that reason, an aid to seeing why the analytic/continental dichotomy is simply incapable of being drawn in any principled, consistent or rigorous way. However, there is more than one kind of creativity that stands to gain from an opening up of those boundaries constructed within and around the philosophical domain by the drive to uphold a division of intellectual labour that first seeks to seal philosophy off against alien, discipline-threatening intrusions and then assigns its various sub-branches each to its own strictly circumscribed sphere of special expertise. Indeed it would be just another example of the same bad dichotomising habit of thought if one connected any signs of new-found creativity or freedom from those earlier curbs and constraints with the growing extent of 'continental' influence on a once resistant but now more receptive analytic tradition. Equally significant is the evidence that many analytically trained philosophers are nowadays questioning that earlier, highly restrictive conception of their own proper role in relation to the various particular concerns – including the natural-scientific – that still provide much of their subject matter but which are no longer taken, in the Lockean-positivist manner, as assigning a strictly subaltern status to any such discourse on or about them. Thus the increased measure of speculative licence – in a strictly non-prejudicial sense of the word – goes along with an increased readiness to allow philosophy the scope to exercise its critical-reflective powers beyond the sorts of territorial imperative that hitherto governed its conduct. I trust that my book will give further impetus to that welcome development by bringing out some of the ways in which a philosophically informed treatment of otherwise very diverse topics can at once throw a new and revealing light on those topics from an unfamiliar angle and work to strengthen our nowadays perhaps rather faltering sense of philosophy's continued claim to attention. These are subject areas that invite such scrutiny precisely in so far as they leave unanswered certain questions that their own specialist practitioners have neither time, patience nor (be it said) the philosophical training to address at adequate length and depth.

V

However, this is all getting to sound too much like piece of pre-emptive self-advertisement so I shall now leave off my general introduction and move to a series of brief chapter synopses. Chapter 1 – 'How *Not* to Defeat Scepticism: Why Anti-Realism Won't Do the Trick' – is the chapter that links most directly to my earlier work defending a causal-realist approach to issues in epistemology and philosophy of science. Since later parts of this book presuppose the validity of that approach as a matter of enabling presupposition for various specific lines of argument it is the best starting-point even for readers who then decide to jump around. Here I examine one particular response to the challenge of epistemological scepticism that has recently enjoyed some success in terms of widespread uptake and influence, though not, I shall argue, by adequately meeting that challenge. It is the position espoused by those who reject the idea of objectivist or recognition-transcendent truth and instead adopt an anti-realist stance according to which truth is always 'epistemically constrained', i.e. subject to the scope and limits of human knowledge. On their account truth-talk is best replaced by talk of 'warranted assertibility', or that which our statements, conjectures and hypotheses are rightfully taken to possess just so long as they are borne out by our best evidence to hand or range of best available proof-procedures. This is thought to provide the only possible non-question-begging answer to scepticism since the latter most often gets a hold through a kind of regular rebound effect whereby the inherently frustrated quest for some intelligible formulation of the realist/objectivist claim flips over, so to speak, and produces an outlook of (at any rate purported) wholesale epistemological doubt. That is to say, scepticism achieves the semblance of a knock-down argument by pressing its point that if truth is indeed recognition-transcendent or epistemically unconstrained then *ipso facto* it must lie beyond the utmost reach of human cognisance. Only by bringing it safely back within range of our perceptual, cognitive, or intellectual powers – redefining it in terms of epistemic warrant – can truth be cut down to practicable size and knowledge re-establish its purchase on reality.

Chapter 1 explains what I take to be wrong with this anti-realist line of argument when marshalled against the threat of wholesale epistemological scepticism and also, for similar reasons, when advanced as a putative checkmate defence against relativism in its various (wholesale or other) forms. Here again the proposed treatment turns out to be not so much a genuine cure or prophylactic but rather a particularly virulent strain of just the same sceptical malady. This effect comes about through a basic confusion between ontological and epistemological issues, and also – I suggest – through the anti-realist habit of conflating metaphysics with epistemology in such a way as to ignore certain crucial lessons imparted by modal realists like Saul Kripke and the early Hilary Putnam. Indeed, the anti-realist position itself very easily leans over into scepticism and relativism once it yields vital ground by renouncing the prime objectivist axiom that truth might always elude the compass of best judgement or optimised epistemic warrant. Anti-realism then comes down to the assertion, with whatever technical refinements, that we can only mean by 'truth' whatever now passes muster or in future might enjoy that status as judged by our present-best- or future-best-achievable methods of proof or ascertainment. From here it is no great distance to the whole current range of conventionalist, descriptivist, constructivist, framework-internalist, paradigm-relativist, 'strong'-sociological, late-Wittgensteinian and suchlike variants on the basic sceptical theme. I conclude that anti-realism is both ill-conceived as a matter of positive doctrine and wholly incapable of doing its work as a means of defence against scepticism and relativism.

Chapter 2 considers what is (or what should be) meant by the description 'great' philosophy and then offers some broadly applicable criteria by which to assess candidate thinkers or works. On the one hand are philosophers in whose case the epithet, even if contested, is not grossly misconceived or merely the product of doctrinal adherence on the part of those who apply it. On the other are those – however gifted, acute or technically adroit – to whom its application is inappropriate because their work cannot justifiably be held to rise to a level of creative-exploratory thought where the description would have any meaningful purchase. I develop this contrast with reference to Thomas Kuhn's distinction between 'revolutionary' and 'normal' science, and also in light of J. L. Austin's anecdotal quip – apropos Leibniz – that it was the mark of truly great thinkers to make great mistakes, or (on a less provocative interpretation) to risk falling into certain kinds of significant or consequential error. My chapter goes on to put the case that great philosophy should be thought of as involving a constant (not just occasional) readiness to venture and pursue speculative hypotheses beyond any limits typically imposed by a culture of 'safe', well-established, or academically sanctioned debate. At the same time – and just as crucially – it must be conceived as subject to the strictest, most demanding standards of formal assessment, i.e. with respect to basic requirements of logical rigour and conceptual precision. Focusing mainly on the work of Jacques Derrida and (at greater length) Alain Badiou I suggest that these criteria are more often met by philosophers in the broadly 'continental' rather than the mainstream 'analytic' line of descent. However – as should be clear – the very possibility of meeting them, and of their being jointly met by any one thinker, is itself sufficient indication that this is a false and pernicious dichotomy.

Chapters 3 and 4 see a shift of focus toward matters of practical as well as theoretical concern, but again by way of some central issues in current academic debate. In Chapter 3 I present a critical review of the quarrel between partisans of two, on the face of it sharply conflicting movements of thought. On the one hand are ranged the thought experimentalists, or those who uphold some version of the 'armchair' philosopher's traditional appeal to truths of reason or a priori grounds of knowledge. On the other are found their more empirically minded opponents who urge that we ought to abandon such delusory ideas and instead practise a different form of 'experimental philosophy'. This latter is conceived very much on the model of the social sciences and involves a survey of opinion on various topics conducted across a sample group of respondents including, though by no means restricted to, the community of expert or specialist philosophers. Here I examine the interests at stake between these two camps and suggest some reasons – among them a number of tenacious dichotomies and (pseudo)-dilemmas – why the issue has acquired such a high profile in recent debate. Thus it picks up on all the problems bequeathed by Descartes, Kant and a long line of thinkers, both empiricists and rationalists, who have endorsed some version of the mind/world, concept/intuition, form/content, a priori/a posteriori, or (for that matter) rationalist/empiricist distinction. I argue that a strongly naturalised approach to epistemology and philosophy of mind – as opposed to the weaker and still dualism-prone variety advanced by Quine – is the only way that philosophy will achieve (what it surely wants and needs) a fully-fledged naturalistic monism capable of laying those problems to rest. In the process it would also leave behind that kindred dualist misconception that would suppose the existence of a deep divide between experiments carried out in the first-person apodictic 'laboratory of the mind' and experiments conducted on the basis of third-person evidence or enquiry.

Chapter 4 takes up some closely related issues by examining various aspects of the 'extended mind' (EM) thesis proposed by David Chalmers and Andy Clark. Their claim is that various items of extra-cranial equipment (ranging from diaries, memos and note-books to calculators, laptops and iPhones) are so closely bound up with the mental processes of those who habitually use them that they must – on a 'parity principle' – count as parts or integral components of the users' minds. Opponents of the thesis typically object that minds don't have parts, that the devices in question are themselves products of human ingenuity and that intentionality – the mark of the mental – cannot be attributed to notebooks or iPhones without falling into gross confusion. In response the advocates of 'strong' EM run a range of arguments, mostly of the slippery-slope kind, in order to press their point that there is no way to draw a firm or principled line between 'internal' and 'external' modes of mental extension or cognitive enhancement. My chapter reviews the current debate, start-ing out from a position of broad sympathy with the EM thesis but then raising problems with it from a phenomenological as well as an ethical and socio-political standpoint. I conclude that its advocates have been too much concerned with prosthetic devices of a physical or material kind and have thereby been led to underestimate the role of human interpersonal, collective and social exchange as a source of enhanced or expanded mental powers. By way of pointing up this missing dimension of the EM argument I briefly trace a history of thought – from Spinoza to Negri and other recent theorists – which lays chief stress on the idea of 'multitude' as a means of breaking with the entrenched individualism of Western post-Cartesian philo-sophic thought.

Chapter 5 pursues this emergent 'continental' drift in a direction that happily manages to combine a great number of my principal interests, among them music, politics, literary theory and philosophi-cal aesthetics, at least in the non-traditional forms it has adopted in response to various shrewdly aimed critiques from Marxist and other dissident perspectives. Here I take political song as the single most challenging (hence most revealing) topic for any ontology of music. Political songs – those with genuine and lasting social impact – are on the one hand maximally context-specific or geared to particular historical occasions while on the other hand capable of somehow maintaining that impact in later, often very different historical circumstances. I address this seeming paradox from a range of perspectives, among them Frank Kermode's reflections on 'the classic' and Jacques Derrida's discussion of speech-act 'iterability'. Another main source is Alain Badiou's highly innovative thinking about the relationship between being and event. In particular I cite his idea of 'transitory ontology' and his understanding of how great advances – whether in mathematics, science, politics or the arts – come about through a mode of proleptic or premonitory grasp despite the limits of present-best knowledge or practical realisation. Such are those breakthrough occurrences that mark the advent of a new ontological dispensation and which thus constitute a further stage in the unfolding dialectic of being and event that Badiou describes in his book of that title. Political song is of special significance in this context since its highly elusive ontological status goes along with a strong political charge and a temporal-modal orientation toward the realm of future possibility.

Chapter 6 offers a critical review of the Speculative Realist movement that emerged in the wake of Quentin Meillassoux's book *After Finitude* (French publication 2006; English translation 2008) and was then developed in various, often divergent or conflicting ways. It is a movement remarkable both for the extraordinary rapidity with which it has been taken up, debated and acquired a veritable canon of much-cited texts – chiefly through websites and other electronic media – and for what would previously have struck most qualified observers as a wildly improbable combination of attributes. These are the facts that it is (1) French in origin, (2) decidedly 'continental' in its chief points of reference, and (3) a full-fledged objectivist realism which forcefully abjures all forms of so-called 'correlationist', i.e. post-Kantian, subject-oriented epistemology. This latter the speculative realists see as having given rise to the whole range of likewise unacceptable since overtly or covertly anti-realist positions that emerged in the wake of the latter-day turn toward language – alternatively 'discourse', 'paradigm', 'episteme', 'framework', 'conceptual scheme', 'language game' or cultural 'life-form' – as (supposedly) the ultimate horizon or limiting condition of knowledge and truth. All the same this uncompromising realism has often gone along, as in the second, more extravagantly 'speculative' part of Meillassoux's book, with some far-fetched and unwarranted (indeed philosophically insupportable) ideas which, if taken at anything like their literal force, would totally undermine the realist case or show it up as merely a fig-leaf doctrine.

I suggest that the problem has resulted from these thinkers' conspicuous failure, or refusal, to engage with certain highly germane developments in the 'other' (analytic) line of descent. More specifically, they have ignored the conceptual resources nowadays on offer from those varieties of strong (ontologically grounded) causal realism that have lately mounted a vigorous challenge to correlationist assumptions, and all the more so when conjoined with a historically and scientifically informed account of inference to the best explanation. Elsewhere, and tending to confirm this diagnosis, the exponents of SR have a habit of simply listing or enumerating objects of assorted shapes, sizes, sensory appearances, observable behaviour, etc., as if the mere fact of their multifarious existence were enough to clinch the realist case without much thought as to what makes them objects of just that kind with just that range of attributes. Thus, ironically, they give every sign of reverting to a Humean state of scepticism with regard to the prospects of delving deeper into the depth-structural or dispositional make-up of those various realia and thus getting further along toward a genuine and substantive rather than a merely notional or abstractly conceived realism. This impression is borne out by the fact that Hume comes in for a wildly heterodox, in its own perverse way ultra-objectivist but in the end realism-incompatible reading in the second part of Meillassoux's *After Finitude*. I therefore suggest – reversing the emphasis of previous chapters – that this curiously out-of-character development on the continental scene is in need of some input from the analytic side if it is going to develop in a properly realist way and not give in to the temptations of its own somewhat overwrought speculative leaning.

VI

Chapter 7 takes us onto literary-philosophical ground by offering some tentative answers to three (as I consider them) closely related questions. The first question asks: what is it about Shakespeare that has so sharply polarised responses between those, the vast majority, who count him a creative genius of the first rank and those, a tiny but vocal minority, who either (like Dr Johnson) endorse that estimate with large reservations or else (like Ludwig Wittgenstein) profess to find it in most respects simply incomprehensible? The second question asks: what is it about the writings of Jacques Derrida that provokes such extreme hostility among certain philosophers – in particular those of a broadly 'analytic' persuasion – that they see fit to denounce his works, very often on the basis of minimal or second-hand acquaintance? The third question asks what these two negative responses might have in common and hence what they might indicate concerning the marked commonality between Shakespeare's and Derrida's challenge to the claims of 'ordinary language' (or common-sense judgement) as an ultimate court of appeal.

I go on to examine the particular ways in which their writing raises problems for any such normative conception and does so, moreover, through the kind of creative-exploratory language that is no less conceptually precise for its breaking with conventional or acculturated modes of expression. Hence my focus on Wittgenstein's strangely ambivalent attitude to Shakespeare, or his constant veering about between high disdain for the conventional estimate spouted by 'a thousand professors of literature' and a nagging sense of the Shakespearean 'sublime' as something quite beyond his own comprehension. Despite the generic differences between them – differences all too easily ignored by those (like Rorty) who claim Derridean warrant for the idea of philosophy as just another 'kind of writing' – I put the case for this Shakespearean aspect of Derrida's work as showing how philosophy and literature can enter into a close and productive yet sufficiently character-preserving relationship. Thus when literary critics refer somewhat vaguely to Shakespeare's plays as possessing an uncommon depth or subtlety of 'philosophic' grasp and when philosophers speak (approvingly or otherwise) of Derrida's 'literary' style their claims can best be seen in terms of this asymptotic convergence. What unites them is a shared recognition – all too easily obscured by routine deference to the authority of 'ordinary language' – that the virtues of intellectual depth and conceptual precision may well go along with linguistic inventiveness of the highest order.

Indeed I have come to think that philosophy generally, and not just philosophy of language, would gain a great deal in terms of intellectual creativity and freedom from ruling conceptions of the way things ought to be done if it managed to find room for some of those insights achieved by the best, that is to say the most linguistically responsive as well as analytically acute literary critics. It is just this projected encounter that has oriented much of my thinking here and in other recent work having to do with those sundry vexing dualisms – prototypically 'analytic'/'continental' – that have done so much to skew and distort the currency of present-day academic philosophy. Above all they have given rise to the entrenched idea that any proposal along these lines must come either from a 'literary' quarter, that is, from someone keen to reverse the traditional post-Platonic order of priority between philosophy and literature, or else – what amounts to the same thing – from a Rortian standpoint according to which philosophy *just is* a 'kind of writing' altogether on a par with poetry, fiction or the more creative ('strong-descriptivist') sorts of literary criticism. My point is that there is no rational incentive to adopt this 'post-philosophical' or, more specifically, this post-analytic line of talk if one accepts that conceptual-linguistic analysis of a high order can perfectly well go along with a high degree of linguistic (and to that extent) conceptual creativity. This is also why William Empson looms large in Chapter 7 – and indeed in much of my thinking since undergraduate days – as a marvellous exemplar of what literary criticism can be when it conjoins both these powers with a further gift for their inventive deployment across a great range of literary and other contexts.

Most likely it was Empson's expansive conception of the literary critic's role, followed up by my early (to begin with largely baffled) reading of Derrida, that set me against the kind of narrowly professional ethos according to which the limits of one's specialism are not only the limits of what one can legitimately talk about but also the imperative boundary-markers for anyone presuming to discuss, comprehend or (above all) criticise one's views. I consider this idea to have done great damage to philosophy as practised across a wide range of its currently accredited subject areas. On the contrary: philosophers can and should turn their attention to any topic that (1) engages their (preferably intense or passionate) interest, (2) poses one or more significant philosophical issue(s), and (3) may additionally have the potential to change people's sense of what counts as a topic that satisfies descriptions (1) and (2). At times such an approach might seem to push things just a bit too far beyond the personal toward the downright idiosyncratic. Still I would want to hold my ground on this and say again that condition (1) is non-negotiable for anyone who wishes to philosophise in a more than merely academic way, while the standards laid down by (2) should properly be open to revision in light of some new and, at first appearance, unsuitable candidate for treatment. Should philosophy lose sight of this possibility, or close ranks against the discussion of non-approved themes or ideas, then it will surely become ever more subject to that law of sharply diminishing returns that goes along with over-specialisation in topics dictated very largely by its own professionally driven agenda. It will also run the risk – unfortunately all too present in an academic culture so much given over to 'research' interests driven by the next assessment exercise – of turning into what George Orwell described as a 'smelly little orthodoxy'.

I trust that my introduction will have gone some way toward convincing the reader that philosophy is under no obligation to beat its own bounds in the currently accepted way, and second that a philosopher's interests can hang together – make up a coherent and intelligible sequence of thought – despite taking on a pretty wide range of topics. Indeed, this book is meant as something of a manifesto for the nowadays professionally outré idea that it is the bringing to bear of critical-reflective intelligence across subject areas, rather than the exclusive concentration on this or that locus of presumed special expertise, that is likely to produce the best results in terms of philosophical creativity and mind-transformative (as distinct from piecemeal problem-solving) power. Whether it succeeds as a putting-into-practice of its own agenda is of course entirely for the reader to decide. Meanwhile I should like to thank my colleagues and postgraduate students in Cardiff for having so often, whether knowingly or not, helped me get past some sticky point of argument or sparked off some new line of thought. There are a great many people to whom I am indebted in various respects for the way it has turned out and the fact of its ever having reached publication. I shall therefore – albeit with some misgivings – not list them individually but trust (casting scepticism properly to the winds) that my and their mind-worlds are sufficiently in touch for them to know very well who they are.

It is, or once was, conventional practice to insert a caveat at this point to the effect that 'any mistakes that remain are my own' or – where the item in question looked like causing a fuss – 'all opinions expressed here are those of the author'. I guess that applies especially to this Introduction, and perhaps to some of my more jaundiced (let us rather say detached and predominantly critical) remarks about the current, as I see it far from healthy, state of Anglophone professional-academic philosophy. Anyway I hope that those in broad agreement will not be put off by the more polemical or grouchy bits and that those who roundly reject my views will feel themselves spurred to put up an invigorated case for the defence.

Note: I have not provided bibliographical details for all the authors or works referred to here since most of them are discussed in subsequent chapters and the relevant information can be tracked down easily enough through the index and endnotes. The only references provided for this Introduction are therefore to passages of direct quotation and to those works (rather few) that don't come in for treatment or conspicuous mention later on. Actually I am a bit of a stickler for references, as the reader will soon find out, although it does strike me – as a matter of general practice – that some of the formalities could well be dropped now that all the relevant information can in most cases easily be tracked down in a few seconds via Google Scholar or other online resources.)

Notes

1. See especially Gottlob Frege, review of Edmund Husserl's *Philosophie der Arithmetik*, trans. E.-H. W. Kluge, *Mind*, Vol. LXXXI (1972), pp. 321–7; also Michael Dummett, *Origins of Analytical Philosophy* (Cambridge, MA: Harvard University Press, 1994); Dagfinn Follesdal, 'Husserl and Frege: a contribution to elucidating the origins of phenomenological philosophy', in Leila Haaparanta (ed.), *Mind, Meaning and Mathematics: Essays on the Philosophical Views of Husserl and Frege* (Dordrecht and Boston: Kluwer, 1994), pp. 3–47.
2. Stephen Hawking and Leonard Mlodinow, *The Grand Design* (New York: Bantam Books, 2010).
3. W. V. Quine, 'Two dogmas of empiricism', in *From a Logical Point of View*, 2nd edn (Cambridge, MA: Harvard University Press, 1961), pp. 20–46, at p. 43.
4. For more detailed discussion of these developments see Christopher Norris, *Resources of Realism: Prospects for 'Post-analytic' Philosophy* (London: Macmillan, 1997), *On Truth and Meaning: Language, Logic and the Grounds of Belief* (London: Continuum, 2006), and *Fiction, Philosophy and Literary Theory: Will the Real Saul Kripke Please Stand Up?* (London: Continuum, 2007).
5. Norris, *Quantum Theory and the Flight from Realism: Philosophical Responses to Quantum Mechanics* (London: Routledge, 2000).
6. See especially Jürgen Habermas, *The Theory of Communicative Action*, 2 vols, trans. Thomas McCarthy (Boston: Beacon Press, 1984 and 1987) and *The Structural Transformation of the Public Sphere*, trans. Thomas Burger (Cambridge: Polity Press, 1989).

7. See, for instance, Richard Rorty, *Consequences of Pragmatism* (Brighton: Harvester, 1982), *Objectivity, Relativism, and Truth* (Cambridge: Cambridge University Press, 1981) and *Objectivity and Truth* (Cambridge University Press, 1994).

8. Gilles Deleuze and Félix Guattari, *What Is Philosophy?*, trans. Graham Burchell and Hugh Tomlinson (London: Verso, 1994).

9. G. E. Moore, 'A reply to my critics', in P. A. Schilpp (ed.), *The Philosophy of G. E. Moore* (La Salle: Open Court, 1968), pp. 535–687; also C. H. Langford, 'The notion of analysis in Moore's philosophy', ibid., pp. 321–41.

10. For evidence of what I take to be this mutually beneficial effect, see various essays collected in Norris and David Roden (eds), *Jacques Derrida*, 4 vols (London: Sage, 2002).

11. See, for instance, Edmund Husserl, *Logical Investigations*, trans. J. N. Findlay, 2 vols (New York: Humanities Press, 1970) and *Ideas: General Introduction to Pure Phenomenology*, trans. W. R. Boyce Gibson (London: Collier Macmillan 1975); Jacques Derrida, '"Genesis and Structure" and phenomenology', in *Writing and Difference*, trans. Alan Bass (London: Routledge & Kegan Paul, 1978), pp. 154–68 and *La problème de la genèse dans la philosophie de Husserl* (Paris: Presses Universitaires de France, 1990); T. W. Adorno, *Against Epistemology: A Metacritique*, trans. Willis Domingo (Oxford: Blackwell, 1982); and – for an early indication of the analytic backlash – Gilbert Ryle, 'Phenomenology' and 'Phenomenology versus *The Concept of Mind*', in Ryle, *Collected Papers*, Vol. 1 (London: Hutchinson, 1971), pp. 167–78 and 179–96.

CHAPTER 1

How Not *to Defeat Scepticism:*
Why Anti-realism Won't Do the Trick

I

With the exception of doughty defenders such as Joseph Margolis there are rather few philosophers nowadays who would happily sign up to the relativist cause in anything like an overt, programmatic or doctrinally explicit way.[1] The reason for this reluctance is plain to see since the chronicle of mainstream Western philosophy from Plato and Aristotle down is very largely the record of those who deemed themselves serious, rational, truth-seeking, disciplined, rigorous or intellectually and vocationally qualified thinkers and who took this to require that they espouse a position at the maximum possible distance from their relativist Others. These latter have gone under various pejorative names from time to time – whether 'sophists' for Plato or 'postmodernists' for his avatars in the present-day analytic camp – but their trademark signatures have remained pretty much unchanged.[2] Thus the history of relativism, at least as told from this antagonistic standpoint, is the history of so many temporally indexed, technically or idiomatically diverse but nonetheless deeply kindred variations on the basic theme that 'man is the measure'. Just as Plato derived considerable philosophic mileage from his set-piece ripostes to the sophists in numerous contexts of debate from logic, metaphysics and epistemology to ethics and political theory so present-day philosophers draw a great deal of intellectual and moral sustenance from their claim to be carrying on the good fight that Plato took up from Parmenides and which has since then figured centrally in philosophy's elective self-image as a discourse specialised in the pursuit of reason and truth.

Of course this leaves room for much finessing of arguments on both sides.[3] Anti-relativists strengthen their position by striving to close as many loopholes as possible in the adversary case while relativists strive to shore theirs up by explaining how the opposition have got them wrong, whether unwittingly or (more often) through deliberate misrepresentation. Such is, for instance, Margolis's claim that the put-downs have typically issued from a travesty or plain distortion of that Protagorean claim about man being the measure.[4] If we give up the straw-man version of that thesis which takes it to say that 'truth' is whatever this or that individual makes of it, and instead more charitably take it to say that humankind collectively constitutes the relevant tribunal, then (he argues) we shall not be so easily won over by the standard anti-relativist case. To which of course the opposite party responds with a more-or-less refurbished statement of that case which denies that there is a genuine difference – a difference worthy of philosophic note – between the (supposed) point-scoring travesty of relativist thought and the version put forward as a corrective to it. That is to say, for the realist or the rationalist any move of this sort is sure to leave its proponents in double jeopardy since they will find themselves exposed first to co-option by the advocates of unashamed, full-strength relativism and then – in direct consequence of that – to demolition by philosophers who have not only Plato and his lineal descendants but also (irresistibly) truth and reason lined up on their side. However, such arguments will not impress the relativist so long as he or she takes strength from the claim that has become something of a staple in contemporary re-runs of the ancient quarrel. This is the idea that realism (or objectivism) about truth is inherently self-refuting since it places a strictly unbridgeable gulf between such truth, conceived as recognition- or verification-transcendent, and whatever counts as knowledge (or justified true belief) by our own human, all-too-human epistemic lights.[5]

On this view we can opt for realist (objectivist) truth but with no possible means of knowing, discovering or knowing ourselves to have discovered it. Alternatively we can opt for an anti-realist conception of truth as epistemically constrained or recognition-dependent and hence as lying by very definition within the scope and limits of human grasp. However, this second option, though currently attractive to many, comes only at the far from negligible price of giving up that objectivist idea. For along with it, the realist will argue, goes the highly intuitive as well as scientifically well-attested notion that truth might always turn out to elude our present-best powers of perceptual warrant, cognitive command or probative reasoning in logic, mathematics and the formal sciences. If we endorse the anti-realist line and consent to take 'true', for all practical purposes, as synonymous with '"true" to the best of our capacity for discovering, ascertaining, inferring, proving, or deducing the truth-claim in question' then we shall automatically fail to explain how belief has ever fallen short of knowledge, or how there could ever be partial, i.e. veridical-so-far-as-they-go states of knowledge, or again, how knowledge could ever have made any progress through and beyond such states.[6] The only way we can hang onto that idea, so the realist will urge, is by likewise hanging onto the basic claim that progress comes about through a truth-conducive or truth-approximative movement of thought whereby knowledge replaces an earlier state of ignorance or manages to close the gap between truth and what previously counted as truth according to the verdict of educated opinion, best belief, optimal judgement or widespread agreement among those presumed best qualified to know.[7] These latter kinds of formulation, along with others to similar effect, are more typically adopted by thinkers who incline toward anti-realism as an antidote to epistemological scepticism (since, to repeat, it seems to bring truth safely back within the scope of human attainability) while none the less acknowledging a certain anxiety – a sense of normative deficit or alethic shortfall – with regard to the strict anti-realist claim that truth *just is* whatever counts as truth according to the verdict of present-best knowledge.[8] To be sure, anti-realism promises an end to the sorts of wholesale epistemological doubt conjured up by Descartes' *malin génie* and sundry later variations on the theme. Still it is liable to strike anyone with a reasonably robust sense of everyday or scientific realities as failing to allow for that basic distinction between objective truth and present-best belief which alone makes room for a convincing, philosophically cogent account of how knowledge both accrues and can be known to have accrued.

Over the past few decades a good number of philosophers have devoted a good deal of argumentative effort and ingenuity to the task of resolving this dilemma on terms acceptable to both parties. That is, they have tried to come up with some theory, proposal or formula that would meet the realist demand for something more substantive in the way of specifiable truth-content while at the same time leaning far enough in an anti-realist direction as to characterise truth as epistemically constrained – or redefine it (with Dummett) as 'warranted assertibility' – and thereby render knowledge proof against the slings and arrows of sceptical fortune. These efforts have taken various forms and gone under various names, among them 'internal realism', 'framework realism', 'quasi-realism', the 'natural ontological attitude' and response-dependence (or response-dispositional) theory.[9] What they all have in common, despite certain otherwise significant differences of view, is the idea that fully fledged realism is the last thing needed by anyone who seeks to vindicate the claims of everyday or scientific knowledge since it will always fall prey to a (supposedly) knock-down counter-argument, i.e. that it places such knowledge forever and intrinsically beyond human reach.[10] Hence their diverse but similarly motivated efforts to pre-empt that rejoinder or head off that sceptical threat by devising a middle-ground position that would yield no hostages to fortune – stop safely short of endorsing the existence of objective (recognition-transcendent) truths – but would none the less disclaim any overt commitment to an anti-realist approach. Most often the reason for this latter kind of reluctance is anti-realism's proneness to invite the same variety of charges routinely brought against scepticism on grounds of its purported failure to explain or accommodate our knowledge of the growth of knowledge. That is to say, any whole-hog endorsement of the doctrine would leave its proponent over-exposed to counter-arguments based on the prima facie powerful claim that human enquiry has made certain widely accepted or hard-to-deny scientific advances that cannot be accounted for except in terms of a tendentially progressive or deepening knowledge of the various objects, properties or structures that constitute its topic-domain. Yet it is far from clear, as I have argued elsewhere, that this attempt to strike a viable median stance can avoid leaning over in one or the other direction, that is toward a realism that dare not quite speak its name for fear of sceptical challenge or an anti-realism that is likewise held in check by its need to avoid any full-strength (and hence more plainly problematical) statement of the case.[11]

Usually it is the anti-realist temptation that exerts the greater pull since it seems to offer the best chance of a knowledge-preserving response to the challenge of epistemological scepticism along with its sundry latter-day relativist, constructivist or 'strong'-sociological offshoots.[12] After all, it is that kind of sceptical argument that has formed a kind of ironic or confidence-sapping counterpoint to the claims of science – or everyday knowledge – to be something more than an outlook or mindset grounded in best belief among those believed best qualified to know. If 'internal realism' or one of the above-mentioned substitutes for realism in its fully fledged problem-creating form can perfectly well do the main job (i.e. recapture the argumentative high ground) without drawing too much sceptical fire then by the same token, so advocates maintain, it will manage to do what cannot be achieved by either of its purebred (hence all the more vulnerable) parent doctrines. By somehow splitting the difference between them – avoiding their respective bad liabilities while conserving what is most philosophically attractive or intuitively plausible about each – an approach along these lines can (it is hoped) offer a solution to the single most vexing problem in post-Kantian epistemology and philosophy of science. For Kant it was who first opened up, or who most conspicuously tried and failed to mend, that troublesome rift between mind and world, subject and object, or concepts of understanding and the sensuous intuitions that alone provide them with substantive or determinate content.[13] Moreover, it was Kant whose relentlessly dualist approach – despite his constant protestations to contrary effect – led on to the typecast split between 'analytic' and 'continental' modes of thought, deriving as they do in large part from issues that arise respectively in the 'Transcendental Analytic' and 'Transcendental Aesthetic' of the First *Critique*.[14]

This in turn had the unfortunate long-range effect of closing analytic philosophers' minds to some highly pertinent resources available within that 'other' tradition, chief among them the phenomenological enquiry into aspects of thought, knowledge, judgement and experience that has been so central to mainland European philosophy in the wake of Husserl's inaugural endeavours.[15] Had Kant not deepened the dualist rift in its various manifestations then they might have felt free to go further along the investigative path that was flagged up briefly by some of their number – such as Ryle, Austin and nowadays Dummett – and not been put off by the analytically ingrained idea that any such enquiry must fall prey to some kind of subjectivist or psychologistic error.[16] In which case, to continue this counter-factual line of thought, we should not perhaps have witnessed those sundry reinventions of the Kantian wheel that have characterised recent analytical attempts to move beyond the impasse bequeathed by old-style logical empiricism. That is to say, these thinkers – notably John McDowell – have proposed a selective retrieval of Kant in the hope that his approach to epistemological issues, once relieved of its surplus metaphysical baggage, might yet point a promising way forward from the doldrums into which analytic philosophy was driven by its espousal of a drastically dichotomous conception of mind and world, or again (in the familiar Chinese-box way) of the faculties whereby mind was supposed to acquire its knowledge of the world.[17] Thus McDowell suggests that we switch our attention from Kant's problematical since plainly

dualist talk of bringing 'intuitions' under adequate or answering 'concepts' and instead focus on his notion of 'receptivity' and
'spontaneity' as powers that are so closely intertwined – so strictly
inseparable one from the other – that even to assign them such different names is an artefact of discourse liable to generate further
misapprehension.

However, one is inclined to turn his point around and ask why the
dichotomy in question should be viewed as merely a nominal distinction or an inconsequential *façon de parler*, given that McDowell is
no more able to dispense with it – no further along toward a genuine
working monism – than was Kant when he deployed either this or
his intuition/concept pair. In short, the idea that a happy deliverance
from all those vexing dualities might be had by revisiting Kant (of all
philosophers!) is somewhat like going to Hume in quest of a robust
theory of causal powers, or – more pointedly – to Descartes in hope
of a common-sense riposte to the demon of sceptical doubt. All the
same one can see, just about, why it might have seemed a viable
option in the face of those dilemmas that have plagued the discourse
of analytic philosophy since the heyday of logical empiricism. If
they have lingered on well into the period of widespread retrench-
ment sometimes described as 'post-analytic' this is partly because
they received not so much their wished-for quietus as their deeply
problematical *ne plus ultra* through the wholesale demolition-job on
that movement and its basic presuppositions that Quine undertook
with such iconoclastic relish.[18] In this context the recourse to certain
elements of Kantian epistemology – its claim to have overcome the
sceptical upshot of Humean empiricism and its conjoint challenge
to the purebred rationalist 'way of ideas' – is by no means hard to
understand and might even be welcomed in so far as it reveals an
increased openness to ideas and arguments with their source in the
'other', mainland European tradition. All the same, any notion that
Kant might provide the needful resources for awaking analytic philosophy from its epistemological slumbers – for setting it on course
toward an adequate account of the mind/world or concept/intuition
nexus – is sadly belied by Kant's own failure and that of his present-
day advocates to provide anything like a cogent demonstration
that their various terminological dichotomies are indeed just that,
i.e. matters of language only and by no means indicative of deeper
dualist commitments.

II

I have written elsewhere about the sundry variations on this Kantian theme rehearsed by post-Quinean analytic philosophers, most of them seeking to head off any charge of 'metaphysical' indulgence or over-commitment by purportedly bringing it down to earth through some infusion of pragmatist, contextualist, framework-relativist or naturalistic elements.[19] The upshot, to repeat, is a highly unstable middle-ground or third-way 'solution' which seeks to combine the argumentative strengths of a realist outlook – chiefly its advantageous position with regard to issues of scientific progress and our knowledge of the growth of knowledge – with a nod to the anti-realist quarter or a shrewdly placed concessionary clause when it comes to questions concerning the existence of objective, mind-independent or recognition-transcendent truths. For in the end that stance cannot be maintained except through a precarious balancing act which involves a constant effort to steady the scales through a trade-off between one and the other set of considerations, and a consequent failure to secure any reasonably firm or principled grounds on which to mount the alternative case. Quite simply – and the issue really is quite simple, whatever the epicyclic complexities to which this debate has given rise – *either* there are truths as the realist conceives them, i.e. that may or may not be captured in our various well-formed statements, propositions, hypotheses, conjectures, theorems, predictions, covering-law generalisations and so forth, *or else* that claim must be thought strictly unintelligible since truth cannot possibly exceed the bounds of evidence, proof, epistemic grasp, demonstrative reason, perceptual warrant, documentary record or other such providers of assertoric warrant. In this context *tertium non datur* for the same reason that classical (bivalent) logic accommodates no third truth-value, i.e. no middle category such as might be paraphrased 'neither-true-nor-false', or 'both-true-and-false', or 'located at some intermediate point on the scale (e.g. of probabilities) running from absolute or determinate truth to absolute or determinate falsehood'.[20]

Thus anti-realists, especially in mathematics and the formal sciences, tend to favour a three-valued logic such that unproven conjectures, theorems or hypotheses are thought of as belonging to Dummett's 'disputed class', or the class of statements to which the values 'true' and 'false' have no application. For the realist, on the other hand, it is not just conceivable but downright prerequisite to any thought-procedure capable of bringing about genuine advances in knowledge that truth should be thought of as always potentially surpassing the limits of cognitive or epistemic grasp. So long as the statement in question is well formed, its syntax correct and its constituent terms sufficiently precise then we are justified in claiming to know that it possesses an objective truth-value (that it is either true or false) quite aside from our present-best – or even our future-best attainable – state of knowledge concerning it. This is because there are certain formal proof-procedures or modes of reasoning, chief among them *reductio ad absurdum*, that would lack all demonstrative force were it not for the validity of a classical precept – that of double-negation-elimination – which decrees that 'two negatives make a positive'. That is to say, a statement can be verified (a theorem confirmed, etc.) by showing its negation to entail some false or plainly unacceptable consequence and hence to require that the truth of the statement be acknowledged as a matter of logical necessity.[21] Anti-realists have to forego this argumentative or conceptual resource since, for them, valid reasoning doesn't depend upon adherence to the classical axioms of bivalence and excluded middle, and therefore can – indeed must – get along without any such assurance that double negatives cancel out. Hence the readiness of anti-realists (aka intuitionists) like Dummett to grasp this particular nettle and propose that we switch our preferred way of thinking from the idea of mathematical discovery as a striking out into new and previously uncharted terrain to the idea of it as more like a process of artistic or imaginative creation.

To this way of thinking what typifies a breakthrough moment is not the encounter with objective conditions or constraints on thought – as when, on the realist account, reason confronts a *reductio ad absurdum* or other such logical dilemma – but rather the sense of open-ended possibility that constantly invents new conceptual terrain for its own further exploration. So it is that mathematicians may properly be said to make up the story as they go along, or as the story unfolds at their creative prompting, just so long as that creativity is held in check by a due respect for the scope and limits of human comprehension or a well-attuned sense of what falls within the bounds of warranted assertibility. This latter phrase, rather than 'truth', is the anti-realists' favoured way of talking since it signals their non-commitment to objectivism in any guise – whether as regards the formal, natural or social and human sciences – and hence their invulnerability to the kinds of full-strength sceptical argument that often begin by driving a wedge between objectivist truth and humanly attainable knowledge, and then proceed to skewer the realist on just that (supposedly) for him inescapable dilemma.[22] For the third-way theorist of whatever precise or technical philosophic persuasion any argument along these lines needs tempering by a healthy respect for the findings of science and a robust sense of the various respects in which we can reasonably claim to know – rather than unreasonably call into doubt – the evidence of certain striking advances in our stock of knowledge to date or in the range, depth and explanatory power of our best theoretical accounts of it.

However, it is doubtful (I would say impossible) that any such tempering effect can be had by appealing to a range of realist criteria, no matter how elaborately qualified or hedged around, which belong to a different, indeed a squarely opposed mode of thought and one that the third-way theorist has rejected in order to head off the sceptical challenge. That is to say, they are in danger of ending up with the worst of both worlds by losing whatever notional advantage the anti-realist might wish to claim in this latter regard while leaning far enough in an anti-realist direction to void any token or accommodating gestures with regard to the realist case. It seems to me that this diagnosis applies to a whole large swathe of developments in recent epistemology and philosophy of science, all of which – whatever their otherwise diverse characters – can be shown either to occupy a region of strictly uninhabitable no-man's-land or else to give up their ecumenical claim by surreptitiously embracing a full-strength version of the realist or anti-realist argument.[23] Nowhere is this conflict plainer to see than in the project undertaken by a systematic thinker like Crispin Wright to specify exactly the conditions under which diverse statements or judgements in sundry 'areas of discourse' should be counted either truth-apt (i.e. accountable to standards of bivalent truth/falsehood) or better suited to other, less stringent or perhaps more epistemologically nuanced modes of evaluation.[24] Thus Wright comes up with a range of candidate terms to mark the different kinds and degrees of approximation to objective truth, most prominent among them 'superassertibility' and 'cognitive command'. The former he defines as applying to a statement 'if and only if it is, or can be, warranted and some warrant for it would survive arbitrarily close scrutiny of its pedigree and arbitrarily extensive increments to or other forms of improvement of our information', while in the latter case 'any difference of opinion will be such that there are considerations quite independent of the conflict which, if known about, would mandate withdrawal of one (or both) of the contending views'.[25]

It would seem to be 'cognitive command' that comes closer to conceding the existence of objective (verification-transcendent) truth since it adduces 'considerations quite independent of the conflict' that would serve to settle the issue or restore bivalence, whereas 'superassertibility' clearly stops short of any such decisive concession to the realist since it locates the furthest limit of our quest for truth at the point where some statement, theory or hypothesis has passed every available test for veracity and fared adequately under such testing. Any room for 'truth' on this account can be stretched only so far as to define it in optimized epistemological terms and thereby render it pretty much synonymous with a Peircean or limit-point pragmatist conception of 'truth at the end of enquiry'.[26] Yet Wright's conception of 'cognitive command' also turns out to be hedged around with qualifying clauses that keep it from ever quite crossing that crucial line between 'truth to the very best of our knowledge' or 'truth near as dammit, epistemically speaking' and 'truth as objective and therefore as always potentially transcending our utmost powers of proof or ascertainment'. After all, in his own careful phrasing, the sorts of 'consideration' that would force one or both parties in dispute to shift argumentative ground are factors that would have this effect only 'if known about', rather than – as the realist or objectivist would insist – placing their previous beliefs in the wrong whether or not such corrective knowledge was within epistemic ken.

Of course the passage might be understood as implying no such thing but rather as addressed purely to the epistemological issue (i.e. the issue of what is 'known about' and what kinds of claim are licensed by that knowledge) and hence as taking no position, realist or anti-realist, on the question of objective truth. However, in view of Wright's general acceptance that anti-realism has set the terms for debate, it seems fair to conclude that those hedging clauses are there because they offer a readily available line of defence against any notion that he might be yielding ground – or capitulating outright – to a realist conception of truth as ontologically distinct from whatever state of knowledge happens to prevail within some given (no matter how expert) cognitive community. To this extent he is typical of many current thinkers, especially in the response-dispositionalist camp, who take it for granted that the burden of proof rests chiefly on those who seek to defend such a realist stance rather than on the anti-realist whose arguments are often of a highly refined or philosophically sophisticated character although (or perhaps just because) they go so strongly against the intuitive, common-sense or everyday-practical as well as orthodox scientific grain. Moreover, that assumption nowadays runs so deep – mainly in consequence of the 'linguistic turn' across manifold branches of philosophy – that it has led some proponents to extend the remit of response-dispositional or kindred compromise 'solutions' even to the realm of mathematics, logic and the formal sciences where they are likely to encounter maximum resistance from a realist or objectivist position.[27]

There is no such readiness for compromise about Dummett's intuitionist philosophy of mathematics, i.e. his claim that, here as elsewhere, the limits of 'truth' must also be the bounds to what lies within reach of mathematical knowledge, ascertainment or demonstrative proof. This sort of argument has gained further credence from its fitting in neatly with the Wittgensteinian conception of language as the basis of communal understanding, and moreover of communal understanding as the ultimate horizon of intelligibility and final court of appeal when it comes to issues of knowledge and truth.[28] What sets Wright's thinking somewhat apart from that currently widespread nexus of ideas is his determination not to let go of certain basic realist precepts, above all the claim that truth cannot be reduced *tout court* or without remainder to that which communally counts as such according to received or prevalent epistemic norms. His resistance comes mainly from a clear conviction – in company with a good many advocates of 'realism' in various internal, framework-relative or likewise qualified forms – that full-strength anti-realism gets so far out of touch with scientific as well as everyday conceptions of knowledge and truth that there must be some alternative which stops well short of that pyrrhic outcome yet yields no hostages to sceptical fortune by endorsing the opposite (i.e. full-strength realist) thesis. However, Wright's determination not to make either mistake – to steer a judicious course, Odysseus-like, between those perilous extremes – has the effect of skewing his project very markedly toward the anti-realist pole. After all, the appearance of even-handedness is something that it shares with Dummett's express policy of testing the realist and anti-realist options across the widest possible range of subject areas, suspending any prejudice either way, and thus finding out, through a case-specific method, which approach best suits some given region of discourse. For of course it is just the realist's point that these fine distinctions of epistemic warrant – such as Wright's 'superassertibility' and 'cognitive command' or Dummett's allowance for the different criteria applying to different regions – are pertinent in this context of debate only to the extent that truth has already been redefined, in anti-realist terms, as epistemically or evidentially constrained. In which case any effort, however scrupulous, to make allowance for the various kinds and degrees of such constraint can only strike the realist as far from even-handed since it starts out from this basic assumption that full-strength (objectivist) realism is simply not on the cards for serious philosophic purposes.

All the same Wright's commitment to a tentative way of proceeding is more genuine – more open to the various claims and counter-claims on both sides – than Dummett's for the most part very definite espousal of an anti-realist standpoint which he clearly regards as the default position and as capable of trumping the realist opponent on metaphysical as well as on logico-semantic grounds. What chiefly accounts for this difference is Wright's deep unease with what he plainly regards as the strong likelihood that anti-realism will be pushed by some of its adherents in the direction of an outright (and to him just as plainly unacceptable) outlook of socio-cultural linguistic relativism. With Dummett, conversely, there seems to be no such anxiety even as concerns those touchy subject areas, like historical discourse, where anti-realism – or the idea, as he puts it, that 'gaps in our knowledge' are equivalent to 'gaps in reality' – might be thought to have some decidedly worrisome, not to say disastrous implications.[29]

Indeed it is clear from some of his more explicit statements in this vein that Dummett sees the realist as actually much likelier to find herself drawn in a relativist or sceptical direction by having to confront the realism-generated rift between objective, recognition-transcendent truth and humanly attainable knowledge. Moreover, as I have said, his programme finds its point of departure and its most favoured source of (supposedly) clinching examples in the philosophy of mathematics where anti-realism equates with the intuitionist principle that truth extends just so far as the limits of demonstrative, formal or constructible proof. Wright is less inclined than Dummett to treat anti-realism as belonging to a technical sphere of debate largely separate from issues around cultural-linguistic relativism, or indeed as offering the best (since metaphysically and logically most cogent) anti-relativist line of defence. Still it is apt to strike any reader of his book *Truth and Objectivity* that the title is something of a misnomer since 'objectivity' pretty much drops out of the picture or comes to signify something more like 'the attempt to be as impartial, judicious, or "objective" as one can'. The kinds of truth-claim that most occupy his interest are plausibly located somewhere on a scale that runs from the wholly or largely response-dependent to those which pass muster only on condition of their being shown to meet the most stringent demands of epistemic warrant. Even with the latter sorts of case what we have is not 'realism' in any sense of the term that would satisfy thinkers who count themselves philosophically committed to that position, i.e. who take it that there is always the possibility of a coming-apart between objective, recognition-transcendent truth and 'truth' to the best of presently existing or even best-attainable knowledge.

III

As I have said, Wright is well aware of the twin dangers that attend any overly dogmatic or insufficiently critical adoption of the anti-realist stance. Thinkers who veer that way will either be pushed so far out on a logico-metaphysical limb as to lose touch with the commonplace experience of knowledge-acquisition or else feel obliged to endorse some weaker but none the less philosophically disabling internal-realist, framework-relativist or other such compromise position. What is going on in such cases, Wright's among them, is a constant swinging back and forth between epistemological and metaphysical issues whereby the desire to avoid falling into the sceptic's or the relativist's well-laid trap gives rise to an ultra-cautious or risk-averse mindset when it comes to the prospects for narrowing the gap between knowledge and truth. The basic thought is: let us take just as much as we need from anti-realism (i.e. its supposed capacity for blocking sceptical or relativist arguments at source) but reject any version of it that threatens to cross the Maginot Line between metaphysics and epistemology.

However, I suggest, this strategy most often turns out to have just the opposite effect since the two sorts of issue cannot be so firmly or safely held apart. Rather the result, most often, is that anti-realism – even when adopted in a low-strength or diluted form – sets the terms for debate and effectively decrees that any talk of 'truth' will have to be justified by recourse to epistemic norms. From which it follows that any realist thesis concerning truth (i.e. any argument that might be mustered against relativism on that basis) cannot go beyond the emollient concession that 'realism' has to be construed always relative to this or that conceptual scheme, ontological framework, metaphysical worldview, Wittgensteinian 'language game' or communal 'form of life'. Thus anti-realism, like response-dependence theory,

purports to offer an escape route from the travails of epistemological
scepticism but does so – if at all – only at the cost of rendering all
truth-claims 'internal' to some such scheme and hence just as open
to the realist's charge of evading the issue as regards the existence of
objective (epistemically unconstrained or recognition-transcendent)
truths. What promises salvation from these sorts of merely artificial or hyper-induced problem turns out to constitute another such
problem and one that is all the more vexing for its claim to have
transposed the whole debate into a different, scepticism-proof key.

There are two distinct issues with respect to this promiscuous
running together of metaphysical and epistemological concerns. One
is the way that it induces thinkers of a broadly realist/objectivist persuasion but impressed by the resourcefulness and ingenuity of certain
sceptical arguments to plump for a 'solution' that abandons the
mine-strewn terrain of epistemology and instead takes comfort from
the metaphysical idea that knowledge is in no way tied to the reality
or otherwise of that which (nonsensically) purports to transcend the
scope and limits of knowledge. The second is its tendency to side-
track debate from particular, sometimes well-documented episodes in
the history of science and other disciplines where truth would prima
facie seem to be centrally involved and redirect interest to issues of
a logico-semantic-metaphysical character which leave little room
for detailed engagement with the relevant kinds of truth-seeking or
knowledge-conducive procedure. Together they provide good reason
for concluding that anti-realism is a natural ally of relativism rather
than a strictly irrefutable means of showing that relativism is misconceived or downright nonsensical since knowledge cannot possibly
come apart from truth or vice versa. For of course this line of argument is distinctly double-edged, pointing as it does with equal (indeed
greater) plausibility to the relativist claim that truth *just is* whatever
counts as such according to currently accepted norms of knowledge
or epistemic warrant. Prima facie there would seem strong warrant
for the case that anti-realism blocks the sceptical or relativist lines
of argument at source by making it simply inconceivable – a kind
of transcendental illusion – that knowledge could ever be decoupled
from truth, or objectivity from that which decides the standards of
'objective', truth-seeking enquiry within some given community of
knowers. Yet of course it is just that possibility that realists need to
maintain if they are not to go the way of those various compromise
settlers whose solutions to the problem do rather obviously court the
charge of throwing out the baby with the bathwater.

No doubt there is a sense – albeit an unsatisfactory and even philosophically disreputable sense – in which the issue between realism and anti-realism comes down to a matter of intellectual temperament. Then we should just have to treat it as one of those endlessly divisive philosophic topoi where no answer or solution can ever be had since the whole debate stems from a clash of intuitions whereby it is self-evident either that there must exist truths (a vast number of them) beyond the furthest range of our present or future-best cognitive grasp or else that quite simply it doesn't make sense to assert any such claim since, after all, we are unable to specify any-thing regarding their nature, content, entailment-relations, or (most crucially for the anti-realist) their means of recognition/verification. This seems to be the gist of a curious passage by Dummett where he pretty much concedes that his own four-decade-long programme of research – a matter, as he often claimed, of even-handedly exploring the applicability of realist or anti-realist approaches to different areas of discourse – might in fact answer to needs or inclinations that fall well outside the range of philosophic accountability as defined in his own more characteristic logico-semantic-metaphysical mode. Thus:

> [r]ealism about the past entails that there are numerous true propo-sitions forever in principle unknowable. The effects of a past event may simply dissipate . . . To the realist, this is just part of the human condition; the anti-realist feels unknowability in principle to be simply intolerable and prefers to view our evidence for and memory of the past as constitutive of it. For him, there cannot be a past fact no evidence of which exists to be discovered, because it is the exist-ence of such evidence that would make it a fact, if it were one.[30]

This applies not only to historical statements but also to a great many subject domains where the issue works out in similar terms. On the one hand is a truth-based or realist conception of enquiry according to which present-best belief can always fall short of knowledge and present-best knowledge fall short of truth in certain (presently unknowable) respects. On the other hand is an anti-realist conception according to which neither of these claims can stand up philosophically since they both propound a strictly unintelligible, i.e. objectivist (verification-transcendent or epistemically unconstrained) doctrine of truth. Certainly it spans the full range from empiri-cally based investigative disciplines, via those dependent mainly on archival research or documentary record, to the natural sciences and thence to mathematics and logic where Dummett's arguments were first honed and where they find their most congenial – as well as (to many) their most strongly counter-intuitive – field of application.

That temperament – even intellectual temperament – should be thought to play a role in such deep-laid differences of view is of course an idea much likelier to find favour among psychologists or cultural historians than philosophers, especially those of an analytic mind whose antennae are hypersensitive to any hint of 'psychologism' or subjectivism in the treatment of such issues.[31] And indeed, at least if the realist is right, then there is a truth of the matter with respect to the issue between realists and anti-realists which has absolutely nothing to do with temperamental leanings in either direction or with the sorts of sentiment that find voice in the passage from Dummett cited above. Whether anti-realism lends support to the contrary claim that such leanings should be thought of as playing a role – a legitimate role – in deciding one's outlook on issues like these is a question not so easily answered since it seems to receive very different answers from Dummett. That it does point that way is strongly suggested by his talk of the anti-realist finding it simply 'intolerable' to suppose that there may be truths about the past that are 'unknowable in principle', and of their 'preference' for deeming our knowledge somehow 'constitutive' of past events. Still there is a clear enough sense in which Dummett's project asks to be taken on its philosophic merits – more precisely: on its claims to logico-semantic and metaphysical correctness – rather than taken as a mode of oblique self-revelation or as belonging to a genre of oddly displaced confessional narrative.

However, to set against that, there is the evidence from Dummett's acknowledged mentor in the philosophy of mathematics, the intuitionist Brouwer, that in this domain at least the idea of objectivity is one that can very well be dispensed with and replaced (if there is the need for an alternative motivating mindset) by the idea of mathematical discovery – for instance, the devising of a new proof procedure – as closely analogous to emotional experiences such as that of falling in love.[32] Nor is one obliged to ignore the various signs in Dummett's work, especially his giving credence (from an anti-realist viewpoint) to the idea of prayer as having some power to influence the course or affect the outcome of past events, that his project may itself be motivated in part by certain predisposed – or at any rate far from neutral – theological commitments.[33] However, this need not after all be taken to imply that the debate between realists and anti-realists in the end comes down to a clash of opposing temperaments and, beyond that, must be counted incapable of any resolution on reasoned, principled or other than personal/preferential grounds. For the realist does put up a range of distinctive philosophical arguments – those that I have rehearsed at various points in the course of this chapter – for not so counting it and for supposing, on the contrary, that realism has considerations in its favour that go beyond mere temperamental affinity or affective disposition on the part of this or that respondent. Rather the case has everything to do with its passing muster by standards that philosophy (rather than psychology) is best equipped to provide, and which also look to science (rather than, say, the sociology or cultural history of changing views on this topic) for their appropriate means of assessment and validation.

Of course this argument will cut no ice with those in the opposite camp for whom any talk of realism or truth – let alone objectivity – is just a sign of the utterer's being in the grip of a deluded meta-physical idea, one that leads not only to the endless frustration of its own impossible quest but also, very often, to the point of a reactive giving up on that quest and a consequent retreat to epistemological scepticism. Once again the anti-realists can be seen to follow Kant, in this case his parable-like cautionary tales in the First *Critique* concerning the various perils to which thought is subject if it leaves the safe ground of attainable knowledge where intuitions are reliably 'brought under' adequate concepts.[34] Then it is prone to strike out into regions of speculative *terra incognita* where pure reason may engage with issues of the highest importance for ethics, politics or theology but where knowledge (understanding) should properly fear to tread if it is not to become lost in the travails of empirically ungrounded and conceptually undisciplined metaphysical enquiry. If there is any confusion on this cardinal point – any tendency to think that these deployments of speculative reason should or could be expected to yield some advance in our determinate knowledge of ourselves or the world – then that hope is predestined not only to a state of permanent non-fulfilment but also to the role of a perpetual temptation or seductive power over thought.

It is here, I suggest, that modern anti-realism takes its cue from Kant, albeit at a large doctrinal remove (approaching these issues as it does from a standpoint informed or in large part defined by the lat-ter-day linguistic turn) and, to all appearances at least, without any-thing like Kant's burden of surplus metaphysical baggage. However, one may doubt whether the much-vaunted turn to language as a bottom line or ultimate horizon of enquiry has not brought along with it many of the same issues and problems – some of them distinctly metaphysical in character – that both preoccupied Kant as a matter of express philosophic concern and arose to complicate the tenor of his arguments despite and against their avowed intent. Thus anti-realism shares Kant's desire to beat the bounds of knowledge, or of cognitive intelligibility, by decreeing certain otherwise enticing ideas to be strictly beyond the pale, chief among them the realist idea that we can somehow have *knowledge* concerning the existence of objective, epistemically unconstrained or recognition-transcendent truths. Moreover, it makes that cautionary case by way of an argument – the hard-worked anti-realist thesis that talk of 'objectivity' is inherently self-stultifying since mortgaged to a wholly unattainable and hence scepticism-inducing conception of truth – that finds its closest analogue in Kant's warning of the perils that our quest for knowledge is sure to run into if it seeks to overstep the limits of phenomenal (sensory) cognition and establish truths pertaining to the realm of noumenal reality, or the supra-phenomenal 'thing in itself'. Where Kant deems this a sure way of falling into metaphysical error, or of conjuring strictly insoluble (pseudo-)problems through a misuse of powers belonging to the exercise of reason in its speculative mode, the anti-realist issues a similar caution concerning the strictly insuperable barrier that thought encounters when it struggles to conceptualise an objective, mind-independent, recognition-transcendent reality which *ipso facto* lies altogether beyond its utmost cognitive or epistemic reach.

IV

Nowadays there are many philosophers of a broadly naturalistic bent who would see nothing more in all this wire-drawn metaphysical (or anti-metaphysical) argumentation than an expression of certain foregone commitments or predilections with their source in some corresponding state or condition of the subject's mind/brain.[35] All the same, and whatever the occasional evidence of temperamental bias in the writing of those on either side, we are not (as I have said) reduced to treating the issue between realists and anti-realists as in the end just a matter of personal preference and therefore as incapable of any resolution on reasoned and principled philosophic grounds. For there is a great difference – all the difference in the world, one is tempted to say – between realist arguments from the evidence of scientific progress or our knowledge of the growth of knowledge and, on the other hand, a Dummett-type anti-realist avowal of finding it somehow 'intolerable', that is, a notion quite simply too disturbing, demeaning or not to be borne that there might exists truths (historical, natural-scientific, mathematical or whatever) that exceed the furthest bounds of human proof or ascertainment. Those who espouse the anti-realist line on the grounds of its avoiding the standard range of sceptical (anti-objectivist) arguments will need to confront the more sizeable challenge of explaining how the everyday or scientific evidence can point so clearly to a realist interpretation, that is, unless they wish to explain that evidence away by falling back to some notion of miracles or cosmic coincidence.[36] And if, as so often, they pin their hopes of deliverance from all these pesky problems on a doctrine of truth as recognition-dependent or epistemically constrained – a doctrine that claims the notional advantage of bringing it safely back within epistemic bounds – then this will carry costs (among them the necessity of devising some implausibly complex or baroque theory of empirical or assertoric warrant) which may very well strike most observers as simply not worth the effort.

At any rate the variety of scepticism in question is so hugely generalised and so much at odds with every aspect of our lived experience as well as our grasp of scientific history and method as to look a very papery sort of tiger by comparison with the problems that anti-realists and others of a kindred persuasion tend to create for themselves when obliged to come up with answers to the range of typical realist rejoinders. Such is, for instance, Bas van Fraassen's perversely ingenious argument for a form of constructive empiricism that would have us treat observation-statements concerning readily visible, i.e. macroscopic, objects as permissibly bearing a realist interpretation but would deny that title to any object that exceeded the compass of unaided (or moderately aided) human perceptual powers, whether by reason of its smallness, vastness, remoteness, celerity, evanescence or other such elusive properties.[37] Thus on his account – absurdly, from a realist standpoint – we should have every reason to credit the reality of a small planetary moon viewed from close up through a spaceship window, perhaps with the help of an optical telescope, but not the reality of that same moon when viewed through even the best designed and most expertly engineered radio-telescope. Or again, we might properly call a micro-organism 'real' so long as it showed up with reasonable clarity under an optical microscope but not if its viewing required the use of an electron microscope or other such sophisticated piece of equipment, no matter how reliable its operation and how well-proven its working principles despite the technological complexities involved.

It is the latter point that anti-realists (or constructive empiricists) most often exploit in making their case for a suspension of belief in the reality of items on a scale beyond the cognisance of naked or moderately enhanced human perception. However, it is then left open to their adversaries – among them instrumental realists such as Ian Hacking – to remark, sensibly enough, that unaided perception has seldom been a good (and more often a downright misleading) guide in matters scientific, especially when joined to a common-sense-intuitive worldview that enshrines the dictates of received, e.g. Ptolemaic, wisdom as if in truth they involved nothing more than straightforward perceptual self-evidence.[38] Moreover, as Hacking points out, we may often be much better off relying on sophisticated equipment whose design features and modus operandi its users understand pretty well – in a jointly theoretical and practical way – than making 'reality' dependent on our own, highly fallible senses or on the use of only such instruments (rather primitive ones at that) which happen to fit van Fraassen's oddly specified constructive-empiricist bill.[39] These are the kinds of anti-sceptical argument that bank on a knowledge and a detailed understanding of real-world situated human enquiry, whether in the natural sciences or in other, perhaps less specialised regions of investigative thought where the various practices of hypothesis-construction, theory-building, obser-vation, prediction, confirmation and falsification also have their legitimate place. In this respect they stand squarely opposed to that whole line of thought which takes anti-realism (or some variation on the theme) as the sole means of defence against full-strength episte-mological scepticism. In addition they provide far stronger eviden-tial, argumentative and principled grounds for advancing the realist claim than anything yet brought up to support the anti-realist idea of its being somehow inconceivable that truths should exist beyond our epistemic ken, or that portions of reality might lie forever outside the furthest bounds of human exploration.

The latter thesis seems to be advanced most often in that curiously bipolar form – a strongly marked, sometimes overt temperamental bias together with arguments of a highly metaphysical character albeit conducted very much in the formal or logico-semantic mode – which typifies Dummett's thought. On both counts there is some-thing very odd, and something that realists will think altogether off the point, about a manner of reasoning that arrives at such extraordinary (not just heterodox or counter-intuitive) conclusions on the basis of a readily professed aversion to the idea of truths that are not (or cannot be) known. Thus the commitment to anti-realism may be thought to follow logically enough granted certain highly questionable premises but gains absolutely nothing thereby in terms of scientific or everyday-practical warrant. After all, his case for anti-realism stands up against the standard range of realist rejoinders only provided Dummett is correct in stipulating his three requirements for a statement to possess genuine assertoric force, i.e. that it be uttered by someone so placed as to meet the conditions for acquiring, recognising and manifesting an ability to deploy said statement with adequate probative or epistemic warrant under the right sorts of warrant-constitutive circumstance. Those requirements can themselves be justified solely – if at all – by the basic anti-realist premise that truth be cashed out in terms of warranted assertibility, and the latter construed as entirely dependent on our various linguistic transactions or modes of communicative discourse. Yet, as realists are wont to retort, there is a strange sense of inverted priorities about this readiness of some philosophers to adopt a highly speculative argument from a field rife with doubts and disagreements like that of philosophical semantics rather than those other, more tried and tested kinds of reasoning – such as inference to the best explanation – that find their home ground and chief source of evidence in the natural sciences.[40]

As should be clear by now, I find myself somewhat bemused by the prominence of anti-realism in recent analytic debate. Beyond that – in areas outside the strict domain of anti-realism as defined in Dummettian (logico-semantic and metaphysical) terms – I am equally struck by the extent to which a movement of thought with so technical a basis in philosophy of logic and language, so clearly marked if subliminal an appeal to certain dispositions or temperaments, and (above all) so tenuous a hold on the structure and contours of reality has managed to dictate such a sizable swathe of the broader philosophical agenda. Thus it is largely in response to anti-realism in its purebred Dummettian form that many thinkers about issues in epistemology and philosophy of science – including some erstwhile proponents of a strong realist position – have felt themselves obliged to back off under pressure and thereafter espouse some scaled-down or framework-relative version of (quasi-)realism that meets the anti-realist's self-imposed requirements for meeting the sceptic's likewise self-imposed since far from realistically credible challenge. It seems to me that what we have here is an instance of philosophy giving way to the lures of a certain metaphysical worldview – in this case a negatively inflected one with drastic implications for the scope and capacities of human knowledge – that takes a cue from the Kantian critique of pure or speculative reason in its strictly illegitimate (knowledge-claiming) role.

However, the problems that I have noted already with respect to Kant's argument are present in spades when modern anti-realists extend that critique, with highly problematical results, to the realm of epistemology where Kant was quite insistent that sensuous intuitions could indeed match up with (or be 'brought under') concepts of understanding. For their case then amounts to a vote of no confidence in the power of human intellect not only to conceive the existence of truths beyond its present-best epistemic grasp but also to conceive its own claims to truth or its present-best state of knowledge as possessing any more than empirical warrant or justification by the standards prevailing in this or that communal-linguistic context. Indeed it is fair to say that this whole chapter of developments has taken rise from a persistent confusion between metaphysical and epistemological issues – as likewise between matters of *de re* and *de dicto* reference and truth – which could never have gone so far had the thinkers concerned paid more heed to the specifications on just that score issued by modal realists like Kripke and Putnam in their writings of the 1970s.[41] Thus they (the anti-realists) should have learned from these exponents of the 'new' causal theory of reference how vital it is from both a realist and an anti-sceptical viewpoint to maintain the greatest possible degree of clarity with respect to such basic distinctions. What is always apt to happen if they are ignored or softened up is that truth becomes subject to the scope and limits of knowledge, and knowledge in turn to the scope and limits of present-best conceivability.

At this point any hope of securing the pass against scepticism and/ or relativism will surely be undermined. The result is not so much to lift that threat by driving out the wedge between knowledge and truth but rather to drive it in all the more firmly by equating 'truth' with one or other of those currently available scaled-down substitute notions such as – in ascending order of strength – communal agreement, rational consensus, best judgement, optimised epistemic warrant, Peircean truth at the end of enquiry and Wright's aforementioned high-spec notions of 'superassertibility' and 'cognitive command'. For these all have the marked disadvantage (at least when adopted, as they most often are, with a view to blocking sceptical arguments at source) that they signally fail – or point-blank refuse – to recognise that present-best belief may sometimes come apart from knowledge and present-best (even future-best) knowledge fall short of truth in certain respects. Thus even the most expert, intelligent, perceptually acute, open-minded, well-informed, evidentially constrained, self-critical and epistemically virtuous knower (or community of knowers) must always be in the situation of sensibly disowning any claim to have the last word in issues of knowledge and truth. More precisely: they will either accept, with the realist, that *not all truths are known* – since on this view there is nothing paradoxical or self-contradictory about claiming to know that there exist verification-transcendent or recognition-transcendent truths – or else side squarely with the anti-realist and deny flat out that such a claim can make any kind of metaphysical or logical let alone epistemological sense.

If they seize the latter horn then this option has some surely less than welcome entailments. Chief among them is the consequence of exiling truth – on whatever precise understanding of that term – to a realm where its very existence becomes problematic to the point of ineffability, rather than (as the realist/objectivist would have it) just asking us to grant, in very un-mysterious fashion, that there are many truths of all sorts that we don't yet know and might never find out. Thus anti-realism takes us back to the idea – the strikingly Kantian, not to say Platonic, idea – of truth as having its habitation in some noumenal domain beyond the utmost grasp of a faculty of knowledge wherein concepts are tied to sensuous intuitions and (on the anti-realist account) shrunk to the dimension of cognitive-epistemic warrant. Anti-realism then begins to look very much like a negative or sceptically motivated version of the tendency of thought that Kant ascribed to the unrestrained high gyrations of pure reason.[42] This is a version that replaces the veto on a seeking after knowledge of cognitively inaccessible truths with the outright denial that thought can have access even to those items of knowledge (i.e. syntheses of concept and sensuous intuition) which for Kant provided the paradigm instance of humanly attainable cognitive grasp. So it is that an enterprise – that of anti-realism – one of whose chief motives was to render knowledge proof against sceptical attack turns out to constitute a form of scepticism all the more powerful (though all the more subject to challenge on principled philosophic grounds) through its promiscuous conflation of metaphysical and epistemological themes.

At any rate there is no good reason to endorse an anti-realist meta-physical position (or one of its epistemologically angled derivatives) which can yield only a notional defence against the equally notional threat of global scepticism, and which moreover brings along with it such a large burden of additional self-imposed problems.

Notes

1. For modern defences of a relativist position (however hedged around with qualifying clauses), see, for instance, Nelson Goodman, *Ways of Worldmaking* (Indianapolis: Hackett, 1978); Joseph Margolis, *The Truth about Relativism* (Oxford: Blackwell, 1991) and *Pragmatism Without Foundations: Reconciling Realism and Relativism* (Oxford: Blackwell, 1986); Hilary Putnam, *Reason, Truth and History* (Cambridge: Cambridge University Press, 1981); Richard Rorty, *Objectivity, Relativism, and Truth* (Cambridge: Cambridge University Press, 1991).

2. For some representative lines of attack, see Simon Blackburn, *Truth: A Guide* (Oxford: Oxford University Press, 2005) and Paul Boghossian, *Fear of Knowledge: Against Relativism and Constructivism* (Oxford: Oxford University Press, 2006).

3. Among recent contributions to this debate, see Maria Baghramian, *Relativism* (London: Routledge, 2004); Stuart Brock and Edwin Mares, *Realism and Anti-Realism* (Chesham: Acumen, 2007); Martin Hollis and Steven Lukes (eds), *Rationality and Relativism* (Oxford: Blackwell, 1982); Robert Kirk, *Relativism and Reality: A Contemporary Introduction* (London: Routledge, 1999); Christopher Kulp (ed.), *Realism/Antirealism and Epistemology* (Lanham, MD: Rowman & Littlefield, 1997); Larry Laudan, *Science and Relativism: Some Key Controversies in the Philosophy of Science* (Chicago: University of Chicago Press, 1990); Robert Nola, *Relativism and Realism in Science* (Dordrecht: Kluwer Academic, 1988).

4. Margolis, *The Truth about Relativism*, op. cit.

5. See especially Michael Dummett, *Truth and Other Enigmas* (London: Duckworth, 1978) and *The Logical Basis of Metaphysics* (London: Duckworth, 1991); also Michael Luntley, *Language, Logic and Experience: The Case for Anti-realism* (London: Duckworth, 1988); Gerald Vision, *Modern Anti-Realism and Manufactured Truth* (London: Routledge, 1988); Neil Tennant, *The Taming of the True* (Oxford: Clarendon Press, 2002).

6. For further argument to this effect, see Christopher Norris, *Truth Matters: Realism, Anti-realism and Response-Dependence* (Edinburgh: Edinburgh University Press, 2002); also William P. Alston, *A Realist Conception of Truth* (Ithaca, NY: Cornell University Press, 1996);

Michael Devitt, *Realism and Truth*, 2nd edn (Princeton: Princeton University Press, 1997); Jerrold J. Katz, *Realistic Rationalism* (Cambridge, MA: MIT Press, 1996).

7. See, for instance, D. M. Armstrong, *Truth and Truthmakers* (Cambridge: Cambridge University Press, 2004); Devitt, *Realism and Truth*, op. cit.; Jarrett Leplin (ed.), *Scientific Realism* (Berkeley and Los Angeles: University of California Press, 1984); Peter Lipton, *Inference to the Best Explanation*, 2nd edn (London: Routledge, 2004); Stathis Psillos, *Scientific Realism: How Science Tracks Truth* (London: Routledge, 1999).

8. See, for instance, Crispin Wright, *Truth and Objectivity* (Cambridge, MA: Harvard University Press, 1992) and *Realism, Meaning, and Truth*, 2nd edn (Oxford: Blackwell, 1993); also John Haldane and Crispin Wright (eds), *Reality, Representation, and Projection* (New York: Oxford University Press, 1993); Norris, *Truth Matters*, op. cit.

9. See notes 1, 3, 5 and 8, above.

10. For a detailed exploration of this line of argument, see Michael Williams, *Unnatural Doubts: Epistemological Realism and the Basis of Scepticism* (Princeton: Princeton University Press, 1991).

11. Norris, *Truth Matters* and *On Truth and Meaning* (see note 6 above).

12. For examples of relativism in its 'strong-sociological' mode, see David Bloor, *Knowledge and Social Imagery*, 2nd edn (Chicago: University of Chicago Press, 1991); Harry Collins, *Changing Order: Replication and Induction in Scientific Practice*, 2nd edn (Chicago: University of Chicago Press, 1992); Steven Shapin and Simon Schaffer, *Leviathan and the Air-Pump: Hobbes, Boyle, and the Experimental Life* (Cambridge: Cambridge University Press, 1995).

13. Immanuel Kant, *Critique of Pure Reason*, trans. N. Kemp Smith (London: Macmillan, 1964). On these troublesome aspects of Kant's epistemological legacy, see Frederick C. Beiser, *German Idealism: The Struggle Against Subjectivism, 1781–1801* (Cambridge, MA: Harvard University Press, 2002).

14. For further discussion of this Kantian aftermath, see Norris, *Minding the Gap: Epistemology and Philosophy of Science in the Two Traditions* (Amherst: University of Massachusetts Press, 2000).

15. See, for instance, Edmund Husserl, *Formal and Transcendental Logic*, trans. Dorion Cairns (The Hague: Martinus Nijhoff, 1969) and *Experience and Judgment: Investigations in a Genealogy of Logic*, trans. James S. Churchill and Karl Ameriks (Evanston: Northwestern University Press, 1973).

16. For a detailed account, see Norris, *Language, Logic and Epistemology: A Modal-realist Approach* (London: Macmillan, 2004).

17. John McDowell, *Mind and World* (Cambridge, MA: Harvard University Press, 1994).

18. Norris, 'McDowell on Kant: redrawing the bounds of sense' and 'The Limits of Naturalism: further thoughts on McDowell's *Mind and World*', in *Minding the Gap*, op. cit., pp. 172–96 and 197–230.

19. See notes 6, 14, 16 and 18, above.

20. See Neil Tennant, *Anti-Realism and Logic* (Oxford: Oxford University Press, 1987); also Dummett, *Truth and Other Enigmas* and *The Logical Basis of Metaphysics* (note 5, above).

21. Tennant, *Anti-Realism and Logic*, op. cit.; also Susan Haack, *Deviant Logic: Some Philosophical Issues* (Cambridge: Cambridge University Press, 1974).

22. See Williams, *Unnatural Doubts*, op. cit.; also Dummett, *The Logical Basis of Metaphysics*, and – for a dissenting (realist) view – Norris, *Truth Matters*, op. cit.

23. Norris, *On Truth and Meaning* (see note 6, above).

24. See especially Wright, *Truth and Objectivity*, op. cit.

25. Ibid., pp. 48 and 103.

26. C. S. Peirce, *Selected Writings of Peirce*, ed. Justus Buchler (London: Kegan Paul, Trench, Trubner, 1940).

27. See Norris, *Truth Matters*, op. cit.

28. Ludwig Wittgenstein, *Philosophical Investigations*, trans. G. E. M. Anscombe (Oxford: Blackwell, 1958).

29. Dummett, *Truth and Other Enigmas*, op. cit.; also – for a critique of Dummettian anti-realism on ethico-political as well as epistemological grounds – Christopher Norris, 'Staying for an answer: truth, knowledge and the Rumsfeld creed', in Norris, *Epistemology: Key Concepts in Philosophy* (London: Continuum, 2005), pp. 18–41.

30. Dummett, *The Logical Basis of Metaphysics*, op. cit., p. 7.

31. For a critical account of this anti-psychologism in its more extreme, dogmatic and at times philosophically disabling forms, see Norris, 'Who's afraid of psychologism? Normativity, truth, and epistemic warrant', in *On Truth and Meaning* (London: Continuum, 2006), pp. 12–40.

32. Thus Brouwer has no time for what he takes to be the thoroughly erroneous idea that 'mathematics, when it is made less formal, will pay for it by a loss of "exactitude", i.e., of mathematical truth'. So far from that, 'for me "truth" is a general emotional phenomenon, which . . . can be coupled or not with the formalistic study of mathematics' (cited by Karen Green, *Dummett: Philosophy of Mathematics* (Cambridge: Polity Press, 2001), p. 91). See also Dummett, *Elements of Intuitionism* (Oxford: Oxford University Press, 1977). Although Dummett would surely never lend his name to such cloudy sentiments it is all the same reasonable to suppose that, in his case as in Brouwer's, there is a more than incidental link between the two (i.e. the specialist mathematical and everyday colloquial) senses of 'intuition'.

33. These theological overtones come out most markedly in Dummett's discussions of the temporal paradoxes that were first formulated by J. M. McTaggart (with more than a little help from Zeno), and which have lately been revived by, among others, those who interpret quantum mechanics as entailing some form of time-reversal or backward causation. Thus Dummett's prime instance of how it can make sense (or offend against no basic principles of right reason) to entertain this idea is the case of a father who knows that a battle has already taken place in some remote region but who has no detailed knowledge of the outcome and therefore prays that his son should not have been killed. See Dummett, 'Can an effect precede its cause?', 'Bringing about the past', and 'The reality of the past', in *Truth and Other Enigmas*, op. cit., pp. 319–32, 333–50 and 358–74.

34. Kant, *Critique of Pure Reason* (op. cit.), 'Transcendental doctrine of elements', Part II, Division II, Book II, Ch. I.

35. For a critical survey of various naturalising trends in epistemology and philosophy of mind – including both 'hard-line' and 'moderate' variants – see Norris, *Re-Thinking the Cogito: Naturalism, Reason, and the Venture of Thought* (London: Continuum, 2010).

36. On the 'no-miracles' argument in support of scientific realism, see especially J. J. C. Smart, *Philosophy and Scientific Realism* (London: Routledge & Kegan Paul, 1963); also Richard Boyd, 'The current status of scientific realism', in Garrett Leplin (ed.), *Scientific Realism* (Berkeley and Los Angeles: University of California Press, 1984), pp. 41–82 and Wesley C. Salmon, *Scientific Realism and the Causal Structure of the World* (Princeton: Princeton University Press, 1984).

37. Bas van Fraassen, *The Scientific Image* (Oxford: Clarendon Press, 1980); also (for a critical assessment) Norris, 'Anti-realism and constructive empiricism: is there a (real) difference?' and 'Ontology according to van Fraassen: some problems with constructive empiricism', in *Against Relativism: Philosophy of Science, Deconstruction and Critical Theory* (Oxford: Blackwell, 1997), pp. 166–95 and 196–217.

38. Ian Hacking, *Representing and Intervening: Introductory Topics in Philosophy of Science* (Cambridge: Cambridge University Press, 1983).

39. Hacking, 'Do we see through a microscope?', *Pacific Philosophical Quarterly*, 62 (1981), pp. 305–22; also G. Maxwell, 'The ontological status of theoretical entities', in H. Feigl and G. Maxwell (eds), *Minnesota Studies in the Philosophy of Science*, Vol. 3 (Minneapolis: University of Minnesota Press, 1962), pp. 3–27 and C. J. Misak, *Verificationism: Its History and Prospects* (London: Routledge, 1995). For a range of views on this topic see P. M. Churchland and C. M. Hooker (eds), *Images of Science: Essays on Realism and Empiricism, with a Reply from Bas C. van Fraassen* (Chicago: University of Chicago Press, 1985).

40. See Gilbert Harman, 'Inference to the best explanation', *Philosophical Review*, 74 (1965), pp. 88–95, and Peter Lipton, *Inference to the Best Explanation*, 2nd edn (London: Routledge, 2004). See also Devitt, *Realism and Truth*, op. cit., for the argument that there is something quite literally preposterous ('putting first what should come after') about questioning so eminently robust a theory as scientific realism on a pretext thrown up by so highly contestable a range of theories as those that go under the heading of 'philosophy of language'.

41. These arguments find their classic formulation in Saul Kripke, *Naming and Necessity* (Oxford: Blackwell, 1980) and Hilary Putnam, 'Is semantics possible?', 'The meaning of "meaning"', and 'Language and reality', in *Mind, Language and Reality* (Cambridge: Cambridge University Press, 1975), pp. 139–52, 215–71 and 272–90. For further discussion from a variety of viewpoints see Leonard Linsky (ed.), *Reference and Modality* (Oxford: Oxford University Press, 1971); Stephen Schwartz (ed.), *Naming, Necessity, and Natural Kinds* (Ithaca, NY: Cornell University Press, 1977); David Wiggins, *Sameness and Substance* (Oxford: Blackwell, 1980).

42. See notes 13 and 34, above.

CHAPTER 2

Great Philosophy: Discovery, Invention and the Uses of Error

I

Jonathan Bennett reports J. L. Austin as having once remarked, apropos an idea of Leibniz, that 'it is a very great mistake', but that 'only a very great philosopher could have made it'.[1] One could pursue this comment in various directions, among them its bearing on Austin's work and what it tells us – when strategically placed upfront in his essay 'Spinoza's Error' – about Bennett's project of rational reconstruction as applied to sundry great philosophers in the Western canon. Austin, one can safely say, would not for one moment have extended to himself or his own philosophical practice the sort of generous licence for getting things wrong in a big, brave, intellectually ambitious and hence inherently error-prone way that he here extends to Leibniz. 'Ordinary language' philosophy as practised most influentially by Austin is, after all, a close-focused and meticulously disciplined enquiry into the manifold possible mistakes that result from our not taking adequate note of how language functions in everyday contexts of usage.[2] Not for him the idea that there might be some honour – some special claim to greatness – in the readiness to risk falling into error or (conceivably) downright nonsense in pursuit of some grand but ultimately false or untenable thesis. Rather it is the business of philosophy to eschew such well-documented sources of large-scale systematic, speculative, or – as the charge sheet typically runs – 'metaphysical' error. Best stick to the kinds of common-sense though often highly nuanced and even revelatory wisdom enshrined in our everyday linguistic transactions.

So if greatness in philosophy is thought to entail the possibility of being greatly or grossly in error then Austin will have none of it. Indeed he spends a good deal of time putting his case that big theories are almost sure to go off the rails and produce bad or morally repugnant results in so far as they aspire to an order of systematic grasp that allows the setting aside of any guidance supplied by that

communal-linguistic tribunal. For Austin this is the original sin of
all philosophy – whether in the grand metaphysical tradition or the
echt-analytic, hence staunchly anti-metaphysical mode – that thinks
to prove its specialist credentials by presuming to correct or refine
everyday usage and its associated modes of thought. As he famously
wrote in this deflationary mode:

> Our common stock of words embodies all the distinctions men
> have found worth drawing, and the connections they have found
> worth marking, in the lifetimes of many generations; these surely
> are likely to be more numerous, more sound, since they have stood
> up to the long test of the survival of the fittest, and more subtle, at
> least in all ordinary and reasonably practical matters, than any that
> you or I are likely to think up in our armchairs of an afternoon – the
> most favoured alternative method.[3]

However Austin then goes on to qualify – even retract – this handsome
compliment to ordinary language by conceding that, in the interests
of clarity and intellectual hygiene, one might need to 'prise' words
off their customary referents or communally sanctioned contexts of
usage. Only thus, he suggests, can philosophy bring its critical tools
to bear on those other, more wayward or error-inducing tendencies
to which language is occasionally prone. Hence the requirement
for 'ordinary-language' philosophy to maintain a proper balance
between, on the one hand, its deference to everyday commonplace
talk – what sets it apart from logicist or revisionist approaches in the
analytic line of descent from Frege and Russell – and, on the other, its
need to point out those occasional untoward tendencies.

The same tension is often felt in other movements of thought
within modern philosophy, most evident in cases where they have
self-consciously or programmatically taken the 'linguistic turn'
but visible also among those – like P. F. Strawson – more disposed
toward a scaled-down version of older (e.g. Kantian) philosophical
concerns.[4] Thus it tends to emerge where a broadly descriptivist
desire to have done with the large-scale speculative or systematising
drive of earlier 'metaphysical' schools goes along with a residual
corrective impulse that is nowadays very often focused on language
as its reassuring taproot back to a sense of communal grounding.
With Austin it is a matter of intellectual temperament – expressed
through a highly distinctive, sometimes ironic, sometimes teasingly
allusive (and elusive) 'literary' style – which enables him not so much
to resolve or reconcile that tension but rather to deploy it as a source

of heightened linguistic-analytic perspicacity. Still his work keeps very firmly to a conception of philosophy's proper remit that would draw a clear line against treating itself to the kind of indulgence that he somewhat whimsically extends to Leibniz. Moreover, Austin's philosophical practice has this much in common with the practices of other (broadly speaking) analytic philosophers, whatever their specific differences of interest, method or approach. Thus it rests on the shared assumption that, at least for all normal purposes, the philosophical virtues simply *cannot* go along with a liability to error or to risk transgressing the bounds of a decently restrained and methodical approach. Or again – where this conception is most markedly at odds with various 'continental' developments – it is taken pretty much for granted that one major part of philosophy's role is to guard against just such perilous venturing out onto the inherently suspect and error-strewn paths of 'metaphysical'-speculative thought. All very well, so the implication goes, for a thinker such as Leibniz to make certain big philosophical mistakes since he and his contemporaries laboured under the twin disadvantage of not having taken the linguistic/analytic turn and, for that reason, being chronically prone to just such seductive illusions. However – it continues – there is simply no excuse for present-day philosophers to persist in conjuring the same illusions through a more-or-less wilful failure to learn from those hard-won lessons concerning the scope and limits of their enterprise.

When Bennett cites Austin on Leibniz as a prelude to his own essay on Spinoza the comment acquires a somewhat sharper ironic edge or a critical force that is strikingly absent from Austin's genial remark. No doubt this is partly due to pre-acquaintance with Bennett's well-known manner of proceeding with the great dead philosophers of Western tradition, namely his idea of 'collegiality' as the right sort of mindset in which to approach those thinkers.[5] What it involves, briefly stated, is the treatment of them as collocutors in a shared and to that extent trans-historical debate within which their arguments are up for assessment according to standards predominantly set by our own (presumptively more adequate, advanced or unillusioned) ways of thought. 'Collegial' might seem an odd term for what tends to work out as a distinctly slanted or, in argumentative terms, strikingly one-sided dialogue. Thus Bennett's genuine respect for his great precursors and his occasional passages of unstinting praise for their moments of precocious insight are very often undermined – as happens to spectacular effect when he gets to Book V of Spinoza's

Ethics with its appeal to the (seemingly) mystical-intuitive 'third kind
of knowledge' – by subsequent expressions of regret, disappointment
or outright exasperation when their arguments go off the rails as
judged by present-day analytic criteria.[6]

At any rate 'collegiality' of this sort has much in common with
the activity of rational reconstruction as practised by a thinker like
Bertrand Russell, that is to say, what analytic philosophers tend to do
when they take time off for a dip into the history of ideas. Certainly
it seems a far cry from anything in the nature of a two-way dialogical
exchange or – in hermeneutic parlance – an open encounter of interpretative horizons where there is no such presumption concerning the
manifest superiority of present-day methods and ideas. 'In [Austin's]
paradoxical remark', he suggests, 'there is at least this much truth: a
philosopher can be led into error by the very power of his thought,
making serious mistakes that he might not have made if he had seen
less and probed less deeply.'[7] Nor is it merely coincidental that the
particular case of such power-driven error that Bennett has in mind is
'Spinoza's profoundly wrong view that what we ordinarily call error
is really a species of ignorance'. One main tenet of the ultimately
Kant-derived analytic outlook that Bennett shares is the belief that
philosophers go badly wrong if they ignore those strict boundary-
conditions enjoined upon the exercise of speculative thought by the
need to keep it from laying claim to an order of knowledge – Kant's
'intellectual intuition' – that would purport to yield direct, epistemically unmediated access to reality and truth.[8] In so doing it would not
only tempt pure reason into error by supposing it to offer the kind
of knowledge that requires sensuous intuitions to be brought under
adequate concepts but also leave knowledge a prey to sceptical doubt
by seducing it into speculative regions beyond the terra firma of cognitive grasp. Moreover, it would have the morally deleterious effect
– Kant's great bugbear and also the gravamen of all those 'Spinozism'
charges bandied about at the time – of pointing to a monist (whether
pantheist or materialist) conception of mind/nature that left little
room for traditional ideas of free will and responsibility.[9]

It is not hard to detect an echo of those fierce controversies two
centuries back in Bennett's flat refusal to countenance the Spinozist
doctrine according to which truth and error are functions of relative
knowledge or ignorance rather than errors ultimately brought about
by some more or less culpable failure to pursue the right (analytically
accountable) process of reasoning. It is the same root conviction that
leads Bennett, more firmly than Austin, to distance himself from any

too ready endorsement of the notion that 'greatness' in philosophy can plausibly go along with a proneness to the sorts of 'error' attendant on the over-extension of speculative thought. More precisely: what he wants to rule out for all good philosophical purposes is the idea that thinking might sometimes achieve remarkable and otherwise unattainable insights through a mode of understanding – tantamount to 'intellectual intuition' – that by its very nature involved a certain risk of non-trivial error. Hence Bennett's suggestion that indeed it is the very 'power' and 'depth' of Spinoza's thought, or its consequent failure/refusal to abide by the rules of proper conduct analytically defined, that leaves it exposed to errors whose 'greatness' he is strongly inclined – unlike Austin – to reckon on the negative rather than the positive side. Beyond that his attitude captures one aspect of the no doubt exaggerated but still institutionally salient rift between 'analytic' and 'continental' philosophy. Thus it highlights the difference between a tradition based on something very like the standards of Kuhnian 'normal science' and one that respects them – as a matter of logical, evidential, argumentative or broadly rational warrant – while receptive to the kinds of 'revolutionary' thinking that don't so much break with those standards but rather redefine them in sometimes radical ways.[10] Such is typically the continental readiness to risk a great deal, including (possibly) the charge of egregious error, for the sake of pursuing certain heterodox ideas that press well beyond the limits of currently accredited philosophical discourse.

II

It is in this sense, I shall argue, that Austin's mildly double-edged remark about Leibniz – together with Bennett's rather less charitable application of it to Spinoza – may offer us a way to make better sense of that often crudely typecast analytic/continental dichotomy. If recent commentators have tended either to treat it with suspicion or to reject it outright then this is undoubtedly a good thing since the labels were up to now used for the most part with polemical or self-promoting purposes in view and with no very adequate or definite sense of just what they properly referred to.

Any approach along national, historical, or geo-cultural lines is sure to hit the buffers early on because, as is well known, a great many of the founding figures in analytic philosophy – among them Frege, Wittgenstein, Carnap, Tarski, Hempel and Reichenbach – were mainland European (mostly German or Austrian) by birth and

in terms of intellectual background, training and allegiance. Nor is
there much help to be had from the sorts of broad-brush contrast that
used to be drawn with regard to the pervasive influence of Husserlian
phenomenology on continental developments from Heidegger and
Sartre down – even where that influence has been most strenuously
resisted – as opposed to the strongly logicist cast of most analytic philosophy after Frege and Russell. This version of the story has its roots
in the famous crossing of paths when Frege reviewed Husserl's early
work on the philosophy of mathematics and took it to task for the
cardinal sin, from an analytic standpoint, of 'psychologism'.[11] The
charge was later echoed by Gilbert Ryle when he underwent a drastic
and highly vocal change of mind after writing some well-informed
and broadly approving essays on Husserl and Heidegger.[12] However,
it had dubious or very partial warrant – despite its well-documented
impact on Husserl's later thought – and has since then been steadily
chipped away at to the point where it only stands up, if at all, when
hedged around with numerous and large qualifications. Thus analytic thinkers such as Michael Dummett have adopted a moderately
ecumenical stance which grants Husserl a fair claim to have travelled
some way along the Fregean path toward clarity on issues of language, logic and truth although not as far along – or with such sure
compass bearings – as Frege himself.[13] Meanwhile other scholarship,
some of my own work included, has done more to complicate the
received (analytic) picture both by showing how deep the affinities
run in certain crucial respects and how difficult it is to specify exactly
rather than gesture at the differences involved.[14]

Least of all can this be achieved by taking the word for the deed –
or the label for a strict and exclusive trademark – so that work within
the mainstream Anglophone tradition would *per definiens* count as
'analytic' in a proprietary, i.e. non-'continental', sense of the term.
That idea, explicit or not, has for too long served as a handy device
whereby members of the analytic guild could at once certify their
own credentials and preclude admission – or the right to a hearing
– for those deemed to belong outside it. Such was the pretext for
Ryle's volte-face with respect to Husserl, for the logical positivists'
allergic response to any language bar their own ultra-regimented discourse, and again – even less excusably – for John Searle's stubborn
refusal to engage with Derrida's arguments on the topic of speech-
act theory in a properly attentive or responsive way.[15] What these
and other kindred episodes have in common is the straightforward
presumption that, at least when it comes to the business of logical

(or rational) argument, analytic philosophy is *by very definition* the place one should look for instances of best practice. At the same time this serves to reinforce the idea that 'continental' philosophy, as its opposite number, may safely be supposed – without much in the way of careful investigation – to exemplify the contrary features of (to rehearse the standard charge sheet) obscurity, indiscipline, logical confusion and stylistic self-indulgence. Thus the kind of licence extended to Leibniz by Austin, and more grudgingly by Bennett to Spinoza, is very firmly withheld as a matter of general policy by analytic philosophers when addressing the work of their present-day 'continental' counterparts. Indeed one can best explain this switch of attitude by following out the implications of a 'collegial' approach to the great dead philosophers as defined by Bennett. On his account, as on Austin's, 'greatness' is achievable for the mighty dead along with or despite their 'great mistakes' just on condition that they have been dead long enough to enter a plea of ignorance with respect to the signal advances that philosophy has achieved since taking the jointly analytic and linguistic turn. However, so the unspoken premise goes, that claim amounts to no more than a piece of gratuitous wordplay with the adjective 'great' when it is extended to thinkers – like Derrida – who can have no possible justification for entering any such plea.

What this amounts to is a kind of reverse statute of limitations, or rule of historically increasing liability with the passage of time and the presumptive accrual of knowledge and expertise. One might compare the line of argument whereby Kierkegaard, in *The Concept of Irony*, deemed it acceptable (ethically warranted) for Socrates to practise his ironic strategies because he antedated the good-faith-demanding event of Christ's incarnation yet unacceptable (ethically and religiously remiss) to continue such a practice, like the romantic ironists of his own time, in the temporal wake of that event.[16] So likewise we may justifiably incline to attribute the errors of Leibniz or Spinoza to the power, indeed the 'greatness', of their thought but only on condition of making that allowance for their blameless non-possession of certain lately arrived at truths concerning the scope and limits of philosophical enquiry. I should not for a moment wish to deny that philosophy can make progress and that this progress may sometimes – perhaps most often – consist in the salutary recognition that certain sorts of truth-claim or erstwhile relied upon modes of reasoning were either fallacious or prone to overestimate their own powers and prerogatives. However, this does absolutely nothing to legitimise the fixed idea, among many analytic philosophers, that present-day 'continental' thinkers – or those most typically accorded the title – must surely be labouring under some such delusion (though without the same kind of excuse or extenuating circumstance) simply by reason of having attracted that label. That they might have achieved genuine greatness not *despite* but precisely *in virtue of* transgressing the in-place analytic norms, and moreover by risking commensurately 'great' errors when judged by those same standards, is on this view an idea beyond the limits of rational (let alone logical) conceivability. Yet it is my contention that by far the most impressive philosophical achievements of the past quarter-century have demon-strably come about through a combination of the speculative reach that has typified much continental work with the formal precision and logical rigour which, on the received view, should be thought of as the hallmark analytic virtues.

It is in just this sense that I am here interpreting the Austin-Bennett notion that 'greatness' – no matter how qualified or ironised in their usage of the term – may often go along with a heightened pos-sibility of error. That is to say, such a project will risk running up against problems, contradictions or paradoxes that leave it with a choice between three alternative responses. The first – and basically the line of least resistance – is to revise certain of its premises or procedures on a conservative principle of damage-limitation which seeks to restore formal consistency by removing all trace of those symptomatic stress points. The second, somewhat more adventurous path is to question whether certain axiomatic or taken-for-granted rules such as those of classical logic (i.e. bivalence, excluded middle and non-contradiction) might after all be up for revision, or even to outright suspension, should they meet with such a weight of (say) quantum-physical evidence as to warrant that move. This idea has found support from a good many philosophers, among them Quine and Putnam, who take it that science – more particularly physics – is our best source of guidance in such matters and therefore that if sci-entists find it most convenient to change their logical axioms or pro-cedures rather than question the physical evidence then logicians had much better follow suit.[17] However, this problem-avoidance strategy has problems of its own, including a large (and self-disabling) nor-mative deficit and a consequent failure to explain how major shifts or advances in scientific thinking could ever occur on such a basis of tweaking, bending or simply vetoing the logical 'rules' in response to observational anomalies.[18] In other words option two is really not so very different from option one since it amounts to just another line of least resistance, albeit with a more radical-sounding programme attached.

Only by moving to the third option can thinking hold itself open to the radical advances that may possibly result when such problems – of aporia, conceptual deadlock or self-referential paradox – are no longer managed through some crisis-avoiding technique of renormalisation or Quinean pragmatic redistribution of truth-values across the whole fabric of currently accredited knowledge. That option consists in pressing them to the *limit and beyond* through a range of formal (logico-semantic or mathematico-logical) procedures that allow for the kind of epochal development – the access to a new and hitherto strictly inconceivable order of truths – typified by events like Cantor's set-theoretical breakthrough. This latter is taken as a paradigm case by Alain Badiou, one of those thinkers – along with Derrida – whom I had chiefly in mind when offering the above characterisation of a thinking that would match in formal rigour what it showed in the way of speculative creativity. Derrida and Badiou are my primary warrants for the claim here advanced that there exists a whole genre of continental philosophy that not only comes up to the standards set by work in the mainstream analytic tradition but surpasses those standards precisely in so far as it ventures into territory marked firmly off-limits in orthodox analytic terms. These thinkers constantly essay those limits by way of an exploratory procedure – one with its closest formal analogue in Cantor's set-theoretical technique of diagonalisation – which allows them to reveal not only the aporias or stress points but also the prospect of taking such presently intractable problems as a stimulus for just the sort of radical rethinking that led Cantor to his great discovery.[19]

So my suggestion here is that major philosophical achievements necessarily involve an exceptional combination of inventive/speculative boldness with the capacity to pass in critical review any far-reaching theories or hypotheses thereby produced. In Derrida's case it produces a series of now canonical readings that press classical logic to the point of its encounter with a deviant (e.g. 'supplementary', 'differer*a*ntial' or 'parergonal') logic that takes its lead from certain prominent terms in the writing of (respectively) Rousseau, Husserl and Kant.[20] However, this has primarily to do with the logical syntax of the text in hand – and indeed of any discourse beyond a certain level of complexity – rather than with those particular terms and their meaning as it might be given by a purely semantic, thematic or text-specific analysis. In Badiou's case it is a matter of showing – through a closely-worked and meticulously reasoned engagement with set-theoretical developments from Cantor down – how the dialectic of being and event (or ontology and that which comes to disrupt and transform some existing ontological scheme) can be seen at work in every major advance in the scope of mathematical, scientific, philosophical, artistic and even political enquiry.[21]

My recourse to the word 'even' just now was no doubt a reflex accommodation to the prevalent idea, strongly endorsed by the standard analytic division of labour, that intellectual hygiene requires a rigorous demarcation between the formal sciences (principally mathematics and logic), the physical or natural sciences and those other disciplines where the terms 'social science' or 'human science' should be taken with at least a pinch of logical-positivist salt. However, that defensive reflex finds absolutely no warrant in either Derrida's or Badiou's work. On the contrary: among their greatest achievements is the way that they have managed – Badiou more explicitly – to formalise a range of topic-areas (including various specific topoi within the realms of art, politics and ethics) that are conventionally viewed, at least by analytic philosophers, as neither requiring nor permitting such treatment.[22] Moreover, the formal procedures involved are of the sort developed by mathematicians and logicians in response to certain well-known problems encountered during the early twentieth century with the attempt by thinkers like Frege and Russell to place mathematics on a wholly consistent or contradiction-free logical basis. That project famously ran up against Russell's discovery of the paradox – more strictly, the aporia or logically intractable dilemma – that arose in the case of self-referential or self-predicative expressions such as 'the set of all sets that are not members of themselves'. A further blow to the confidence of mathematicians, with their newly raised foundationalist hopes, was Kurt Gödel's incompleteness theorem to the effect that no formal system could be both consistent and complete, or again, that any formal system powerful enough to generate the axioms of basic arithmetic or first-order logic will contain at least one axiom unprovable within the system itself.[23] However, these findings, despite their problematical nature, were also germane to other developments – mostly with their source in Cantorian set theory – which not only found room for such (on the face of it) downright paradoxical or aporetic results but deployed them as a spur to ever more powerful methods and techniques for advancing mathematical knowledge.

Most significant here, since basic to all of them, was the process of 'diagonalisation' by which Cantor demonstrated the existence of infinite sets larger than that of the integers or natural numbers, i.e. sets that were uncountable or non-discrete (like the real numbers) and therefore precluded any one-for-one pairing with the integers. That procedure had much in common with Russell's way of arriving at his paradox of self-predication since in both cases it is a matter of applying certain conditions, such as those of set-theoretical membership, and showing how they generate a contradictory or aporetic outcome. However, it is at just this point that Badiou takes issue with Russell over the latter's idea of how best to resolve the problem, or how best to prevent the set-theoretical dilemma from wreaking havoc with the rational foundations of mathematics and logic alike. Russell's solution – famously – was to posit the existence of a hierarchy of formal languages and decree that the offending items (self-predicative sentences like 'the set of all sets that are not members of themselves') be subject to rigorous regimentation such that any looming paradox is resolved by the expedient of drawing a sharp logical distinction between first-order and second-order levels of discourse. Thus any appearance of self-predication can always be finessed, or stopped from doing harm, by invoking that distinction and reconstruing the (on this account pseudo-)paradox as merely a product of the failure to observe the mandated formal boundary between language and meta-language. For Badiou, as I have said, this solution falls short of the rigour required of any adequate set-theoretical or indeed any adequate philosophical address to the issues involved. Indeed, he counts it among the most damaging instances of that widespread pragmatist or constructivist tendency in present-day thought which always seeks to accommodate any problematical instances – anything of an exceptional, paradoxical, anomalous, contradictory or logically recalcitrant nature – just so long as its threat can be neutralised or its disruptive potential disarmed by some such face-saving move.[24]

To this way of thought there is a standing presumption in favour of the working principle that any contradictions can always be managed through the saving recourse to some metalinguistic means of conflict resolution such as the Russellian hierarchy. That strategy is open to the obvious objection that it creates an infinite (and arguably vicious) regress from one to another level, so that any solution thereby to be had is endlessly deferred and hence merely notional. However, Badiou's objection cuts deeper and concerns not only certain technical issues in the philosophy of logic and mathematics but, by analogy with those, two rival conceptions of human enquiry and agency with implications (among them political implications) far beyond that specialist sphere. Or again, more to the point: what he proposes is the radically different orientation according to which my phrase 'far beyond', and the whole idea of logic and politics as conceptually worlds apart, would show up as nothing more than a parochial prejudice engendered by a failure to think the logic of politics with sufficient rigour and precision. Thus Badiou's first charge against constructivism in all its mathematical, political and other (e.g. ethical or artistic) guises is that it always leaves room for various kinds of pragmatist fall-back strategy, and hence for the refusal to pursue contradictions to their ultimate (potentially transformative) upshot. Whence his second main charge: that constructivism always involves the premature appeal to some notion of presently achieved – or at any rate presently achievable – completeness, unity, totality or comprehensive grasp. This may, as with Russell's stopgap remedy, be a regulative notion or limit-point idea and therefore subject to the kind of indefinite deferral from one meta-level to the next that would seem to resist any tendency toward premature closure. Nevertheless, Badiou argues, it offers the temptation of a ready-made solution at every such juncture along with the undesirable effect of discouraging thought from any strenuous pursuit of truths beyond the compass of present-best knowledge.[25]

Constructivism thus has much in common with philosophical doctrines such as pragmatism, instrumentalism, fictionalism and ontological (conceptual-scheme) relativism. That is to say, it advises that we respond to logico-mathematical problems and anomalies – just as Quine recommends in the case of 'recalcitrant' empirical data – by making adjustments here or there in the total 'fabric' of currently accepted belief. Depending on a range of pragmatically weighted considerations such as simplicity, empirical adequacy and overall (fabric-wide) coherence these adjustments can be made at any point between the observational periphery and the innermost core of supposedly invariant logical axioms or putative laws of nature.[26] In the former sort of case one might seek to save some particularly cherished or deep-laid core item by pleading observational error or the limits of available technology. In the latter, conversely, one might hang on to some theoretically unaccountable or logically anomalous observation-statement by electing for a change of prevalent theory or, at the limit, of logical system. As I have said, Badiou rejects this entire set of notions in favour of a rigorously axiomatised approach that takes consistency – rather than completeness – as its governing principle despite what might seem its contrary commitment, as a matter of set-theoretical precept, to the absolute priority of inconsistent over consistent multiplicity. It is concerned not with maintaining the idea of some workably unified and paradox-free totality but rather with pressing contradictions or logical anomalies to the point of decisive advance where 'paradox turns into concept'. At such points thinking achieves the kind of conceptual breakthrough marked by epochal events such as – prototypically – Cantor's set-theoretical revolution in the mathematics of infinity.

III

Thus the case with mathematics, logic and the formal sciences bears a more than remote or merely fanciful relation to the case with politics. With each it is a matter of certain procedures – having their paradigm in Cantor's method of diagonalisation – which allow for the existence of anomalous, uncounted, inconsistent or paradox-generating elements within any given (quasi-)totality, elements that figure nowhere in the currently prevailing count-as-one or state of knowledge with regard to some existing situation. With each it is precisely what remains unperceived or beyond the furthest powers of present comprehension that may at length turn out, after the occurrence of a future (presently unforeseeable) event, to have held the potential for some major advance. Moreover, with each it is solely by way of such set-theoretically specified formal procedures with their source in just such signal advances from Cantor down that one can later – with the warrant of informed hindsight – account for the discoveries in question. Where Badiou decisively breaks new ground, and lays claim to the more than honorific title of great thinker, is by accomplishing the conventionally unthinkable passage from a close and meticulously reasoned engagement with these issues in mathematics and logic to a sustained and historically specific engagement with issues in political theory. This he is able to achieve by occupying both domains at just the point where some given mathematical or social-political ontology comes up against its limit of consistent formalisation, which in turn gives rise – after some more or less extended period – to an event that radically reconfigures the pre-existent situation. This is all worked out in mathematical detail, and with further reference not only to political but also to artistic (notably poetic) revolutions, in the course of Badiou's magisterial opus *Being and Event*.

What emerges to most striking effect through his deployment of set-theoretical formalisms and proof procedures is the historical or temporal dimension whereby such revolutions come about. Thus a truth-event can pass almost unnoticed, or its impact scarcely register, at the time of its first occurrence and only later – through the active or 'militant' fidelity of subjects who work to sustain it – exert the kind of long-range transformative effect that suddenly and unpredictably issues in an epochal paradigm-change. Again, this applies equally – with the same degree of formal-demonstrative rigour – in the case of politics as in that of mathematics, logic and the formal sciences. Just as Cantor's breakthrough was obscurely prefigured in the often baffled or balked attempts to cope with the concept of infinity, or the related aporias of the one and the many, by earlier thinkers from Plato and Aristotle down so likewise the history of failed, abortive or repressed revolutions presages the event that might always arrive to vindicate their so far unrealised promise. What gives this claim its demonstrative force – as distinct from though closely allied to its power of passionate conviction – is once again the high degree of formal, i.e. logico-conceptual, precision with which Badiou argues his case and the way that this allows him to move with no sense of impropriety or conceptual strain between two such (on the standard view) disparate domains as logic and politics. That this is possible at all, he argues, is a result not only of Cantor's inaugural discovery but also of the various subsequent advances in set-theoretical thinking that came about through Cantor's having opened up what Hilbert famously described as the 'mathematicians' paradise' of set theory.[27] Such was the really decisive break with previous orthodoxy, that is, with the doctrine of various thinkers since Plato and Aristotle, that the one necessarily precedes and encompasses the many and that any mathematical or philosophical thought on this topic must – on pain of descending into nonsense – have to do with merely virtual or potential rather than actual infinities.

Indeed, the very notion of a 'logic of politics' or – even more so – a 'politics of logic' might justifiably have been written off as a mere category-mistake in the absence of just those post-Cantorian conceptual resources that allow Badiou the theoretical space to develop his thematically diverse though tightly integrated lines of argument. Thus it is only on the basis of Cantor's power-set theorem that Badiou can advance his case for the precedence of inconsistent over consistent multiplicity, the ubiquitous excess of *parts* over *members* in any given set, and the equivalent discrepancy between those multiples that count as *belonging* to it and those (necessarily more numerous) multiples that are *included* as subsets of it. This is also expressed, in Badiou's elective terminology, as that which occurs when *presented* elements are subject to the process of second-order *representation*, or again, when some existing *situation* – whether of present-best mathematical knowledge or of 'representative democracy' as currently conceived – is likewise subject to a more inclusive re-count that yields the *state of the situation*.[28] The latter may thus be defined as what results from the addition of all those non-presented, non-belonging or non-member multiples that were excluded from the original count-as-one through restricted knowledge, ideological filtering or the deficit structural to all past and present forms of 'actually existing' democracy. Nevertheless it is the wager of the faithful subject that those excluded multiples may yet emerge, most likely as a result of intensifying conflict or the growing weight of unresolved problems and dilemmas. Such are the anomalies, or 'excrescences', that will surely be produced by any application of the count-as-one when carried out under limits imposed by the above-mentioned kinds of restriction or partiality. This exposure of the 'state of the situation' may then bring about a full-scale crisis of representation and a consequently heightened pressure for change that is no longer containable within existing structures of accredited knowledge or political-institutional power. It is likely to first break surface at certain 'evental sites' where there is seen to exist some especially acute or urgent case of the excluded multiple, i.e. some hitherto ignored range of unresolved mathematical dilemmas or some drastically marginalised social group (like the *sans-papiers* or undocumented migrant workers) that constitutes a now unignorable challenge to the regnant status quo.[29]

Badiou's great achievement is to have brought all this within range of a highly complex yet lucid and rigorously worked-out range of formalisms that are no doubt liable, on first acquaintance, to strike analytic philosophers as wildly speculative or downright implausible yet which could only be denied the title 'analytic' on a narrowly parochial understanding of the term. This applies especially to his arguments in favour of a strictly extensionalist approach to set-theoretical ontology, that is to say, one that interprets the relevant terms, concepts and relations purely on the basis of their referential scope and without any appeal to semantic or intensional properties. To be sure, extensionalism is normal fare for most set-theoreticians – as indeed for philosophers like Quine with a taste for 'austere desert landscapes' rather than luxuriant climes – since it promises to eliminate all those pesky ambiguities and instances of opaque reference that natural language is heir to.[30] Besides, it is presupposed by the Zermelo-Fraenkel system of set-theoretical axioms which are nowadays taken as pretty much standard and which Badiou himself uses for exploratory as well as expository purposes. However, the extensionalist commitment is clearly doing extra work in the context of Badiou's joint engagement with issues in the logico-mathematical and the socio-political spheres. Thus it serves to reinforce his commitment to a universal or generic rather than particularist or identity-based conception of that which gives human beings their claim to political justice or adequate representation. So there exists at the very least a strong elective affinity between extensionalism as applied in mathematics, logic and the formal sciences and the orientation in politics – call it generic-egalitarian – that takes individuals all to count equally irrespective of their differences in class, gender, status, creed, ethnic origin or other such marker (chosen or imposed) of distinctive personhood. If the alternative (intensionalist) approach to set theory lacks the kind of clear-cut analytic grasp and freedom from referential opacity possessed by its extensionalist counterpart then identity-politics – the nearest equivalent of intensionalism in political thought – lies open to a similar criticism. That is to say, it lacks the conceptual resources whereby to maintain that generic idea of humanity and of the requisite conditions for social and political justice quite aside from all merely social, cultural or ideological factors.

Again, what might seem a technical issue in the philosophy of set theory turns out to have large and far from merely suggestive implications for our thinking about politics. In both cases we are confronted with the choice between an intensionalist (basically constructivist) approach where the multiples in question are defined or specified according to some given distribution of pre-assigned features, predicates or properties and an extensionalist (generic) approach where no such differential criteria apply. Here it is worth noting – though limits of space preclude anything more – the crucial importance of that term 'generic' as an index of Badiou's primary commitments across the entirety of his work to date. In formal (mathematical) terms, the generic is that which plays a decisive role in some ongoing truth-procedure or process of investigative thought on account of precisely that trait, i.e. of its pertaining to each and any multiple that falls within its extensional scope irrespective of whatever defining or individuating attributes that multiple might presently be taken to possess. In political terms the generic is that which pertains indifferently to each and every human being irrespective of their socially or culturally assigned attributes. Thus it signifies both the dominant orientation of Badiou's choices among the available range of set-theoretical procedures and his kindred conception of politics as a space where conflicting interests, values and priorities are subject to critical assessment on conditions other than those laid down by the dominant count-as-one and its tally of inclusions and exclusions. This is why he comes out so strongly against the various forms of identity-politics that would equate the emancipatory interests of this or that oppressed, subaltern or marginalised group with their self-proclaimed 'difference' vis-à-vis other sectors of society. To Badiou, such ideas – whether advanced in the name of gender, class or ethnic affiliation – should rather be seen as inherently anti-egalitarian since premised on a hierarchical distinction between those who do and those who don't lay claim to the relevant differential traits. Hence also, as I have said, his choice of a set-theoretical system (based on the Zermelo-Fraenkel axioms) that involves absolutely no reference to intensional properties or attributes.

Badiou's usage of the term 'generic' – and his deployment of it in certain well-defined mathematical and other contexts – derives from the work of Paul Cohen whose 1962 work *Set Theory and the Continuum Hypothesis* he takes to be a work of epochal (or evental) significance second only to Cantor's inaugural discovery.[31] The book's primary concern is with Cantor's famous and much-debated claim that there exists no set with cardinality between that of the integers, i.e. the natural or counting numbers, and that of the real numbers, i.e. the continuous (non-discrete) range including all the positive and negative integers, fractions, irrational numbers, decimals, etc. This is also to say that there is nothing intermediate between a set and its power-set, a thesis whose truth or falsehood – or again, more to the point, its lacking any proof one way or the other by the best methods to hand – is central to Badiou's entire line of argument. Thus where Cantor produced a formal demonstration that the truth of the continuum hypothesis (the non-existence or impossibility of any intermediate set) was compatible with the standard Zermelo-Fraenkel axioms Cohen subsequently managed to prove that its untruth (the existence of such a set) was equally compatible with them. Although the two proofs are not strictly contradictory – since each asserts only a negative claim which leaves room for the other's truth – they do bring about a situation (one that still obtains despite

various post-Cohen attempts to resolve it) where any way forward
will necessarily involve an element of choice or decision. In order
to proceed beyond this dilemma and use it as a spur rather than an
obstacle to thought the set-theorist will need to take a stand – adopt
a rationally argued and motivated even if strictly non-demonstrable
stance – as to whether or not Cantor's hypothesis be granted validity
and added to the basic Zermelo-Fraenkel axioms.

IV

There are several reasons why these twin results (the Cantor and
Cohen proofs) have great importance for Badiou's project. One is the
support they offer for his claim – a central thesis of *Being and Event*
– that formal rigour of the kind required in advanced mathematical
or logical reasoning is by no means at odds with, and may indeed
be inseparable from, a maximal degree of subjective commitment
on the part of its practitioners. Such commitment has to go beyond
the mere willingness to entertain certain hypotheses, conjectures or
unproven theorems for what they are worth – in instrumentalist-
fictionalist terms – as a matter of their likely or possible heuristic
yield. Rather it concerns what Badiou describes as the process of
'subjectivation' by which certain truths seize upon certain thinkers
whose commitment thereafter requires that they combine the utmost
degree of disciplined investigative thought with the readiness to stake
their entire life's work on a wager concerning the veridical status of
those so-far unproven hypotheses.[32] This is because, if thinking is to
achieve any notable advance upon some pre-given state of knowledge, then the truth-claims in question must unreservedly be taken as
valid – subscribed to with a force of passionate conviction – so that
their implications can be followed through to the furthest extent and
with the greatest conceptual rigour.

Hence the second reason for Badiou's attachment to the Cantor/
Cohen dilemma concerning the continuum hypothesis: that it leaves
no room for certain prejudicial and grossly reductive conceptions of
truth. Just as it shows the subject to have a rightful place in procedures of formal-scientific reasoning so likewise it brings out the false
and artificial character of any ranking-order (such as, prototypically,
that proposed by the logical positivists) that equates truth with objectivity and objectivity, as if by very definition, with the total rejection
of any involvement on the part of subjects whose very existence qua
truth-seekers depends on precisely that involvement. Badiou makes

the point rather neatly by reference to Plato's purported set-piece demonstration in the *Meno* of how mathematical truths – in this case the truth of Pythagoras' Theorem – necessitate *both* the existence of objective truth-values that might always happen to exceed the limits of human knowledge *and* (by no means incompatibly with that) the involvement of a subject actively committed to finding them out.[33] Indeed this is one of the major points on which Badiou parts company with most analytic philosophers of mathematics. These latter tend to treat it as a great mystery – or at any rate a huge dilemma in the way of any objectivist (Platonist) conception of mathematics – that if truths are objective then *ipso facto* they might always stand beyond reach of human cognition or attainment. And yet, so this argument goes, if we take the anti-realist/intuitionist line of least resistance and decree that such truths *just are* coextensive with the scope of existing or (more liberally) limit-point-attainable human knowledge then objectivity goes straight out of the window along with any workable conception of that which we don't yet know yet are striving to discover.[34] So the Cantor/Cohen dilemma stands out as a singularly apt illustration of the error of this way of thinking and the fact that certain kinds of truth-oriented subjectivity can perfectly well go along with a commitment to the existence of truths exceeding the compass of present-best knowledge.

This is, to repeat, Badiou's main objection not only to anti-realism, intuitionism, constructivism and other such forms of (as he sees it) mathematical truth-avoidance but also to the various kindred modes of thought that have lately captured the high ground across otherwise disparate areas from philosophical semantics to historiography, epistemology and philosophy of science.[35] However, it is clearly not enough by way of decisive rebuttal that he should hold them up to supposed refutation through Plato's patently stage-managed dialogue or allude to their deleterious effect on the kinds of motivation that typically impel thinkers to conceive some means of truth-attainment that transcends the limits of present-best knowledge. After all, if the realist's case stops there, then the anti-realist might well be right in counting it a product of wishful thinking or – perhaps more charitably – another example of the way that thinking is apt to go when it posits the existence of truths surpassing the scope and limits of human knowledge. However, this brings us to Badiou's third and most decisive reason for attaching such importance to the negative result of Cantor's and Cohen's deliberations concerning the continuum hypothesis. It has to do with Cohen's concept, technique or methodology of 'forcing', that is, the formal procedure whereby he established not only that negative result but also – Badiou maintains – its far-reaching implications within and beyond the philosophy of mathematics. The method of forcing is one that explains how there *are and always must be* truths that are currently unknown or for which no proof is to hand and yet the existence of which will later become symptomatically detectable – no doubt with the benefit of hindsight – through a grasp of just what had previously worked to render them invisible. It involves an operation whereby the mathematician moves, as in Cantor's 'diagonal' technique, from one to another, more adequate or informative state of knowledge through a technique that involves the addition of certain elements to the original set and a 'filtering' system that selects all and only the generic elements, or those that partake of a truth-procedure indifferent to variations of meaning or context.

Again one can see how the ontological (= set-theoretical) aspects of Badiou's thought find a precise analogue in his political thinking. Thus they mirror his insistence that the central issues – those of justice, equality, participant access and effective representation – have to do with what pertains universally to human subjects and not to any distinguishing traits of gender, culture, language or any other such notionally salient category. However, Cohen's invention/ discovery of forcing has a further special significance for Badiou since it offers a formal, i.e. a logico-mathematically specified, means of explaining how truth can exceed the compass of present-best knowledge while none the less intelligibly forming a part – albeit an as yet unrecognised part – of what constitutes that knowledge. In other words it holds out the distinct possibility of an answer to the famously intractable question of how theory-change could ever come about, or advances in knowledge occur, given the natural tendency of thought to fall back upon established cognitive routines or habitual modes of reasoning. That problem was raised with particular force by Kuhn's paradigm-relativist conception of scientific knowledge and (at least arguably) of scientific truth, a conception that seemed to make paradigm-change nothing more than a process of random epistemic drift or – as ultra-Kuhnians like Richard Rorty would have it – just a product of boredom with the old dispensation.[36] As we have seen already, the same problem arises with Quine's brand of conceptual-scheme relativism according to which ontologies are as many and various as the schemes that sustain them and statements should therefore be reckoned true or false just in so far as they happen to fill some given ontological bill. Again, it is hard to see how any scientist or mathematician could be rationally motivated – as distinct from culturally, ideologically or psychologically inclined – to give up some regnant set of beliefs in favour of some heterodox set that counted as unscientific or downright irrational by currently accepted standards.

Clearly there is a sense in which the very concept of 'discovery' involves the idea of a break with foregone habits of thought or of stepping outside and seeing beyond some presently existent range of beliefs. If this fact is unaccounted for by the Quine/Kuhn doctrines of ontological relativity and radical meaning-variance across paradigms – so that talk of truth or advances in knowledge becomes problematical or downright naive – then it is the doctrines that consequently stand revealed as suffering from a drastic rationality and normativity deficit.[37] On the other hand upholders of a realist-rationalist view have undoubtedly had their work cut out in producing something better than the kind of knock-down argument that simply appeals to the massive self-evidence of techno-scientific advance and the equally massive miracle or 'cosmic coincidence' required if all those (mostly) high-functioning technologies don't work on (at any rate something very like) the causal-explanatory principles discovered by scientists to date.[38] Despite their near-invincible force as a matter of common-sense inductive reasoning these arguments are subject to all the sophisticated (not to say sophistical) lines of response that sceptics have honed over the past two millennia whenever their opponents fall back on any form of the appeal to inductive warrant. What they lack – necessarily so, given that ultimate ground of appeal – is the conceptual rigour and the *strict*, i.e. formally demonstrable, self-evidence of a procedure that starts out from certain explicit axioms and thereafter proceeds from stage to stage in a sequence of deductively valid reasoning.

Of course this invites the rejoinder, again a staple of sceptics through the ages, which holds that such reasoning can have no traction on issues outside mathematics, logic and the formal sciences. Deductive validity, so the case runs, is uniquely the mark of arguments whose structure is purely tautological, whose conclusion is 'contained in' their premises, or whose self-evidence comes of their conveying no substantive or informative content. However, there are two lines of response then open to the rationalist-realist. One, with its source mainly in the philosophy of natural science, argues on the strength of specific case studies for a better informed and more conceptually adequate conception of the logic of scientific enquiry.

On this account there is something very wrong – albeit a remarkably long-standing and philosophically deep-laid error – about that overly sharp distinction between logical and empirically informed reasoning, or indeed the formal and the natural-scientific modes of truth-testing. Although they have tended to specialise out and develop different technical registers they have a shared point of origin in the investigation of nature and the resultant need for procedures and disciplines – notably those of logic and mathematics – whereby to make best explanatory or predictive sense of those phenomena. In which case philosophy needs to break with the mindset bequeathed by its dualism-touting precursors, from Hume to the logical positivists, and adopt the kind of naturalised rationalist outlook that would treat those problems as so many needless pseudo-dilemmas. Such is the basic motivation of post-positivist thinking, well exemplified by Philip Kitcher's idea of natural 'affordances' as offering a hold for the jointly conceptual-logical-mathematical and perceptual-empirical-explanatory grasp of salient real-world objects, processes and events.[39] It is also a conception closely aligned to the current revival of interest in arguments for abductive reasoning or inference to the best explanation.[40] What they have in common is the clear determination to rid philosophy of that bedevilling notion that there must exist a problematical gap between Humean 'relations of ideas' and 'matters of fact', or again (in logical-positivist terms) purebred deductive logic and everything pertaining to the matter of empirical or observational warrant.

Thus the first line of response to any sceptics who may be over-impressed by Quinean or Kuhnian ontological relativism is one that stresses the grounding of logic (and a fortiori of mathematics) in certain rationally discoverable aspects or structures of physical reality. That is to say, it dissents from Frege's famous logicist critique of those, like J. S. Mill, who would treat logic as empirical through and through, yet dissents not in order to uphold Mill's ultra-empiricist position but rather to reject the very terms of that debate as yet another variant of the old fake dilemma.[41] The second response – most fully developed by Badiou – is one that starts out from the other (rationalist or logicist) standpoint but which likewise refuses to think of this as a choice between alternative or somehow conflicting priorities. Like Parmenides and Spinoza – in other respects two thinkers with whom he is profoundly at odds – Badiou takes it as axiomatic that 'the order and connection of ideas is the same as the order and connection of thoughts'.[42] In this respect he is a thoroughgoing rationalist and monist for whom (as often emerges to forceful effect) the two greatest disasters to have befallen modern philosophy are the Kantian critical-idealist turn with its demotion of ontology in favour of epistemology and then, following directly from that, the latter-day turn toward language or discourse as purportedly a better, more accountable and less metaphysically laden mode of enquiry. In both cases, according to Badiou, the effect has been its progressive degradation through the readiness of philosophers to substitute knowledge-within-human-limits (or the limits of communal expressibility) for objective truth, ontologically conceived as that which might always transcend or surpass those limits. For Badiou, the truth in question – that which philosophers have long attempted to deny or conceal – is the ubiquitous excess of inconsistent over consistent multiplicity, as shown by Cantor's set-theoretical breakthrough to a working concept of the infinite, and the infinitely multiple orders of infinity, that had been strictly unthinkable up to then. With that epochal further passage from the countable to the uncountable, e.g. from the infinity of integers to the infinity of real numbers, mathematics took the leap that philosophers from Parmenides and Plato down had resisted almost as a qualification for being or becoming a philosopher.

Hence, as I have said, Badiou's radical departure from the Parmenidean conception of being as the all-comprehensive One which renders multiplicity the merest of illusions, a doctrine that Zeno famously sought to vindicate with his ingenious sophistical paradoxes of time and motion. In thinkers such as Plato and Spinoza, a symptomatic reading is able to show that this truth invariably leaves its mark in the tensions and torsions of their argument, and all the more so in texts – most notably Plato's *Parmenides* – where that argument engages expressly with themes of the one and the many.[43] What then shows up, through their manifest failure to resolve or suppress the resultant paradoxes, is the strict impossibility of holding thought to a conception of being that would bring multiplicity under the rule of some ultimate, i.e. consistent and exceptionless, instance of the count-as-one. Thus Badiou has nothing but admiration for Socrates' (and Plato's) dogged and intrepid wrestling with problems which here take him into regions of thought where a thinker less committed to the quest for truth, or more dogmatically wedded to his own beliefs, would prudently have feared to tread. To this extent Plato goes further toward an effective, albeit unwilling anticipation of Cantor's discovery than those later thinkers – Leibniz among them – who, despite their greatly more advanced powers of math-ematical grasp, were captive to certain metaphysical ideas (such as the intrinsic dominance of the one over the many) which they took to stand beyond rational challenge. Although Badiou doesn't say so in *Being and Event*, which is organised on largely chronological-developmental lines, it is possible to read Plato's quarrel with himself in the *Parmenides* as a remote prefiguring of just those advances in the working-through of set-theoretical problems and paradoxes that would lead from Cantor's formulation of the power-set theorem to Cohen's invention/discovery of forcing. What links them is just what Badiou finds wanting in Aristotle, Leibniz, Spinoza and other expo-nents of a plenist ontology. That is, these thinkers fail to allow for the subtractive element – the inconsistency or uncounted multiple – concealed by every instance of a given or in-place unifying count. On the one hand this constitutes a structural lack or unperceived deficit in some present-best state of knowledge while on the other it signals the future possibility, as always granted the active intervention of dedicated subjects, that a truth-procedure will be set in train and a consequent advance in knowledge come about.

V

This is why the Cohen 'event' is of such decisive importance for Badiou, ranking as it does – in his estimation – with Cantor's inau-gural discovery.[44] It provides the first adequate formalisation, in set-theoretical terms, of what he sees as the only viable account of how theory-change occurs despite and against the weight of received or orthodox belief. In this way – by approaching the issue via mathematics (and hence, Badiou claims, via the discourse on and of fundamental ontology) – Cohen's technique of forcing achieves what could not be achieved by those empirically and inductively based arguments, such as 'no miracles' and 'cosmic coincidence', that had a good deal of common-sense-intuitive clout but lacked any means of formalisation and could hence be made out to beg certain crucial questions. More than that, it holds the promise of marking a break with that entire history of thought from Kant to the basically post-Kantian travails of recent analytic epistemology and philosophy of language that has occurred – on Badiou's diagnosis – in consequence of the widespread retreat from ontology as philosophy's primary since truth-oriented task or vocation. Forcing offers a formal, set-theoretically derived account of the operations involved in passing from one state of knowledge to another, more advanced state of knowledge even if by means of procedures whose logic becomes intelligible only in retrospect, i.e. from the more advanced situation. In so doing, he claims, it offers a uniquely cogent and powerful means of resolving some of the deepest-laid problems of modern philosophy. These latter run all the way from Kant to Carnap, and thereafter range from the terminal dilemmas of logical positivism/empiricism to the above-discussed normative deficit afflicting philosophy of science and epistemology in the Quinean-Kuhnian wake. Forcing thus becomes the form ultimately taken by a rigorous logico-mathematical statement of what it would require in order for theory-change – or the process of knowledge-acquisition – to become both rationally accountable and capable of assessment in terms of trans-paradigm advancement. Such changes would no longer be subject to relativisation in the Quinean-Kuhnian or, at the limit, the Rortian neo-pragmatist manner which takes them as always specific or internal to some given conceptual framework, ontological scheme, scientific paradigm or descriptive vocabulary.[45] Rather they would be subject to the kind of exploratory, speculative, yet none the less analytically rigorous investigation that has characterised the development of set-theoretical thought.

Here we return, and not before time, to my framing topic which (you may recall) had to do with Austin's passing quip about the close kinship – at any rate the frequent correlation – between great philosophy and the proneness to commit great mistakes. Or perhaps I should rather say 'great errors', bearing in mind the distinction drawn by Paul de Man in a penetrating essay on the various swerves from textual fidelity – some of them quite flagrant – in Heidegger's exegeses of Hölderlin.[46] While the word 'mistake' is most aptly used in cases of carelessness, confusion or inattentive reading the imputation of 'error' is best reserved for those other, more symptomatically revealing sorts of case where a 'strong' interpreter misreads on account of some predisposed will to find a meaning attuned to her or his motivating interests. Such, de Man claims, is Heidegger's way with Hölderlin and such de Man's practice of deconstructive reading in certain instances (among them this Heidegger commentary) when driven by his own sorts of motivating interest or imperative. With Badiou it is not a question of errors wilfully committed, far less of mistakes unwittingly fallen into, but rather the mark of a thinker whose very ambition and speculative range lays his work constitutively open to the risk of going – so to speak – off the rails of a secure methodology or a pre-set agenda of the type favoured by most analytic philosophers. In other words he is not doing 'philosophy of mathematics' as practised by those who conventionally take it that this is by very definition an activity conducted at a distance from, and with no valid claim to participate in, the first-order activity of advanced or creative mathematical thought. Where that approach tends to focus on a handful of topics, such as the issue between realism and anti-realism or the rule-following debate, Badiou works on the opposite principle: that although philosophy has to operate at a certain clearly marked remove from mathematics it none the less has to *think mathematically* at least to the extent of adopting certain as yet unproven axioms and pursuing their consequences with the utmost rigour. That principle – strikingly remote as it is from the mainstream-analytic norm – can be seen to stand as the enabling condition for any project, like his, that not only takes mathematics as the source of any adequate critical ontology but which aims on that basis to rethink the very possibility of radical (as distinct from incremental or piecemeal) advances in the realms of science and politics.

My talk of rails (and coming off them) in the above paragraph may well recall themes from the later Wittgenstein, in particular some much discussed passages from the *Philosophical Investigations*. There he talks about a certain conception of reasoning, or formal rule-following, which mistakenly supposes correctness in such matters to consist in nothing more than the prescribed application of this or that algorithmic procedure laid down in advance like a 'super-rigid rail'.[47] However, there is a great difference between the lesson that Wittgenstein draws from this metaphor and its relevance when used, as here, by way of suggesting what sets Badiou's thought so decisively apart from mainstream philosophy of mathematics. For Wittgenstein, the super-rigid rail fallacy – the error of thinking that rules can be applied in a purely mechanical way without the least exercise of intelligence or reflective judgement – is one that gives rise to a typically philosophical pseudo-dilemma that can be resolved only by opting out of philosophy as presently practised or conceived. It entails *either* the vicious regress of rules for the application of rules for the application of rules (etc.), *or* the equally vicious circularity of rules that are self-sufficient since self-regulating, *or* (his preferred option) the saving recourse to a communitarian idea of correctness that makes it nothing other or more than a matter of best judgement among those communally deemed best qualified to know.

Hence Saul Kripke's famous (purported) demonstration that

Wittgenstein is right, that rules such as $2 + 2 = 4$ or for continuing a given numerical series are indeed communal at bottom, and that therefore the best one can have is a far from comforting 'sceptical solution' to Wittgenstein's profoundly troubling sceptical problem.[48] Nothing could be further from what I meant when I said that Badiou's thinking about/through mathematics is not rule-governed – or rail-governed – in the sense that applies to so many analytic treatments of the subject. Wittgenstein goes straight from that problem, or pseudo-problem, to a conception of mathematics and logic that would ultimately find no room for standards of formal rigour and conceptual precision aside from the communally sanctioned role of such talk in the relevant 'language game' or 'form of life'. Badiou draws just the opposite conclusion from what he takes to be the inherently limited – since always at a certain point aporetic or paradox-prone – character of any formal system beyond a certain level of complexity, including those systems that play a strictly indispensable role in the discourse of post-Cantorian set theory. Of course this much has been accepted as a matter of established logico-mathematical truth since Gödel proved his incompleteness theorem, and – to broadly comparable effect – since Russell discovered his set-theoretical paradox. However, Badiou's distinctive way of following out its philosophical as well as mathematical implications is something that finds absolutely no equivalent in the analytic uptake of those same developments. Here they typically register, with thinkers like Quine or Putnam, as factors that must surely be reckoned with in any adequate survey of the field or methodological, i.e. meta-procedural, account but which all the same need not – perhaps should not, on pain of incoherence – affect the very logic of their treatment at that basically expository level.[49]

Nor is this an idle worry since, as I have said, there is indeed a problem – albeit the reverse sort of problem – when one asks how to square the express commitments of these logical revisionists with the fact that they have to argue in accordance with the precepts of classical logic in order to advance their case with any degree of logical force. Still the case is very different with Badiou since his entire approach is such as to reject that idea, deep-laid within the analytic tradition from logical positivism down, of a necessary and principled distinction between first-order and second-order or logical and meta-logical concerns. Even where the distinction comes under strain or seems to collapse – as occurs, in different ways, with the later Wittgenstein and in Quine's 'Two Dogmas of

Empiricism' – it leaves behind, as I have said, the meta-problem of a drastic normative deficit. This is where Badiou strikes out in such a different and vastly more promising direction. So far from collapsing these orders of discourse into a pragmatist, ontological-relativist or framework-internalist approach – the preferred options of Quine and later Putnam – he takes it that the philosophical discourse on mathematics can and should incorporate into itself all those developments, including Gödel's and Russell's results, that have turned out to complicate the precepts of classical logic. And again, so far from relaxing or simply letting go those precepts he shows how they must continue to operate even (or especially) where they are brought up against the sorts of paradoxical or aporetic outcome that signal their limits of consistent application.

It is at just these cardinal points – points of crisis and imminent breakdown, though also of potentially transformative advance – that thought bears witness to the unpredictable irruption of that inconsistent multiplicity that always inhabited the count-as-one but only now visibly threatens to disrupt its operation. Yet it is also, and crucially, an absolute requirement for any formal demonstration of the processes involved that this be conducted with the strictest regard to those standards of logical consistency and rigour – classical standards such as bivalence, excluded middle and (of course) non-contradiction – that alone make possible and serve to validate that procedure. After all the same conditions apply in the case of a result like that of Gödel's incompleteness theorem where it would seem that if the proof-procedure goes through, i.e. is taken to show that no logical system can be proven both exhaustively valid and fully consistent, then that very upshot is enough to undermine the result thus arrived at. Yet of course the proof is nowadays near universally accepted as having indeed both established the truth of the theorem and done so by means that satisfy those rigorous conditions despite what appears the self-refuting character of any claim to that effect. That it carries such a force of logical self-evidence is due to the mode of jointly demonstrative (formal) and speculative reasoning that it shares with Badiou's *Being and Event* and also, as I have argued at length elsewhere, with Derrida's work.[50] Here likewise it is matter of those deviant, non-classical, paraconsistent or non-bivalent logics that are found to inhabit the texts of philosophers from Plato to Husserl and to raise kindred issues in that regard, yet the workings of which cannot be revealed – or shown up as specifically departing from the classical norm – except on condition of those texts being read in strict accordance with just that norm. Moreover, as with Badiou's exegetical chapters in *Being and Event*, this critical engagement with earlier thinkers involves just the kind of speculative reach combined with logical-conceptual rigour that has typified mathematics during its periods of most intensive or revolutionary activity.

I hope it will be clear by now what I take to be the relevance of Austin's remark about philosophical greatness and great mistakes to the much discussed but still largely unanswered question of how to distinguish 'continental' from 'analytic' philosophy. Even if one tends to wince at Slavoj Žižek's jacket-copy for one of Badiou's recent books – 'A Plato or a Hegel walks among us!' – the claim is not ludicrous when applied to Badiou or Derrida in the way that it would be if applied to any analytic philosopher after Russell. I have argued that this has chiefly to do with the way that these thinkers manage to combine an extraordinary degree of speculative energy and formal inventiveness with a singular strength of analytic grasp that doesn't so much restrain or temper those qualities as focus them all the more sharply. In Badiou's case, to repeat, it is a matter of adopting certain ground-breaking axioms that lack any conclusive proof yet which offer themselves with a force of conviction – a powerful if at present obscurely motivated force – which warrants their pursuit into uncharted regions of thought and the wager on their truth as potentially open to discovery through the advent of some currently unknown proof-procedure. Cohen's 'forcing' is precisely the formal articulation and generalised statement of this approach to mathematical problem-solving which finds its most striking example in Cantor's technique of diagonalisation and subsequent set-theoretical advances achieved through the process that Badiou describes as 'turning paradox into concept'. It could even be said to have started out with those ancient aporias of the one and many – or consistent versus inconsistent multiplicity – which so ruffled Plato's dialectical composure in the *Parmenides* and which later (as he shows in *Being and Event*) emerged to kindred disruptive effect in the work of Aristotle, Leibniz, Spinoza and others.

My point is that there is something inherently error-prone, or perpetually exposed to the risk of error, in any thought that proceeds by wagering the truth of its central hypotheses, the validity of its axioms or the justification of its working methods on a procedure that not only trusts to the event of their future vindication but requires the kind of unswerving fidelity that holds out even in the face of seeming failure or falsification. What distinguishes this from mere pig-headedness, doctrinal adherence, or downright stupidity is precisely what Cohen's discovery of forcing brought to a high point of formal statement. In short, it involves the regulated introduction of additional axioms selected through a process of filtering that – as explained above – distinguishes generic from non-generic elements, or those capable of playing a role in a genuine truth-procedure from those whose particular (context-specific or intensional as opposed to extensional) status prevents them from so doing. This is why Badiou is able to press so far with his more-than-analogy between mathematics and politics, no doubt at risk of provoking (to say the least) scepticism among rail-following analytic philosophers but with strong support from his working-through of set-theoretical developments from Cantor to Cohen. Thus to simplify massively: just as mathematicians may be required to pursue some hypothesis through the travails of repeated failure to achieve a definitive proof so those who keep faith with 'the communist hypothesis' have to maintain their belief in its possible fulfilment or practical realisation despite all the melancholy evidence to date.[51] Moreover, Badiou's entire project inherits the intrinsic riskiness involved in any reasoning upon axioms beyond the current reach of demonstrative proof. My contention is that Austin got it half-right and that among the preconditions for great philosophy is not so much the propensity for making great mistakes but rather the acknowledged liability to error – sometimes, not always, productive error – that goes along with the capacity for great thinking.

Notes

1. Jonathan Bennett, 'Spinoza on error', *Philosophical Papers*, Vol. 15 (1986), pp. 59–73, at p. 59.
2. See especially J. L. Austin, *Philosophical Papers* (Oxford: Oxford University Press, 1979).
3. Ibid., p. 80.
4. See especially P. F. Strawson, *The Bounds of Sense: An Essay on Kant's Critique of Pure Reason* (London: Methuen, 1966).
5. Bennett, *Learning from Six Philosophers, Vol. One: Descartes, Spinoza, Leibniz* (Oxford: Clarendon Press, 2001).
6. Bennett, *A Study of Spinoza's Ethics* (Cambridge: Cambridge University Press, 1984); see also Norris, 'Catching up with Spinoza: naturalism, rationalism, and cognitive science', in *Re-Thinking the Cogito: Naturalism, Reason, and the Venture of Thought* (London: Continuum, 2010), pp. 139–6, especially pp. 140–3.
7. Bennett, 'Spinoza on error', op. cit., p. 59.

8. Immanuel Kant, *Critique of Pure Reason*, trans. N. Kemp Smith (London: Macmillan, 1964); also – of particular relevance here – Henry E. Allison, *Kant's Transcendental Idealism*, 2nd edn (New Haven, CT: Yale University Press, 2004).

9. For some highly informative discussion, see Beth Lord, *Kant and Spinozism: Transcendental Idealism and Immanence from Jacobi to Deleuze* (London: Macmillan, 2011).

10. Thomas S. Kuhn, *The Structure of Scientific Revolutions*, 2nd edn (Chicago: University of Chicago Press, 1970).

11. See Gottlob Frege, 'Review of Edmund Husserl's *Philosophie der Arithmetik*', trans. E.-H. W. Kluge, *Mind*, 81 (1972), pp. 321–37.

12. Gilbert Ryle, 'Phenomenology' and 'Phenomenology versus *The Concept of Mind*', in Ryle, *Collected Papers*, Vol. 1 (London: Hutchinson, 1971), pp. 167–78 and 179–96; also Leila Haaparanta (ed.), *Mind, Meaning, and Mathematics: Essays on the Philosophical Views of Husserl and Frege* (Dordrecht and Boston: Kluwer, 1994).

13. Michael Dummett, *The Origins of Analytic Philosophy* (London: Duckworth, 1993).

14. See, for instance, Norris, *Minding the Gap: Epistemology and Philosophy of Science in the Two Traditions* (Amherst: University of Massachusetts Press, 2000) and *On Truth and Meaning: Language, Logic and the Grounds of Belief* (London: Continuum, 2006).

15. See Jacques Derrida, 'Signature event context', *Glyph*, Vol. 1 (Baltimore: Johns Hopkins University Press, 1975), pp. 172–97; John R. Searle, 'Reiterating the differences', ibid., pp. 198–208; Derrida, 'Limited Inc abc', *Glyph*, Vol. 2 (1977), pp. 75–176; also Derrida, 'Afterword: toward an ethic of conversation', in Gerald Graff (ed.), *Limited Inc* (Evanston: Northwestern University Press, 1989), pp. 111–54.

16. Søren Kierkegaard, *The Concept of Irony, with Continual Reference to Socrates*, trans. Howard and Edna Hong (Princeton: Princeton University Press, 1992).

17. See especially W. V. Quine, 'Two dogmas of empiricism', in *From a Logical Point of View*, 2nd edn (Cambridge, MA: Harvard University Press, 1961) and *Ontological Relativity and Other Essays* (New York: Columbia University Press, 1969); also Hilary Putnam, *Mathematics, Matter and Method* (Cambridge: Cambridge University Press, 1975).

18. For further argument to this effect, see Susan Haack, *Deviant Logic: Some Philosophical Issues* (Cambridge: Cambridge University Press, 1974) and Jaegwon Kim, *Supervenience and Mind* (Cambridge: Cambridge University Press, 1993).

19. See also Paul Livingston, *The Politics of Logic: Badiou, Wittgenstein, and the Consequences of Formalism* (London: Routledge, 2011) and Norris, *Derrida, Badiou and the Formal Imperative* (London: Continuum, 2012).

20. Derrida, 'Speech and Phenomena' and Other Essays on Husserl's Theory of Signs, trans. David B. Allison (Evanston: Northwestern University Press, 1973); Of Grammatology, trans. Gayatri C. Spivak (Baltimore: Johns Hopkins University Press, 1974); Writing and Difference, trans. Alan Bass (London: Routledge & Kegan Paul, 1978); Dissemination, trans. Barbara Johnson (London: Athlone Press, 1981); Margins of Philosophy, trans. Alan Bass (Chicago: University of Chicago Press, 1982).

21. Alain Badiou, Being and Event, trans. Oliver Feltham (London: Continuum, 2005); also Norris, Badiou's Being and Event: A Reader's Guide (London: Continuum, 2009).

22. See for, instance, Badiou, Manifesto for Philosophy, trans. Norman Madarasz (Albany, NY: State University of New York Press, 1999); Infinite Thought: Truth and the Return to Philosophy, trans. Oliver Feltham and Justin Clemens (London: Continuum, 2003); Theoretical Writings, ed. and trans. Ray Brassier and Alberto Toscano (London: Continuum, 2004); Metapolitics, trans. Jason Barker (London: Verso, 2005); Polemics, trans. Steve Corcoran (London: Verso, 2006); The Century, trans. Alberto Toscano (Cambridge: Polity Press, 2007); Conditions, trans. Steve Corcoran (London: Continuum, 2009); Second Manifesto for Philosophy, trans. Louise Burchill (London: Polity Press, 2011).

23. Kurt Gödel, 'On formally undecidable propositions of Principia Mathematica and related systems', trans. B. Meltzer (New York: Basic Books, 1962); see also S. G. Shanker (ed.), Gödel's Theorem in Focus (London: Routledge, 1987).

24. See especially Badiou, Manifesto for Philosophy, op. cit.

25. See Badiou, Being and Event and Manifesto for Philosophy; also his Number and Numbers, trans. Robin Mackay (Cambridge: Polity, 2008).

26. Quine, 'Two dogmas of empiricism', op. cit.

27. See Badiou, 'Theory of the pure multiple: paradoxes and critical decision', in Being and Event, op. cit., pp. 38–48; also – for an excellent primer – Michael Potter, Set Theory and Its Philosophy: A Critical Introduction (Oxford: Oxford University Press, 2004).

28. See Badiou, Being and Event, op. cit.; also Ethics: An Essay on Evil, trans. Peter Hallward (London: Verso, 2001).

29. See Badiou, Metapolitics, op. cit.

30. Quine, Ontological Relativity and Other Essays, op. cit.

31. Paul J. Cohen, Set Theory and the Continuum Hypothesis (New York: W. Benjamin, 1966).

32. For an earlier text that treats these issues from a different though closely related standpoint, see Badiou, Theory of the Subject, trans. Bruno Bosteels (London: Continuum, 2009).

33. See Badiou, 'Platonism and mathematical ontology', in *Theoretical Writings*, op. cit., pp. 49–58; Plato, *Meno*, ed. J. Seymer Thompson (London: Macmillan, 1901).

34. See especially Paul Benacerraf, 'What numbers could not be', in Benacerraf and Hilary Putnam (eds), *The Philosophy of Mathematics: Selected Essays*, 2nd edn (Cambridge: Cambridge University Press, 1983), pp. 272–94; also W. D. Hart (ed.), *The Philosophy of Mathematics* (Oxford: Oxford University Press, 1996).

35. See especially Badiou, *Manifesto for Philosophy*, op. cit.

36. See, for instance, Richard Rorty, *Consequences of Pragmatism* (Brighton: Harvester, 1982) and *Objectivity, Relativism, and Truth* (Cambridge: Cambridge University Press, 1991).

37. Kim, *Supervenience and Mind*, op. cit.

38. For further discussion of these issues in philosophy of science, see Larry Laudan, *Progress and Its Problems* (Berkeley and Los Angeles: University of California Press, 1977); also Norris, *Against Relativism: Philosophy of Science, Deconstruction and Critical Theory* (Oxford: Blackwell, 1997) and *Philosophy of Language and the Challenge to Scientific Realism* (London: Routledge, 2004).

39. Philip Kitcher, *The Nature of Mathematical Knowledge* (Oxford: Oxford University Press, 1983).

40. Peter Lipton, *Inference to the Best Explanation* (London: Routledge, 1993).

41. J. S. Mill, *A System of Logic* (New York: Harper, 1874), pp. 430 ff.; Gottlob Frege, *Foundations of Arithmetic*, trans J. L. Austin (Evanston: Northwestern University Press, 1974); also Kitcher, *The Nature of Mathematical Knowledge*, op. cit. and Norris, 'Who's afraid of psychologism? Normativity, truth, and epistemic warrant', in *On Truth and Meaning*, op. cit., pp. 12–40.

42. Spinoza, *Ethics*, trans. Edwin Curley (Harmondsworth: Penguin, 1994), Book II, Proposition vii.

43. Plato, *Parmenides*, trans. Mary L. Gill and Paul Ryan (Indianapolis: Hackett, 1996). For further discussion see also John A. Palmer, *Plato's Reception of Parmenides* (Oxford: Clarendon Press, 2002).

44. Cohen, *Set Theory and the Continuum Hypothesis*, op. cit.

45. See notes 10, 17 and 36, above.

46. Paul de Man, 'Heidegger's exegeses of Hölderlin', in *Blindness and Insight: Essays in the Rhetoric of Contemporary Criticism*, 2nd edn (London: Methuen, 1983), pp. 246–66.

47. Ludwig Wittgenstein, *Philosophical Investigations*, trans. G. E. M. Anscombe (Oxford: Blackwell, 1954), Sections 201–292 *passim*.

48. Saul Kripke, *Wittgenstein on Rules and Private Language: An Elementary Exposition* (Oxford: Blackwell, 1982); also Alexander Miller and Crispin Wright (eds), *Rule-Following and Meaning*

(Chesham: Acumen, 2002) and Norris, 'Kripkenstein's monsters: anti-realism, scepticism, and the rule-following debate', in *On Truth and Meaning*, op. cit., pp. 155–202.

49. See note 17, above; also Norris, 'The blank and the die: more dilemmas of post-empiricism', in *On Truth and Meaning*, op. cit., pp. 102–29.
50. Norris, *Derrida, Badiou and the Formal Imperative*, op. cit.
51. Badiou, *The Communist Hypothesis*, trans. David Macey and Steve Corcoran (London: Verso, 2010).

CHAPTER 3

Under Which King, Bezonian? Experimental Philosophy versus Thought Experiment

I

It is no coincidence that the current upsurge of interest in 'experimental philosophy' has gone along with a renewed bout of argument concerning the usefulness (or otherwise) of philosophical thought experiments.[1] 'Gone along with' is perhaps not the best phrase to use in this context since advocates of the two approaches not only form separate academic camps but can be seen to have sharply opposed views of what philosophy properly is and does. Experimentalists in Camp One think that the best thing philosophers can do is stop laying claim to some order of knowledge or insight denied to your ordinary, average, philosophically untrained human being and instead start asking around among a wide range of respondents both inside and (more importantly) outside their own specialist community. 'Experiment' in this sense involves a continued address to the traditional problems of philosophy – problems of metaphysics, epistemology, ethics, aesthetics, political theory and so forth – but pitched in a very different key since it adopts (what it takes to be) the path of empirical enquiry flagged by the social sciences and consults the evidence of popular belief rather than the upshot of 'expert' cogitation. Those in Camp Two see nothing wrong with the way that philosophers have most often set about their task, that is, by conducting thought experiments – 'armchair philosophising', as sceptics have dubbed it – designed to establish the truth of certain propositions or, by logical devices like *reductio ad absurdum*, the truth of some through the manifest falsity of their contrary. Experimentation of this kind depends little, if at all, on empirical evidence as to how people generally tend to think since it locates the source of veridical knowledge in some version of the apodictic appeal to a priori truths, or those self-evident to reason, which has been a central feature of the rationalist tradition from Descartes down.[2]

So the two camps are very far apart and indeed, if recent exchanges are anything to go by, very prone to define their respective profiles as mirror-images of each other. Thus the current high visibility of both is not so much a sign that they might have something deeper in common but rather a sign that the difference between them marks a particularly deep fault-line in the way that philosophers nowadays conceive the scope and limits of what they do. Both parties are apt to voice occasional doubts concerning philosophy's role in a culture so largely given over to science-led conceptions of truth, rationality and method. However, they come up with different diagnoses of why this should be the case and – as we shall see – with contrary prescriptions for heading off the threat. Camp One experimentalists reject not only the idea of philosophers as specialists in knowledge acquisition but also, on a rather different tack, the appeal to an order of knowledge potentially accessible to everyone just in virtue of its being a priori and hence hard-wired, so to speak, into the structure of human perceptual experience and cognitive judgement. Such notions should be junked, so the argument goes, because (1) they are redundant and explain absolutely nothing; (2) they run up against counter-evidence from the diversity of what counts as 'self-evident' across cultures, languages or historical periods; and (3) under cover of a specious universalist appeal to the witness of human knowledge and experience in general they actually rest their case on a specialist (*echt*-philosophical) sense of the issues involved. In short, if philosophers want to stay in a job then they had much better drop their delusory claims to a special, uniquely self-validating kind of knowledge and switch to the less grandiose but more useful business of asking around for a good range of answers to sensibly framed questions. Camp Two experimentalists regard this not only as selling philosophy short – reducing it to a humble sub-branch of anthropology, psychology, linguistics or the social sciences – but also as lamentably failing to grasp what is distinctive (indeed unique) about the philosophical enterprise. If it is not to be squeezed out of existence by those other disciplines – and moreover, if they themselves are not to suffer through a lack of properly informed philosophical input – then it needs to resist the pressures that would make for any such self-delegitimising move.

Nor should this be seen, so the thought experimentalists urge, as merely a form of academic one-upmanship or just another ploy for hanging onto philosophy's traditional role as a well-established 'field' with its own proper range of accredited truth-procedures. On the contrary: when philosophers purport to know certain truths as a matter of a priori self-evidence then they are also – along with such otherwise diverse precursors as Plato, Descartes, Kant and Frege – extending that claim far beyond the realm of intra-philosophical debate. That is, they are invoking a mode of knowledge that can and must be accessible to all human beings (all sentient and sapient members of the species) in virtue of their shared cognitive resources and quite apart from their happening to possess or to lack some measure of trained philosophical expertise. No doubt it is a main part of these philosophers' case that the kinds of rational-intuitive knowledge or judgement here in question can be clarified, sharpened and rendered more accessible to conscious or reflective understanding through the kind of mental exercise involved in the conduct of well devised thought experiments. All the same these logically require the existence of another, less specialised stratum of a priori knowledge toward which the exercise is directed or upon which it practises this expert technique. Even when thought experiments lead into fairly remote or abstruse metaphysical regions (e.g. debates between realists and anti-realists concerning mathematical objects and their mode of existence) there is always that appeal open from the philosopher's presumptively expert judgement to the witness of widely shared rational-intuitive conviction. If philosophers – or for that matter physical scientists – come to think that they have good reason for rejecting what presently counts as self-evident then they will need to do so, in the long run at least, by adducing arguments (or a range of conjoint empirical, theoretical and explanatory grounds) with a stronger claim to enjoy the equivalent status.

Above all, they can and should stand firm on the principle that philosophy has to do with first-order questions concerning such matters as truth, knowledge, consciousness, intentionality, sense, reference and the like, rather than with any second-order question concerning whatever might happen to be the majority opinion on those topics among some sample group of respondents. This case has been put most forcefully by Camp Two thinkers, Timothy Williamson among them, who reject what they consider the trivialising notion – one that held sway in many quarters of analytic debate until quite recently – that the proper or even sole legitimate business of philosophy is that of conceptual analysis.[3] More specifically, they see no justification for the drastic narrowing of philosophic sights that this was commonly taken to require, i.e. the restriction to a purebred strain of analysis which strictly eschewed any backsliding into bad old Kantian synthetic a priori ways of thought. For the ultimate result of this negative ordinance was – or at any rate would surely have been, had its proponents pushed right through with it – completely to deny philosophy's right or competence to pronounce on matters of substantive import beyond that self-enclosed regulative sphere. Once headed in this direction it is not very far to the pyrrhic upshot that G. E. Moore labelled the 'paradox of analysis', that is, the point at which philosophical discourse aspires to the purely self-validating (hence redundant or tautologous) status of the analytic proposition strictly so defined.[4] It can then, by its own lights, have nothing of substance or interest to contribute beyond what is already there – stated or presupposed – in one or another constituent premise. This is why the thought experimentalists are keen to stake their distance not only from empirically minded experimental philosophers but also from those of a contrary persuasion – *echt*-analytic types – whose prescription would, if consistently applied, have a likewise deleterious effect. Thus it would leave no work for philosophy to do beyond the elucidation of pre-existing concepts and the parsing of various set-piece statements along with their validity-conditions.

Of course there has been much debate among philosophers from Kant to the present concerning the question as to whether there exist any genuinely a priori truths, or the further question as to whether, if so, they can have any genuine (synthetic or substantive rather than merely analytic or tautological) import.[5] However, what the thought experimentalists have to assume in order for their arguments to get off the ground is the validity of certain rational intuitions – most importantly, certain synthetic a priori results – arrived at on the basis of logical reasoning from strictly inescapable or self-evident premises. Thus they may, as Williamson argues, on occasion come up with metaphysical truths or discoveries concerning what is necessarily the case with respect to some particular topic-domain (mathematics, physics, temporal relations, causality, free-will, personal identity and so forth) which take the enquirer out beyond anything belonging to her previous stock of knowledge or range of rational-intuitive grasp. Still it is plainly the case that such advances cannot come about by thought-experimental means unless they are in some way potentially 'there' within the cognitive or epistemic ken of suitably placed human subjects. So really there is a sizeable area of agreement between Camps One and Two – the empirical investigators and the thought experimentalists – despite their currently squared-off stance of mutual suspicion or hostility. No doubt they are opposed in some fairly basic ways, chief among them the trademark Camp

One devotion to canvassing philosophically untutored informants as against the Camp Two preference for subjects (basically themselves or fellow members of the profession) trained up in philosophical ways of thought. However, in the end this opposition comes down to something like a rerun of various old debates – most obviously empiricism versus rationalism – which have found a great range of revised, refined or elaborated versions in present-day discussion. Camps One and Two can be seen to take up their contrary positions on ground staked out in advance by sundry antagonists – from Locke contra Descartes to Hume contra Leibniz and thence to any number of current post-Quinean disputes – which have pitched the defenders of common-sense empiricism against their rationalist adversaries.[6] In each case it might well turn out that a bit more patient exploratory digging on ground long trodden into ruts will reveal certain deeper-laid affinities that require a fairly drastic revision of the standard textbook account.

The two factions have at any rate this much in common: that they both make appeal – necessarily so – to one or other side in those various disputes (expert v. lay, rationalist v. empiricist, a priori v. a posteriori, etc.) where the appearance of conflict actually conceals an underlying kinship of method and purpose. Just as the rationalist Descartes has to take for granted the human reliance on a whole range of sensory-perceptual inputs so likewise the supposed arch-empiricist Locke inconspicuously helps himself to enough in the way of innate ideas for his empiricism not to look implausible or downright absurd.[7] Much the same point can be made about the tendency of Camp One and Camp Two experimentalists to quietly swap roles or switch priorities when it comes to explaining, refining and defending their respective positions. Thus the former constantly quiz their subjects on just the sorts of topic – ethics, identity or personhood, language (e.g. the tussle between descriptivist and causal theories of reference), epistemology and a range of metaphysical issues – which require, if those subjects' responses are to carry any weight, not only some form of a priori knowledge but also a distinct aptitude for addressing such trademark philosophical issues. Although they may not be 'expert' in the sense of 'trained up or professionally qualified' they must surely be taken to possess at the very least that degree of adjudicative competence that makes it worth the experimenter's while to consult them as offering evidence appropriate to the case in hand. And conversely, when the Camp Two ('armchair') thought experimentalist thinks to derive certain substantive conclusions from consulting her own philosophically disciplined rational intuitions it can scarcely be on the exceptionalist premise or elitist assumption that these somehow lift her outside and above the realm of everyday knowledge. Both parties have a need to avail themselves of something that in theory is the perquisite of those on 'the other side', but which in truth is common property for any thinker whose ideas are not programmed in advance by this present-day revival of the old empiricist/rationalist debate.

Nor is it really such an outright clincher, as Camp One thinkers typically suppose, that the armchair types can be seen to rest their case on a fallacious or unwarranted appeal to the stability and universality – at any rate the strong uniformity – of human intuitions across differences of historical, geographical and socio-cultural context. No doubt, as many in Camp Two will readily admit, there is evidence that responses do indeed vary from one such context to another along with certain ideas about just what counts – should properly, legitimately count – as a rational intuition. Moreover there may be empirical evidence to show beyond reasonable doubt that these ideas have sometimes, and perhaps very often, varied according to other (e.g. gender-marked) perceptions of the normative standards that distinguish valid from invalid truth-claims.[8] Hence, for instance, Tamler Sommers' typical Camp One claim that thought experiments and the kinds of argument raised in their defence are based on 'empirically implausible assumptions about the stability and universality of intuitions'.[9] Still this offers no genuine support for the Camp One case against any notion that philosophers might somehow excogitate important (substantive or informative) truths simply by taking thought or by deploying resources available only through experiments conducted in the 'laboratory of the mind'. For there is no argument on empirical grounds or from a survey-based conspectus of widely held views that could possibly invalidate the thought experimenter's basic claim, i.e. that an appeal to the considered intuitions of suitably equipped (rational, reflective, sensorily responsive, perceptually unimpaired) subjects is a *sine qua non* of acceptability for judgements of the relevant kind. After all, the Camp One experimentalists are themselves dependent for any claims they can muster on the say-so of experimental subjects – those hauled in to answer the questions – and unless these respondents are given credit for thinking straight and having access to reliably accurate intuitions then the whole line of argument collapses into manifest nonsense. Any probative value attaching to the verdict of this or that informant will depend upon their accreditation as a subject 'presumed to know', at least to the extent of being able to perceive, apprehend and reflectively engage with whatever topic comes up for review.

II

Thus there is something highly questionable about the oft-repeated Camp One claim that an appeal to philosophically 'expert' judgement is really no such thing but instead just a means of boosting philosophers' preferred self-image as purveyors of truths unknown to those without the relevant training or (perhaps) the requisite native intelligence. For the thought experimentalist can easily turn this argument around and make the point that, in philosophy as elsewhere, expertise mostly comes from the further cultivation of perceptual, cognitive or intellectual capacities that are widely shared (even universal) among normally constituted human beings but which some of them develop to a higher degree through specialist training of various sorts. In that case any results produced through a rational, disciplined, well-conducted exercise of speculative thought can surely be held to reflect or embody the kinds of judgement that 'ordinary people' or 'lay philosophers' would reliably produce if persuaded to focus their minds on such matters.

Williamson makes the case very pointedly when he remarks that most people – those with no expert training in philosophy but none the less able to think straight in a range of everyday situations – must in fact be well practised in the art or technique of modal reasoning from counterfactual premises.[10] This they share not only with philosophers but also with historians, physical scientists, sociologists, psychologists, detectives and anyone else (that is to say, all of us) with a practical interest in procedures like inference to the best causal explanation.[11] It involves the very basic human capacity for testing certain explanatory conjectures by conducting a thought-experimental variation on the presumed causal antecedents of some given state of affairs and seeing whether that state of affairs would demonstrably *not* have come about had the alternative (counterfactual) scenario obtained. Instances abound across all those disciplines, in particular history and the natural sciences, where causal factors play a large role and where there is scope for constructing or devising what modal logicians call a 'nearby possible world', i.e. a historical or physical state of affairs that departs from actuality – from the real-world course of events – only in the most relevant (explanatorily crucial) respects.[12] But they are also to be found in a great many everyday situations when people need to figure out why something happened and do so, at whatever level of conscious awareness, by asking themselves if the same thing would have occurred in the absence of this or that antecedent condition. Thus, in Williamson's succinct formulation, thought experiments of the relevant kind are those in which certain (presumptively) valid conclusions are arrived at through a procedure of 'employing deductively valid arguments with counterfactual premises that we evaluate as we evaluate other counterfactuals, using a mixture of imaginative simulation, background information, and logic'.[13] Of course this might make the process sound so highly technical or intra-philosophical that it could scarcely have any bearing on matters of everyday or real-world practical concern. All the same that impression is readily dispelled – so the Camp Two theorists maintain – by reflecting on the way that we normally (and reliably) reason when confronted with certain problem situations or unresolved issues that are such as to require an exercise of rationally motivated speculative thought. By this is meant one that goes appreciably beyond the empirical evidence or anything derivable in terms of straightforward (analytically valid) deductive warrant but which is also – crucially – an exercise constrained by standards of logical consistency and truth.

Hence Williamson's on the face of it implausible claim that the average person is competent in handling a good range of seemingly 'technical' questions having to do with metaphysical possibility, modal logic, counterfactual-conditional reasoning and other topics that more typically preoccupy philosophers. On this view there are two basic claims that the thought experimentalist needs to establish against the experimental philosophers, or those who would reject the very idea that 'armchair' philosophy – as widely practised by a great many thinkers from Plato to the present – can afford us access to truths beyond the trivially self-evident or the tautologies of formal logic. One is the claim that there exists a basic continuity between everyday, common sense or philosophically untrained modes of reasoning and the sorts of relatively specialised argument that take place in philosophy seminar rooms or the pages of academic journals. On Williamson's account we can safely suppose such reasoning to be a commonplace accomplishment since 'the ordinary cognitive capacity to handle counterfactual conditionals carries with it the cognitive capacity to handle metaphysical modality', which in turn explains why human beings in general have an 'overall capacity for somewhat reliable thought about counterfactual possibilities'.[14] This assurance is needed because the thought experimentalist would otherwise be trading in arcane speculations or far-fetched conjectures that lacked any bearing on the sorts of problem that the method purported to resolve. The other – seemingly at odds with that – is the 'expertise defence', as Williamson calls it. On this view expert training of the kind typically acquired in the course of a more or less advanced education in philosophy can and should have the effect of making its practitioners better (more reliable, judicious and accurate) in coming up with the right answers. Moreover, by what might seem an odd twist of paradox, it is just that kind of expertise that warrants the philosopher in claiming to address substantive or first-order issues of (for example) linguistic reference, personal identity, the mind/body problem and so forth, all of which plainly have to do with common-place or everyday aspects of human life. So if philosophers, or some of them, perceive a conflict between these two sorts of claim – the expertise defence and the appeal to widely shared intuitions – then it is perhaps fair to say that the problem is not so much a genuine dilemma as an artefact of present-day intra-philosophical debate.

And indeed there are signs, if one just stands back from the scrimmage, that the two sides have a lot more in common by way of enabling presupposition than either seems ready to concede. Both make much of the analogy with science, or with scientific know-how, as a matter of highly trained practical, observational and hands-on technical skill. This in turn makes the same joint appeal on the one hand to capacities shared by all human beings simply by virtue of their basic situational needs and on the other to capacities developed in pursuit of different, more expert or specialised aims. What the thought experimentalists have to avoid is any suspicion that they might be resting their case on some 'mysterious intuitive faculty' (Williamson's phrase) that would place philosophers, or those claim-ing to possess it, in a class apart from the mass of human beings who can gain such knowledge, if at all, only by some laborious churn-ing of empirical data and conceptual machinery. Here one might catch an echo of Kant's diatribe against those overweening types – illuminati, enthusiasts, self-styled prophets, spirit-seers, apostles of the inner light – whose 'over-mighty tone' was all the more danger-ous for claiming direct or immediate access to a truth beyond the reach of mere workaday reason or the Kantian 'parliament' of the faculties.[15] Behind that there is the rumble of a large edifice caught in its moment of collapse, namely Kant's elaborate 'architectonic' of the faculties which rested on a pair of (as he thought) unshakable a priori or conceptual-intuitive foundations – Euclidean geometry and Newtonian physics – both of which were rudely torn away by mathematical-scientific developments within little more than a century.[16] At any rate it is clear that the thought experimentalists need to steer carefully between the twin perils of an over-regard for non-expert opinion (which would put them out of a job) and an under-regard for it (which might help to boost their professional self-esteem but would put them out of touch with a main source of corroborative evidence).

On the other hand their critics also need to show caution if their arguments are not to come back like a boomerang. They had better not rest their case too heavily on the claim that philosophers have no special expertise in these matters – attractive as this might seem from a populist or anti-elitist standpoint – since the only alternative on offer is the appeal to lay judgement or the kinds of verdict typically arrived at by those without any such specialist training. Since the critics' main point is that philosophers share in the proneness to error exhibited by these ordinary folk – errors brought about by gender bias, class or ethnic prejudice, doctrinal adherence, 'commonsense' presumption, false analogy, perceptual illusion, foregone conclusions and so forth – they can scarcely wish to elevate folkish intuitions to a status of superior authority or intellectual grasp. Having once adopted such a drastically levelling-down approach they would not then be well placed to turn the argument around and seek a means of deliverance in the very place where all these multiplied sources of error have their prime location. Besides, the critics must themselves be relying on a whole range of accredited expert judgements, including some of a distinctly philosophical character, in order to make these various imputations of bias, prejudice, illogicality, etc. In short, there is more than a whiff of double standards about this keenness among Camp One types to skewer philosophers – or thought experimentalists, taken as the purest representatives of the tribe – on the presumed dilemma of expert versus popular knowledge, or philosophy as a specialist hence 'privileged' domain and philosophy as a discourse properly open to investigation by people (psychologists, sociologists, maybe anthropologists) who will have none of this, to their mind, elitist and obscurantist talk. Thus they would have to side either with the armchair exponents of a method hopelessly in thrall to discredited ideas of synthetic a priori knowledge or else with a more egalitarian approach which lets in the folk – including those folk who are doing the empirical investigations – as having just as strong an adjudicative claim. And of course, should the second option be chosen, then its result is to leave the philosopher intellectually as well as professionally high and dry.

If it is not hard to see how the Camp One experimenters exploit this supposed dilemma then it is just as clear where and why their arguments come off the rails. For one thing, all those claims of prejudice, bias, cultural stereotyping, skewed reasoning and so forth can have their intended force only on condition that the claimants endorse certain strictly indispensable standards – of *un*prejudiced, *un*biased or rationally warranted inference – which in turn find their source and justification in arguments of a distinctly Camp Two kind provided by philosophers from Plato and (more significantly) Aristotle down. For another, those standards (if not the supporting arguments) are just as much an inbuilt component of everyday, ordinary discourse and reasoning as they are of the more specialist debates that preoccupy academic philosophers. The sceptics have the issue precisely upside-down when they charge those 'armchair' types – the thought experimentalists – with taking up residence in some remote mental enclave of a priori or rational-intuitive conviction cut off from all dealing with the world of everyday knowledge and experience. Rather, what the thought experimentalists require in order for their basic case to go through is nothing more than the equally basic presumption that the sort of reasoning typically involved in (relatively) abstract or high-level philosophic argument is closely akin to – indeed just a somewhat specialised extension of – the everyday common-sense sort. That the two might come apart, or that there might be some need for choice between them, is merely the misunderstanding that results from an overly polarised conception of philosophy vis-à-vis the various 'practical' or 'real-world' contexts that philosophy (supposedly) scants or neglects in its quest for a higher, more rigorous mode of knowledge. Indeed there is something quite perverse in the lengths to which Camp One experimentalists (remember: those who reject thought experiments and who rely, or claim to rely, on third-person evidence of various sorts) will occasionally go in their fixed determination to discredit the very idea that 'armchair' philosophy might have anything of value to contribute.

As I have said, this comes partly from their tendency to assume that Camp Two types must surely be closet Cartesians, or covert

Kantians, or at any rate travellers on the 'high priori road' toward a reprise of the well-documented misfortunes that philosophy has suffered through hitching its wagon too closely to the star of rational-intuitive self-evidence. But it also results in no small part from a certain kind of misconceived scientism, or a failure to reckon with the fact that the physical sciences have themselves very often – and now more than ever – got along through a variable mixture of hypothesis, theory, observation, experiment, deduction, induction and (on the basis of all these) abductive inference to the best, most rational or adequate explanation. Camp One experimentalism can be seen as working on the mistaken premise that 'scientific' = not only 'empirically constrained' or 'open to corroboration/falsification by the best evidence to hand' but also 'mercifully free of any attachment to the idea that knowledge might be advanced by critical reflection on the scope and limits of rational conceivability'. In so doing it ignores the extent to which the physical sciences have relied on thought experiments – on test procedures carried out in the laboratory of the mind – as a means of establishing certain conjectures or of falsifying others, very often (as with Galileo versus Aristotle on falling bodies) through a *reductio ad absurdum* designed to draw contradictory entailments from the theory in question.[17] Thus the Camp One hardliners seem to espouse a science-led conception of philosophical enquiry that is oddly out of touch not only with the way that science has made some of its major advances but also with the fact, much canvassed by philosophers of science following Quine and Kuhn, that empirical evidence is always in some degree theory-laden and that theories are always underdetermined by the best empirical evidence.[18] Actually the Camp One prejudice is far more typical of social scientists and their retinue among philosophically disenchanted philosophers than it is of physical scientists or, for that matter, philosophers with a well-developed sense of how scientists typically think and work.

The Galileo analogy will not seem so far-fetched or question-begging if one compares the sorts of mental operation involved in his thought-experimental refutation of Aristotle with the arguments advanced in support of their claim by thought experimentalists or defenders of rational intuition as a source of veridical knowledge. Ernest Sosa puts the case in fairly representative terms when he says that the intuitive judgements concerned have a certain distinctive character and have to meet certain likewise distinctive criteria if they are properly to count as such, i.e. as genuine instances of the kind. On his account, 'to intuit that p is to be attracted to assent simply through entertaining that representational content. The intuition is rational if and only if it derives from a competence, and the content is explicitly or implicitly modal (i.e. attributes necessity or possibility).'[19] Williamson makes much the same stipulation, as presumably would any thinker – whether a philosopher of science, a philosopher of mind or an epistemologist with both interests in view – who wished to vindicate the disputed claim for the efficacy and validity of thought experiments. That claim represents them, in brief, as capable of offering veridical insights (or rational intuitions) through a process of thought that bears reliably on issues of real-world applicable truth but which doesn't depend, at least in the first instance, on validation by empirical or observational means.

Thus it fits very nicely with the Galileo example which involved the following classic *reductio*. (1) Aristotle held that heavy bodies fell faster than light bodies owing to their natural tendency to seek out their proper place in the sublunary order of lighter-to-heavier substances. (2) Let us suppose two bodies, one relatively heavy and the other relatively light (say a cannon-ball and a musket-ball) attached securely together and dropped from a certain height (say that of the leaning tower of Pisa). (3) On Aristotle's theory the heavy ball should fall faster than the lighter. (4) However, on Aristotle's theory again, the combination of heavy and light balls should fall faster than either would if they were released separately. (5) The balls are securely fastened one to the other, hence incapable of coming apart. (6) Aristotle's theory thus gives rise to a manifest and strictly inescapable contradiction. (7) It is unthinkable that any true, valid or consistent scientific theory should produce this contradictory result. Therefore (8) Aristotle's theory of how and why bodies behave in a state of free fall must necessarily be false. In Sosa's phrasing this constitutes a perfect example of a 'rational intuition' (the falsehood of Aristotle's claim) which commands 'assent' on the part of 'competent', i.e. logically right-thinking, subjects in so far as they are able to envisage the scenario in question as a matter of sufficiently detailed or adequate 'representational content' and also to interpret that evidence correctly with respect to its modal status as representing a necessary or possible state of affairs. All this – it should be emphasised – before Galileo undertook his 'real', physical experiment with falling objects from the tower and thus provided the empirical back-up for the thought-experimental result.

III

Of course it may be said – and has been said by sceptics in that regard – that this wasn't really a clinching example of rational intuition paving the way to some epochal advance in our scientific knowledge of the physical world. Rather, so they claim, it is an instance of disguised tautology or of question-begging assumptions smuggled in under cover of a seeming appeal to the evidence of jointly a priori and empirical evidence. Still it is hardly deniable that a great many such advances have indeed come about through the combined application, in various ways, of understanding acquired through empirical research or Russellian 'knowledge by acquaintance' and the improved understanding that typically results from the process whereby such knowledge is subject to rational refinement, elaboration, and critique. Indeed any denial of that claim would effectively exclude from the class of scientifically valid theories, hypotheses or conjectures a large proportion that have eventually turned out to transform or revolutionise our grasp of physical reality. Intellectual events of this order cannot be explained or rendered intelligible except through the standing possibility that thought may on occasion – at the onset of some Kuhnian scientific crisis or episode of radical paradigm-change – enter into a complex dialectic with no epistemic guarantees save those borne out through the critical process thus set in train. This dialectic is that which results from the encounter between what had once seemed (or perhaps still seems) a matter of straightforward, intuitive self-evidence and what to begin with imposes itself as a matter of reasoned yet counter-intuitive necessity and only then, as the new thinking takes hold, itself acquires just such a force of apodictic warrant.

In continental philosophy, broadly so called, the process in question is often treated as retaining certain elements of Kantian aprioristic reasoning from the conditions of possibility for knowledge, judgement or experience but now in the form of a 'historical a priori' which admits the possibility that those conditions may undergo certain kinds of rationally motivated change over time.[20] Versions of this historicist turn range all the way from the critical rationalism of thinkers like Bachelard and Canguilhem to the more extreme and, in some formulations, the downright cultural-relativist approach of Foucault's 'archaeologies' and 'genealogies' of knowledge.[21] While Foucault retains the basic idea that knowledge – or what counts as such from one discourse, paradigm or *epistème* to the next – is subject to certain rational constraints, he none the less treats those constraints, and thus 'reason' itself, as subject to all the buffeting winds of historical and socio-cultural change. Thus paradigm shifts, or Foucauldian 'epistemological breaks', are the product of multiple interacting forces that must appear quite indifferent to the interests of truth since no longer held within the bounds of that critical dialectic between a priori intuition and rational critique that Bachelard and Canguilhem take as prerequisite to any conception of progress in the sciences.[22] Meanwhile analytic philosophy of language in the mainly Anglophone tradition underwent a broadly analogous mid-twentieth-century change, one brought about in large part through the influence of Wittgenstein's later writings but also, ironically enough, by the logician Quine's all-out assault on the two last 'dogmas' of old-style logical empiricism.[23] This involved the switch from a basically logic-first, Fregean-Russellian order of priority to an approach wherein language or its various surrogates ('conceptual scheme', 'paradigm', 'framework', 'language game', communal or cultural 'form of life') came to be thought of as the end point of investigation or ultimate horizon of intelligibility. In both cases, continental and analytic alike, there has occurred a very marked switch of emphasis in this respect and a resultant shift toward the idea of language – natural language in its manifold guises rather than any single, logically privileged formal language – as philosophy's very element and the *ne plus ultra* of analytic grasp.[24]

My point in all this is that philosophers sell themselves short and deprive their discipline of crucial resources if they come down firmly on one or the other side in the current, much publicised stand-off between Camp One and Camp Two experimentalists. We are here offered a false choice between two equally restrictive or unpromising agendas. On the one hand are those who wish to deny philosophy any claim to synthetic a priori knowledge after Kant's posthumous comeuppance at the hands of the non-Euclidean geometers and, of course, Einstein as the thinker who carried their formal speculations into the realm of physical theory. In pursuit of this programme the Camp One zealots would deprive philosophy of its critical-reflective resources and put it to school with a drastically reduced, quasi-positivist version of the methods of empirical research. On the other are those who would reject such methods *tout court*, assert philosophy's entitlement to set its own standards of validity and truth, and thus (so opponents will naturally claim) impose what amounts to a cordon sanitaire around their jealously guarded academic patch. No doubt these phrasings are somewhat more extreme than the views overtly expressed or the positions actually taken by philosophers on either side of this dispute. All the same it is one that has polarised opinion to such an extent that each party has been pressured into taking – or affecting to take – just such a jaundiced view of the opposite camp.

By so doing, I suggest, they have cut philosophy off from that reciprocally strengthening since mutually questioning and testing dialectic that has characterised its relationship with science during periods of their closest and most productive interaction. Indeed this whole current show of hostilities between the two camps is a sure indication that philosophy is entering one of its periodic bouts of chronic insecurity not only vis-à-vis the physical sciences but also with regard to its own credentials as a discourse capable of delivering truths beyond the tautologies of formal logic or empirical matters of fact. Indeed it may be seen as a further episode in the history of exacerbated dualisms that started out with the logical-positivist turn against any version of the Kantian synthetic a priori, continued through the yet more emphatic logical-empiricist refusal to countenance any such thing, and was hardly resolved by Quine's pyrrhic victory over what he saw as the residual Kantianism of both precursor movements. 'Pyrrhic', that is, in so far as the sheer thoroughness of Quine's demolition-job had the ultimate effect not only of exposing and thus (by his own lights) discrediting those two last dogmas – the analytic/synthetic distinction and the idea of individual statements as testable one by one against the empirical evidence – but also of ensuring that his own radical-empiricist theory could muster nothing like an adequate range of normative or probative resources. Quite simply, it showed how this was the inevitable end result of a generalised scepticism concerning both the mind's integral capacity for rational-intuitive knowledge or judgement and the extent to which that capacity could be exercised in acquiring knowledge of the physical world through empirically reliably means.

Of course this is just the same impasse that I have described as having been brought about by the current spat between Camp One experimenters with their empirical (or quasi-empirical) research methods and Camp Two thought experimentalists with their reliance on more philosophically traditional, i.e. aprioristic, modes of enquiry. That is, it results from the failure or refusal to see how the two kinds of knowledge are strictly prerequisite each to the other, or involved in a constant dialectical exchange of priorities which makes it impossible to separate out their distinct contributions except as an academic exercise. On the diagnostic view advanced in this chapter there is a long history, stretching back through and beyond Kant, behind the current bout of hostilities. It has always involved that same set of vexing dualisms – mind/body, intellect/senses, concept/intuition, rationalism/empiricism, form/content, truths of reason/matters of fact – that have plagued Western philosophy since its inception but which entered a particularly sharp and problematical phase in the wake of Kant's critical project. What has tended to ratchet up the conflict in recent years is philosophy's exposure to a wider academic, cultural and socio-economic situation where the physical sciences have come to enjoy undisputed pride of place and thus to exert a palpable pressure on those other (mainly arts and humanities) disciplines which cannot lay claim to anything like so impressive a record in terms of manifest, empirically warranted progress. One reaction has been the 'strong' sociology of science, a kind of fight-back movement aimed – by its more combative proponents – to turn the tables and invert the standard order of priority by subjecting scientific methods and truth-claims to sceptical scrutiny in terms of their socially motivated character or ideological conditioning.[25] Understandably philosophers of science, or most of them, have rejected this idea that attack is the best form of defence since, after all, they have a certain vested interest in maintaining respect for those methods and truth-claims, no matter what problems they might turn up in the course of philosophical analysis. Thus the conflict tends to surface in other forms, among them (as I have said) the dispute between empirical experimenters who want to get science on their side by adopting a version of its well-tried investigative protocols and on the other hand thought experimentalists who wish to reassert philosophy's role as a provider of knowledge ideally unencumbered by any such mundane necessities.

No doubt this is something of a caricature since the debate has now been running long enough for each side to have produced a good number of arguments and counter-arguments intended to refute all the obvious objections to their point of view. Camp One types would concede (well, some of them and in a somewhat grudging manner) that the empirical evidence needs to be carefully sorted and assessed, and that the sorting/assessing must involve some specific competence – whether rational-intuitive insight or acquired expertise – beyond the mere recording of responses to questions on the part of sundry respondents. Camp Two types would likewise acknowledge that the other lot do have a point when they advise that armchair philosophers had better get out of the armchair at least once in a while in order to check that their a priori claims are not too far out of line with the best findings of the empirically informed physical, human and social sciences. On the other hand this seeming *entente cordiale* is really no such thing since the two parties are clearly yielding only minimal ground and doing so only with a view to reinforcing their strategic defences. Thus the empiricists rest secure in their belief that apriority or rational intuition will at length turn out, through empirical research, to be a species of illusion best dispelled by yet more empirical research while the thought experimenters take it for granted that any findings thus produced will be wholly worthless in the absence of critical-reflective understanding or insight. However, the dispute would cease to exist if both parties came to accept – in company with thinkers of a naturalising bent across numerous present-day disciplines – that what stands to reason or counts as a priori for us human knowers can and must fall square with what we learn through experience as a matter of rational warrant.[26]

That is to say, it is only through the bad inheritance of Cartesian and Kantian ideas (along with their Lockean-Humean empiricist counterparts) that philosophy has for so long laboured under this compulsion to create all manner of thought-blocking dualisms where it might more sensibly have taken the monist path of a naturalistic rationalism for which those problems simply don't arise. Recent scholarship has begun to show the extent to which Descartes, so often described as the inaugural figure of modernity, can himself be seen to have inherited a range of medieval scholastic baggage including the primary theological imperative to make room for soul (or latterly mind) as a substance categorically distinct from body.[27] Descartes' novelty – and the source of his extraordinary hold on thinkers over the past four centuries, including many of those most determined to resist or escape it – was to give that idea a seemingly knock-down logical, epistemological and hence (on this conception) metaphysical and ontological force. It could then be deployed against any attempt to set philosophy back on the alternative, i.e. naturalistic, path that it might have taken up and developed from Aristotle had it not been sidetracked by the influence of Aquinas and other scholastic theologians. In contemporary terms, as I have said, the biggest recent setback to progress in that direction has been Quine's problematical but none the less hugely influential demolition job on the two last 'dogmas' of logical empiricism.[28] The result of that vigorous debunking exercise was not so much to get shot of those pesky dualist dogmas – basically the whole Cartesian-Humean-Kantian caboodle of mind/body, concept/intuition, a priori/a posteriori, analytic/synthetic and so forth – but rather to leave philosophers chronically unsure of their normative bearings in the radical-empiricist aftermath. Thus philosophical naturalism as Quine conceived it was an inert combination of Humean empiricism in philosophy of mind with Skinnerian stimulus-response behaviourism on the cognitive-psychology side and, truth to say, nothing very much – or nothing at all – when it came to the issue of epistemological warrant.

One consequence of this was to polarise responses to (so-called) philosophical naturalism between tough-minded types who welcomed this anti-metaphysical, no-nonsense reckoning and those of a more rationalist or value-sensitive disposition who deemed it to fall lamentably short in terms of normative justification.[29] Thus the ultimate (if far from intended) result of Quine's 'Two Dogmas' has been more deeply to entrench, rather than demolish, the whole range of dualisms or false dichotomies that logical empiricism – for all its own no-nonsense and anti-metaphysical convictions – inherited from Kant. It is within this highly specific intellectual and institutional-academic context that we need to understand the current falling out between Type One and Type Two experimentalists. They are basically disputing the question: should philosophy have any say over matters of objective or mind-independent truth or should it not now acknowledge, long after time, that the answers to this and many such questions lie in the scientific or at any rate the empirical-experimental-observational domain? Camp One experimentalists of course respond negatively to the first of these proposals and positively to the second, while the pattern is reversed for Camp Two types. All the same – to repeat – this appearance of two diametrically opposed and irreconcilable positions is really no such thing but rather a conceptual illusion brought about by the recrudescence of sundry no matter how qualified, revisionist or scaled-down variants of Cartesian-Kantian dualism. One reason why the two experimentalist camps have emerged with such sharply antagonistic agendas is the lingering presence of this problem – or this veritable morass of problems – that goes right back to the origins, or putative origins, of modern philosophy. Thus the thought experimentalists count themselves defenders of philosophy's right – its *quis juris* claim – to be upholding standards of rationality and truth while the empirical experimenters roundly deny that any such right exists. According to the latter we always do best, in philosophy as elsewhere, when we stick to the low road that keeps us reliably in touch with the local scenery and local inhabitants, and which steers well clear of the intellectual heights where no doubt there are dizzying views to be had but where the air is inherently thin and provisions hard to come by.

IV

I have argued that this whole debate is misconceived and that it signals the latest stage – possibly the end point if philosophical naturalism continues to gain ground – in the history of kindred misconceptions that was kick-started by Descartes and received its most elaborate treatment in Kant's critical doctrine of the faculties. Its most characteristic feature, and that which marks it out as an epochal rather than a short-term or localised occurrence, is the sheer baroque proliferation of dualisms by which philosophers of otherwise diverse persuasion (typecast empiricists as well as typecast rationalists) have been alternately engrossed and repelled.

Perhaps it is the case, as Stephen Boulter has recently urged, that what strike us now as the presuppositions and patterns of inference typical of post-Cartesian modernity should rather be traced back far beyond Descartes to disputes among late medieval theologians over the scope and limits (if any) of God's executive power.[30] This issue seems to have been settled in favour of the view that divine omnipotence meant just that – the unrestricted power to produce any range of counterfactual events, alterations of history, suspensions of physical law, etc. – with the sole emphatic proviso that even God was incapable of bringing about a contradictory state of affairs, i.e. one that would sustain the truth of two contradictory statements with regard to some particular well-defined aspect thereof. So it was, Boulter argues, that non-contradiction became enshrined as the philosophic principle of principles and also that philosophers from Descartes down came to rest a great variety of non-theological arguments on the premise that any counterfactual proposition or thesis, no matter how absurd, could and should be entertained as a candidate for truth just so long as it could be shown to involve no logical contradiction. His examples include not only the various brain-in-a-vat type technical updates on Descartes' experiment in hyperbolic doubt but also G. E. Moore on the naturalistic fallacy (where a distinction between the good and the pleasurable is advanced on grounds of logical conceivability) and Chalmers' famous zombie argument in philosophy of mind (where it is taken as possible, i.e. non-contradictory, that an atom-for-atom replica of me would have none of my sensations, feelings, mental imagery, qualitative states and so forth.[31]

Boulter's point is that we get things wrong – philosophically as well as historically askew – if we give Descartes either ultimate credit or ultimate blame for the way things subsequently turned out for the project of philosophical modernity. Rather, we should see that the roots of all those tenacious dualisms lay in the medieval scholastic attempt to establish God's privileged exemption from every limit on his sovereign power save that imposed by the rule of non-contradiction. Thus, to repeat, divine omnipotence was taken as subject only to the rock-bottom modal requirement that it not be considered within God's capacity to bring about the existence of any event, situation or state of affairs that would entail the simultaneous truth (or falsehood) of two contradictory statements. Of course this principle was the main tenet of Aristotelian logic and, beyond that, of the entire onto-metaphysical worldview that Aristotle bequeathed to his scholastic (medieval-to-early-Renaissance) disciples and that lasted – on the orthodox account – until Descartes achieved the conceptual revolution that spawned philosophical modernity. Not so, Boulter maintains: the Cartesian 'revolution' was no such thing, unless perhaps in the original (etymological) sense of that term which denoted the full-circle return to some earlier, presumptively superseded situation. On this account Descartes didn't so much break new ground as manage to reinstall the scholastic idea that philosophy was chiefly concerned with – that it derived its very *raison d être* from – issues concerning the logical possibility or conceivability of certain (mainly counterfactual) suppositions. Hence the whole range of present-day philosophical debates where on the one side it is a matter, or is made so to seem, of tests carried out in an apodictic realm of a priori concepts and intuitions while on the other it is a question of cutting philosophy down to size by denying that thought experiments of this type could possibly have any import beyond that of a disguised tautology or a mere tail-chasing *petitio principii*. Among the former sorts of argument are all those that the Camp One (empirically minded) experimenters routinely write off as unfortunate examples of philosophy's proneness to set itself up as dispenser of a knowledge somehow arrived at without benefit of inputs from beyond its self-enclosed epistemic sphere. Among the latter are those that Camp Two types reject on grounds of their normative deficit or failure to provide anything remotely adequate in the way of principled justification.

Thus it is often claimed that hard-line naturalisers in epistemology, ontology, philosophy of science and other disciplines are apt to throw normative caution to the winds and settle for a physicalist or causal theory of knowledge acquisition that falls woefully short of the standards set – with whatever detailed differences of view – by numerous philosophers from Plato down. And it is just as often claimed by those naturalising types that their critics have simply missed the point since any relevant (and not merely notional) appeal to standards of knowledge or epistemic warrant must itself be specified in naturalistic terms – or those laid down by present-best methods and explanatory norms in the physical sciences – if it is not to fall back upon the same empty gestures and habitual recourse to hopelessly circular arguments that marred previous rationalist philosophies. Such is at any rate the current state of play, or the all too familiar kind of stalemate situation that has come to typify the exchanges of Camps One and Two. However it is the experimental philosophers, rather than the thought experimentalists, who have lately done most to skew the terms or muddy the waters of this particular debate. Where the former have tended to moderate their claims in response to the problems thrown up after Kant by developments in geometry and physics the latter have exploited those and other issues in order to push through a programme that would find no room for philosophy, at least in any real or substantive sense of the term. By denying its capacity to yield insights or discover truths that have a relevance – even, at times, a decisive import – for more empirically oriented disciplines they risk falling into the same basic error as Stephen Hawking in his recent, much publicised attack on philosophy as having no place in an age when science has come to define what counts as genuine knowledge.[32] That is, they fail to grasp the extent to which their own researches necessarily draw upon a great many concepts, suppositions or hypotheses that have their source in philosophy, or in the kind of thinking (whether by philosophers or philosophically inclined scientists) that raises issues beyond the strict remit of natural-scientific or physical evidence-based enquiry.

So Camp One diehards can always be asked: do you take this point (in which case you will have to concede that your empirically grounded debunking of philosophy has very definite limits) or would you rather stick to your programmatic guns, maintain the irrelevance or plain non-existence of knowledge arrived at through distinctly philosophical (rational-intuitive) means, and thereby effectively own allegiance to a downright naive epistemology? What lays them open to this two-pronged objection is their curious failure – more often, one suspects, their doctrinally motivated refusal – to perceive the philosophically inflected nature of their own most basic methods and procedures. Thus, for instance, they take very much for granted the reliability of testimonial witness, the empiricist priority of experience (not necessarily first-person) over rational excogitation, and the manifest fallacy (wherever it may lie) of any appeal to scientific thought experiments like that of Galileo by way of making good philosophy's claim to certain kinds of synthetic a priori knowledge. At very least they assume the absence of any grounds for supposing that the purported warrant of rational intuition could possibly trump any claim put forward on the basis of experiential say-so. And this, be it noted once more, despite their often declared affinity with Quine's programme of naturalised (actually radical-empiricist) epistemology and despite what Quine paradoxically claimed to derive from that, namely the theory-laden character of all empirical observations and hence the empirically underdetermined status of any observationally based scientific theory. Where Quine stopped short is also the point at which 'experimental philosophy' tends to go off the rails, or where it bumps up against the problems engendered by its failure to think these issues through with sufficient clarity and care. That is, it declines the redemptive next step of espousing a more robust naturalism – such as I and others have lately proposed – that would, unlike the Quinean version, be able to muster an adequate range of rational (i.e. critical and normative) resources.[33]

From that vantage point the quarrel between thought experimentalists and experimenters of the empirically minded investigative type will very likely seem just a whipped-up storm in an academic teapot. More to the point, it will seem just a late, professionally driven rehash of misconceived problems or false dilemmas that are understandably hard to shake off since their roots go deep and extend far back into the history of post-Cartesian or even, if Boulter's conjecture is correct, of pre-Cartesian scholastic thought. It involves the debate over certain highly contestable precepts, among them the validity – and indeed the purported indispensability for philosophical purposes – of arguments from what is logically conceivable (or inconceivable) quite aside from issues of empirical or natural-scientific fact. Perhaps the most striking instance of this is David Chalmers' 'philosophical zombie' thought experiment, taken as establishing the case for a strong form of mind–body dualism and hence as showing that the 'hard problem' of consciousness is indeed just that, i.e. a problem of peculiar difficulty and depth which fully merits its central position in the discourse of (who else?) professional philosophers.[34] On the one side claims of this sort are deemed prerequisite to philosophy's good standing as a discipline able to sustain its vocation – to justify its very existence – against those of the physical sciences or other disciplines with a prima facie stronger entitlement in that regard. On the other it is taken as a sign of philosophy's attachment to a range of misconceived notions (a priori knowledge, rational self-evidence, apodictic warrant, first-person epistemic privilege and so forth) that possess absolutely no authority beyond its own elective domain. I have suggested that philosophy will not get over all these curiously inbred disputes until it gets over their root error, namely the idea that rationalism and naturalism just don't mix, or again that a robustly naturalised epistemology will *ipso facto* find itself woefully short of normative or rational-justificatory warrant.

It is hard to imagine how the current stand-off could ever have happened, given its quite extraordinary remoteness from the way that reasoning actually operates in various branches of the physical sciences. Nothing could be more off the point than this idea that there is somehow a *choice* to be made – a choice with large implications and decisive consequences attached – between the science-led path of philosophical naturalism and, by its own estimation, the philosophy-led path of rationally justified normative standard-setting for the conduct of scientific enquiry. For surely it is the case, contra this curiously Manichaean view, that scientific reasoning has always proceeded through a complicated melange of facts and theories, intuitions and concepts, induction and deduction, a posteriori and a priori modes of knowledge, empirical observation and rational conjecture, or – to bring the lesson right home – physical experiment and thought experiment. So likewise philosophers, even those of a strongly apriorist disposition, must always be willing to check their intuitions (no matter how firm, rationally grounded or seemingly self-evident) against whatever just might turn up in the way of empirical counter-evidence. Any idea that the terms on each side of these various pseudo-dichotomies are clearly separable let alone conflicting or antagonistic is completely out of touch with how the natural sciences work. This is also the way that philosophy needs to work if it is ever to achieve a genuine and decisive rather than merely gestural break with the deep-laid dualist habit of thought that has bedevilled its post-Cartesian (and especially its post-Kantian) history.

V

Nowhere are the damaging effects more sharply visible than in the current dispute over thought experiments and whether or not their epistemic validity is challenged – even nullified – by the rise of experimental philosophy. Granted, there is a puzzle about why results arrived at in the laboratory of the mind, or by purely apodictic means, should possess any degree of probative force when it comes to matters of scientific truth or the nature and structure of physical reality. Yet this is just the same puzzle that the physicist Eugene Wigner famously if rather plaintively evoked in the title of his essay on the 'unreasonable effectiveness of mathematics in the physical sciences'.[35] Of course my analogy here raises all sorts of questions concerning mathematics, the sources of mathematical knowledge and just how far – if at all – mathematical truths are accessible through any kind of a priori rational-intuitive insight. They are questions that have long preoccupied philosophers of mathematics, not least in consequence of Kant's having raised them – all unwittingly – by yielding so many a priori hostages to the fate of subsequent developments in non-Euclidean geometry and non-Newtonian physics. Still it is sufficiently clear that thought experiments of various kinds do have considerable traction on issues concerning the nature, structure and behaviour of items in the physical (mind-independent) domain, just as it was clear to Wigner when he voiced his puzzlement that the effectiveness of mathematics in physics, no matter how apparently 'unreasonable', was none the less a matter of well-established fact. Indeed, if we define 'reasonable' (more reasonably in this context) not so much according to criteria of strict deductive or quasi-deductive warrant but rather in terms of evidentially guided inference to the best, i.e. all-things-considered most rational explanation, then we shall surely have to conclude that this is a case where the *explanandum* is a downright given and the lack (so far) of any adequate *explanans* a patent defect in our current understanding. That is to say, Wigner's acceptance that mathematics *has played and continues to play* an enormous role in the progress of physical-scientific knowledge finds a direct equivalent in the role of those various thought-experimental procedures – from Galileo to Einstein and beyond – that have often preceded and then been strikingly corroborated by the empirical-observational evidence.

Just lately there have been positive signs of a growing convergence between philosophy of mathematics and philosophy of the physical sciences. This has gone along with a marked reaction against the kind of sceptical thinking that typically took hold within a short time whenever philosophers – like Descartes, Kant or the logical positivists – introduced some new problematical set of mind-internal surrogates for the old mind–body or subject–object dichotomy. One index of change has been the strong anti-dualist idea, developed most influentially by Philip Kitcher, that certain intrinsic 'affordances' of nature are such as to allow, facilitate or actively promote the capacities of human cognitive grasp right through from the basic stage of sensory stimulus–response to the level of scientific explanation and theory construction.[36] The affordances shape and nurture the capacities to the extent that both play a productive, rationally intelligible role in the process of discovery by which mind interacts with various aspects of its physical environment and thereby creates new, farther-reaching opportunities for such creative reciprocity. Clearly this yields a sense of the word 'experiment' – of what goes on the mind-expanding and world-disclosive encounter between knower and known – that is far removed from the limiting senses pre-emptively deployed by the standard-bearers of Camps One and Two. Indeed it is a curious reflection on contemporary mainstream analytic debate that so many thinkers should have come to accept the existence of a genuine or substantive issue between thought experimenters and those who espouse a notion of good experimental practice that is arguably more in line with the methods and procedures of natural science. For this is really nothing more than another late showing of that stubborn and multiform dualist mindset that has wrought such a thoroughly mischievous effect on epistemology and philosophy of mind from Descartes to the present.

Notes

1. See for instance – from various, often sharply opposed viewpoints – Kirk Ludwig, 'The epistemology of thought experiments: first-person *versus* third-person approaches', *Midwest Studies in Philosophy*, 31 (2007), pp. 128–59; Edouard Machery, *Doing Without Concepts* (New York: Oxford University Press, 2009) and 'Thought experiments and philosophical knowledge', *Metaphilosophy*, 42: 3 (April 2011), pp. 191–214; Jennifer Nagel, 'Knowledge ascriptions and the psychological consequences of thinking about error', *Philosophical Quarterly*, 60 (April 2010), pp. 286–306; John D. Norton, 'Why thought experiments do not transcend empiricism', in Christopher Hitchcock (ed.), *Contemporary Debates in Philosophy of Science* (Oxford: Blackwell, 2004), pp. 44–66; Ernest Sosa, 'Experimental

philosophy and philosophical intuition', *Philosophical Studies*, 132 (2007), pp. 99–107; Stephen P. Stich, *From Folk Psychology to Cognitive Science* (Cambridge, MA: MIT Press, 2003); Jonathan M. Weinberg, 'How to challenge intuitions empirically without risking scepticism', *Midwest Studies in Philosophy*, 31 (2007), pp. 318–43 and 'On doing better, experimental-style', *Philosophical Studies*, 145: 3 (September 2009), pp. 455–64; Weinberg, Chad Gonnerman, Cameron Buckner and Joshua Alexander, 'Are philosophers expert intuiters?', *Philosophical Psychology*, 23: 3 (June 2010), pp. 331–55; Weinberg, Shaun Nichols and Stephen Stich, 'Normativity and epistemic intuitions', *Philosophical Topics*, 29: 1–2 (2001), pp. 429–60; Timothy Williamson, 'Philosophical intuitions and scepticism about judgments', *Dialectica*, 58 (2004), pp. 109–53; 'Contextualism, subject-sensitive invariantism, and knowledge of knowledge', *Philosophical Quarterly*, 55 (2005), pp. 213–35; *The Philosophy of Philosophy* (Oxford: Blackwell, 2007); 'Philosophical expertise and the burden of proof', *Metaphilosophy*, 42: 3 (April 2011), pp. 215–29.

2. See note 1, above, for representative instances of the kinds of argument advanced by Camp One and Camp Two thinkers. The titles are highly explicit for the most part and thus give a clear indication of where the authors stand with respect to the issue between experimental philosophers and thought-experimentalists.

3. Williamson, *The Philosophy of Philosophy*, op. cit.

4. G. E. Moore, 'A reply to my critics', in P. A. Schilpp (ed.), *The Philosophy of G. E. Moore* (La Salle: Open Court, 1968), pp. 535–687; also C. H. Langford, 'The notion of analysis in Moore's philosophy', ibid., pp. 321–41.

5. For a wide-ranging and perceptive history of this debate, see J. Alberto Coffa, *The Semantic Tradition from Kant to Carnap: To the Vienna Station* (Cambridge: Cambridge University Press, 1991).

6. See Norris, *Minding the Gap: Epistemology and Philosophy of Science in the Two Traditions* (Amherst: University of Massachusetts Press, 2000).

7. See especially Jonathan Bennett, *Learning from Six Philosophers*, 2 vols (Oxford: Clarendon Press, 2003).

8. For a useful brief discussion, see Stephen Stich and Wesley Buckwalter, 'Gender and the philosophy club', *Philosophers' Magazine*, 52 (2011), pp. 60–5.

9. Tamler Sommers, 'In Memoriam: the x-phi debate', *Philosophers' Magazine*, 52 (2011), pp. 89–93, at p. 92.

10. Williamson, *The Philosophy of Philosophy*, op. cit.

11. See especially Gilbert Harman, 'Inference to the best explanation', *Philosophical Review*, 74 (1965), pp. 88–95 and Peter Lipton, *Inference to the Best Explanation* (London: Routledge, 1993).

12. For a range of approaches, see Geoffrey Hawthorn, *Plausible Worlds: Possibility and Understanding in History and the Social Sciences* (Cambridge: Cambridge University Press, 1991); Saul Kripke, *Naming and Necessity* (Oxford: Blackwell, 1980); David Lewis, *Counterfactuals* (Oxford: Blackwell, 1973) and *On the Plurality of Worlds* (Oxford: Blackwell, 1986); Michael J. Loux (ed.), *The Possible and the Actual* (Ithaca, NY: Cornell University Press, 1979); Robert C. Stalnaker, *Inquiry* (Cambridge, MA: MIT Press, 1987) and *Ways a World Might Be: Metaphysical and Anti-metaphysical Essays* (Oxford: Oxford University Press, 2003); David Wiggins, *Sameness and Substance* (Oxford: Blackwell, 1980).

13. Williamson, 'Philosophical expertise and the burden of proof' (note 1, above), pp. 215–16.

14. Williamson, 'Philosophical intuitions and scepticism about judgments' (note 1, above), p. 196.

15. For more on this curious episode, see Norris, 'Raising the tone: Derrida, Kierkegaard and the rhetoric of transcendence', in *Reclaiming Truth: Contribution to a Critique of Cultural Relativism* (London: Lawrence & Wishart, 1996), pp. 73–126; also Immanuel Kant, *Political Writings*, ed. Hans Reiss (Cambridge: Cambridge University Press, 1976).

16. See note 5, above.

17. See especially James Robert Brown, *The Laboratory of the Mind: Thought Experiments in the Natural Sciences* (London: Routledge, 1991) and *Smoke and Mirrors: How Science Reflects Reality* (London: Routledge, 1994).

18. W. V. Quine, 'Two dogmas of empiricism', in *From a Logical Point of View*, 2nd edn (Cambridge, MA: Harvard University Press, 1961), pp. 20–46; Thomas S. Kuhn, *The Structure of Scientific Revolutions*, 2nd edn (Chicago: University of Chicago Press, 1970).

19. Sosa, 'Experimental philosophy and philosophical intuition' (note 1, above), p. 101.

20. For some highly informative commentary, see Gary Gutting, *French Philosophy in the Twentieth Century* (Cambridge: Cambridge University Press, 2001).

21. For an extended treatment of these French developments alongside broadly comparable episodes in analytic epistemology and philosophy of science, see Norris, *Minding the Gap* (note 6, above).

22. See Gaston Bachelard, *The Philosophy of No: A Philosophy of the New Scientific Mind* (New York: Orion Press, 1968); Georges Canguilhem, *Ideology and Rationality in the History of the Life Sciences*, trans. A. Goldhammer (Cambridge, MA: MIT Press, 1988); Michel Foucault, *The Order of Things: An Archaeology of the Human Sciences*, trans. Alan Sheridan-Smith (New York: Pantheon, 1970).

23. Quine, 'Two dogmas of empiricism', op. cit.; Ludwig Wittgenstein,

Philosophical Investigations, trans. G. E. M. Anscombe (Oxford: Blackwell, 1958).

24. For an early representative sampling, see Richard Rorty (ed.), *The Linguistic Turn: Essays in Philosophical Method* (Chicago: Chicago University Press, 1967).

25. David Bloor, *Knowledge and Social Imagery* (London: Routledge & Kegan Paul, 1976); Barry Barnes, *About Science* (Oxford: Blackwell, 1985); Barnes, Bloor and John Henry, *Scientific Knowledge: A Sociological Analysis* (Chicago: University of Chicago Press, 1996).

26. See, for instance, Fred Dretske, *Naturalizing the Mind* (Cambridge, MA: MIT Press, 1997); Alvin Goldman, *Epistemology and Cognition* (Cambridge, MA: Harvard University Press, 1986); Hilary Kornblith, *Knowledge and Its Place in Nature* (Oxford: Clarendon Press, 2002); Kornblith (ed.), *Naturalizing Epistemology*, 2nd edn (Cambridge, MA: MIT Press, 1994); Norris, *Re-Thinking the Cogito: Naturalism, Reason, and the Venture of Thought* (London: Continuum, 2010); David Papineau, *Philosophical Naturalism* (Oxford: Blackwell, 1993); Ralph Wedgwood, *The Nature of Normativity* (Oxford: Clarendon Press, 2007).

27. See especially Stephen Boulter, 'The medieval origin of conceivability arguments', *Metaphilosophy*, 42: 5 (2011), pp. 617–41.

28. Quine, 'Two dogmas of empiricism', op. cit.

29. See, for instance, Jaegwon Kim, *Supervenience and Mind: Selected Philosophical Essays* (Cambridge: Cambridge University Press, 1993).

30. See note 27, above.

31. David Chalmers, *The Conscious Mind: In Search of a Fundamental Theory* (Oxford: Oxford University Press, 1996).

32. Stephen Hawking and Leonard Mlodinow, *The Grand Design* (New York: Bantam Books, 2011).

33. See entries under note 26, above.

34. Chalmers, *The Conscious Mind*, op. cit.

35. Eugene Wigner, 'The unreasonable effectiveness of mathematics in the physical sciences', *Communications in Pure and Applied Mathematics*, 13 (1960), pp. 1–14.

36. Philip Kitcher, *The Nature of Mathematical Knowledge* (Oxford: Oxford University Press, 1983).

CHAPTER 4

Outside the Box: On the 'Extended Mind' Hypothesis

I

Consider, if you will, the sheer variety of (supposedly) non-mental since extra-cranial processes and events that have gone into the making of this book. I am writing it with the aid – more than that: with what feels like the active involvement – of a computer/word-processor linked to the Internet and sometimes providing me with prompts, references, links to relevant online debates and so forth. Besides, what I write even during periods of off-line dedication to 'the writing itself' is inevitably shot through with a great many witting or unwitting allusions to my online reading and is also, crucially, shaped in large measure by this experience of thinking and working in tandem with a whole range of modern technologies. Indeed their influence goes far deeper than their role in merely providing us with more convenient, speedy or well-stocked and ready-to-hand informational resources. Rather it reaches into various regions of our cognitive, intellectual and even our affective lives in such a way as to induce a profound restructuring of knowledge and experience alike.

To think of those technologies as extra-mental – as standing in a merely prosthetic or supplementary relation to the human mind – must in that case be a big mistake and a product of the anthropocentric or human, all-human tendency to draw a categorical line between what transpires inside and outside the skull. Once rid of that prejudice, so the argument goes, we can start getting used to this counter-intuitive yet strictly inescapable truth, namely that the mind is not intra-cranial but engaged in a constant two-way traffic with objects, events and information-sources beyond the individual brain. Moreover this is an active reciprocity – a mutual exchange or feedback loop with continual adjustment on both sides – that finds no place on more traditional (not just Cartesian) conceptions of the mind–world relationship. Quite simply, philosophers have got it wrong and shown themselves prey to mistaken, folk-psychological beliefs by adopting the view, in however philosophically 'sophisticated' a form, that mental processes and events must be thought of as transpiring in a realm quite apart from the various 'external' devices whereby human beings often contrive to enhance their cognitive powers. Thus the various IT resources that I have called upon in writing this book – or throughout its long period of intellectual gestation – are not just so many useful aids or handy adjuncts to processes of thought that would otherwise have gone on largely unaffected by their absence except for some limiting conditions with regard to information access and ease of textual or data processing. Rather they have become so intimately a part of the cognitive process itself – so deeply bound up with every stage in the business of data-retrieval and selection, ideational synthesis, concept-formation, inference, analogy, critical review and so forth – that it is no longer possible to draw any clear or principled line between mental and non-mental or intra- and extra-cranial events. More precisely: any such line-drawing will amount to no more than a stipulative fiat or a last-ditch attempt to conserve some privileged space for the human (i.e. what is conceived as uniquely or distinctively human) against the perceived encroachments of modern techno-science.

Such is the 'extended mind' (henceforth 'EM') hypothesis advanced by a number of vigorous and eloquent present-day advocates, chief among them David Chalmers and Andy Clark. It was their jointly authored essay of 1998 that first set out the hypothesis in its full-strength boundary-shifting form and very quickly produced a wide range of responses for and against.[1] Most prominent among the naysayers were philosophers of mind and cognitive psychologists, like Jerry Fodor, whose disagreement turned on what they diagnosed as the basic error – or category-mistake – necessarily involved in any ascription of mental states, contents, capacities or powers to extra-cranial (and hence, by definition, non-mental) items.[2] For Fodor it is a truth borne out by common-sense judgement and philosophical reflection alike that mental content is 'underived', that is to say *sui generis*, non-dependent and in itself the sole possible source of whatever strictly derivative contents might attach to various kinds of supplementary device.[3] What sense can there be, he asks, in talking about minds as if they had parts – additional parts or the scope for such piecemeal augmentation – so that some of them (maybe through possession of an iPhone) might come to have more parts than others? Is it not the case that our recourse to – even, at times, our reliance on – devices of this sort requires both that they have already been programmed (by ourselves or others) with relevant, reliably sourced information and also that we, the end-users, should believe that information or at any rate take mental note of it? For Fodor, in short, 'externalism needs internalism, but not vice versa [since] external representation is a sideshow; internal representation is ineliminably the main event.'[4] In this respect he stands foursquare with other thinkers, among them John Searle, who likewise regard underived content – or intentionality – as the distinguishing mark of the mental.[5]

This also, of course, sets him squarely opposed to advocates of the EM hypothesis. Their point is to challenge all such ideas of a mental domain whose locus, however problematically, is inside the human skull. On their account the predicate 'mental' stands in need of radical semantic surgery so as to extend its range of application not only beyond the ghost-in-the-machine of Cartesian mind/body dualism but also beyond the individual brain as it figures in the discourse of hard-line eliminativists or central-state materialists.[6] Indeed this proposal goes even further in an anti-mentalist or anti-Cartesian direction than the thoroughly integrated nexus or synthesis of mind/ body that we are urged to endorse – albeit for very different reasons – by continental phenomenologists and analytic strong-naturalists alike.[7] Chalmers and Clark seek to persuade us that a great many items commonly thought of as extraneous to mind-brain are in fact so deeply intertwined with our perceptual, cognitive, intellectual, affective and creative or imaginative experience as to constitute not merely prosthetic devices but integral components thereof. Just as mind reaches out into world through various kinds of applied technology – from the humble notepad and pencil to the iPhone or other such hi-tech marvels – so world reaches deep into mind through the active combination of that same technology with the human aptitude for adjusting to new and sometimes transformative changes in its ambient life-world. Hence the Chalmers/Clark 'Parity Principle', according to which: '[i]f, as we confront some task, a part of the world functions as a process which, if it were done in the head, we would have no hesitation in recognizing as part of the cognitive process, then that part of the world is . . . part of the cognitive'.[8] I would guess that the untypical clunkiness of this crucial sentence has its point in stressing both the knotty imbrication of mind and world and the resistance that this claim tends to generate in many – Fodor among them – by reason of its coming so sharply into conflict with a range of deep-laid intuitive beliefs.

In his book *Supersizing the Mind* Clark offers numerous striking examples of past, present and future-possible developments which he considers to present a powerful challenge to defenders of the inner/ outer dichotomy or suchlike (as he sees them) Cartesian residues.[9] On his account it is not enough for those of an expressly anti-Cartesian persuasion – mind/brain identity theorists or exponents of a thoroughly naturalised epistemology and philosophy of mind – to reject the charge outright. Where they still betray signs of that bad old heritage is in stopping short at an intra-bodily or 'skin-sack' monism which might indeed count as radical in terms of received philosophical wisdom but fails to question the other, more tenacious dualism. That is, they persist in trying to demarcate mental (even if physically embodied) processes from non-mental since extra-bodily means of cognitive enhancement. Clark's book is largely devoted to running a series of slippery-slope arguments – some of them involving extant technologies, others more in the nature of thought experiments – designed to prove just how questionable, or downright arbitrary, that line really is. Thus his point is to provide a whole series of 'intuition-pumps' (in Daniel Dennett's useful phrase) so as to wean us off accustomed ways of thought, whether philosophical or folk-psychological, according to which there just *must* be a difference – a humanly salient or crucial difference – between what goes on inside and outside our skulls.

II

It is important for Clark's argumentative purposes that this claim should extend well back into the history of cognitive enhancement techniques. Thus he makes a strong point of invoking 'primitive' techniques such as pen-and-paper or the sundry mnemonic devices that people have used, down through the ages, to supplement their limited resources of 'internal' memory or their restricted capacity for processes of 'purely' mental computation. (I am making this liberal use of scare quotes, let me say, in keeping with the anti-dualist conviction that motivates the EM hypothesis, since for now I am trying to represent their case without prejudice either way.) If one thing is intrinsic to the human mind it is not the kind of delusive self-sufficiency envisaged by Descartes and his legion of descendents – some of them unwitting or deeply in denial – but rather this capacity for linking up with its environment in adapative, creative and self-transformative ways. This why Clark likes to offer a range of homely examples so as not to be accused of resting his case too heavily on the latest in current technology or on speculative glimpses of a higher-tech future like that which might be opened up by 'cyberpunk' silicon brain implants.

Hence his best-known fictive or thought-experimental case study, that of Otto and Inga, the two art-loving New Yorkers who decide to visit the Museum of Modern Art on 53rd Street. While Inga relies on her memory to get there – on resources 'internal' to her own mind or brain with its range of unaided mnemonic powers – Otto is suffering from a mild degree of Alzheimer's disease and must therefore consult the directions written down in his notebook. Clark's point is that there is no rational or principled, as opposed to ad hoc or arbitrary, way of drawing a line between the two kinds of memory and the two sorts of procedure for getting from A to B. Of course the mentalist/dualist/internalist will raise all the obvious objections, such as the (presumptive) fact that Inga has direct access to her memories as opposed to Otto's indirect access via his notebook, or that Otto has to inspect its content whereas Inga just knows – without the need for any such roundabout means – how to reach MOMA by the quickest route. However, Clark is breezily unimpressed by these and other counter-arguments put up by critics of the EM hypothesis. Where they always beg the question, he claims, is by taking for granted the validity of certain deep-laid yet far from self-evident folk-psychological beliefs.

Still this has failed to convince those who see nothing in the least naive or folkish about the idea that there exists a real (and not merely ad hoc or gerrymandered) boundary between whatever goes on in our heads and whatever goes on in the world outside our heads. Thus Fodor fires a number of sceptical ripostes back at Clark, among them the suggestion that he try this vignette: Inga asks Otto where the museum is; Otto consults his notebook and tells her. The notebook is thus part of an 'external circuit' that is part of Otto's mind; and Otto's mind (including the notebook) is part of an external circuit that is part of Inga's mind. Now 'part of' is transitive: if A is part of B, and B is part of C, then A is part of C.[10] In which case, Fodor continues, 'it looks as though the notebook that's part of Otto's mind is also part of Inga's', with the consequence that 'if Otto loses his notebook, Inga loses part of her mind'.[11] This sounds logical enough and would seem to knock a hole in the EM case were it not for the temporal aspect of the story which allows both circuits (Otto's with his notebook; Otto's mind with Inga's) to be broken once Otto has mislaid that precious item. After all, it is quite explicitly a question in Fodor's narrative of who knows what and when, that is to say, of knowledge acquired by both parties at a certain stage in the proceedings and then lost by one of them (due to his memory deficit) but presumably not by the other (due to her suffering under no such disadvantage). However, Clark ignores this point and focuses instead on what he takes to be Fodor's most substantive objection, namely his above-mentioned argument concerning the 'underived' (self-sufficient or autonomous) nature of mental content as opposed to the 'derived' (dependent or second-order) status of physical prostheses such as Otto's notebook. His rejoinders regularly take the form of turning Fodor's objections around so as to argue that any sense in which Otto's knowledge or cognitive state can rightfully be called 'derivative', 'secondary', 'dependent', 'unreliable', 'indirect', 'error-prone', 'fallible' or whatever, is also – at no great stretch of counterfactual reasoning – a sense that applies equally in Inga's case.

According to Clark, 'both modes of storage can be seen as supporting dispositional beliefs' – Inga's self-accessed data bank no less than Otto's 'external' guide – since Inga also needs to consult her memory, as the phrase goes, and retrieve the relevant items of information for the purpose at hand.[12] Moreover, she has to have confidence in their accuracy and reliability even if that belief is so much a matter of unthinking routine commitment as scarcely to register at the level of conscious or deliberative thought. Thus Inga's reliance on 'unaided' memory is not, after all, sufficient to establish a categorical or even a reasonably clear-cut distinction between her way of getting to MOMA and Otto's reliance on his trusty aide-memoire. The latter is indispensably a part of that single integrated system that makes up Otto the absent-minded though cognitively enhanced way-finder, just as Inga's memory functions as part of a complex system including – as a formative part of its background history – the possibility of error bound up with all recourse to the presumed self-evidence of first-person recollection. Besides, again contra Fodor, Otto's habit of relying on his notebook is one that we should think of as having acquired the force of habit – of 'second nature' – and therefore as being so tightly bound up with his needs, desires, feelings, thoughts, purposes and intentions as to constitute a quasi-automatic response fully on a par with Inga's implicit dependence on memories laid down in her brain. And to Fodor's objection that Otto has to make an extra effort, i.e. that of consulting his written directions, Chalmers for his part responds that the business of remembering – of calling things to memory – can be quite arduous and by no means always so straightforward and uncomplicated as tends to be suggested by talk of 'underived' (mental) as opposed to 'derived' (artificial or prosthetic) content.

Thus '[i]f one denies a dispositional belief to Otto on the grounds that he has to consult his notebook, then one should also deny a dispositional belief to a version of Inga who has to wilfully consult her memory.'[13] One has to assume that Chalmers includes the word 'wilfully' not by way of conceding that Inga's and Otto's situations are different when her memory is functioning normally, quickly or spontaneously but rather as a first stage in getting his opponents to see that in fact the same applies in that case too. After all, it is the habitual or well-nigh 'automatic' character of Otto's mnemonic practice – the fact that it forms so seamless a part of his getting around town – that qualifies the notebook as an integral component of his mental life and not a mere supplement or add-on. Here again the crucial point is that the 'coupling' between man and device be so close, regular, reliable and habitual as to constitute a genuine circuit or feedback loop rather than an ad hoc or every-so-often used and hence less dependable resource. In such cases, according to Chalmers and Clark, there is no relevant sense in which the domain of mental processes and events can be thought to exclude those various 'external' items that enable the mind/brain to function more efficiently. It may yet be objected that inert items such as notebooks or notebook entries, unlike brains, have meaning, purpose or intentionality only through some prior investment of 'underived' mental content, that is, through the directions having been written down – whether by Otto himself or by a helper – with the aim of getting him to MOMA. However, they respond once again that this objection misses the mark since it fails to grasp that the writing-down is just as much a product of that same ubiquitous interaction between brain, world and the various basic or advanced technologies that play a more or less prominent role in the commerce between them.

Another staple of debate is the use of slippery-slope arguments, most often deployed by upholders of the EM hypothesis against those who defend a mentalist or 'intra-cranialist' position. The idea is that Fodorians will always be vulnerable to this type of reasoning since they are trying to fix a line of demarcation where no such line can justifiably be fixed, in which case there will always be a ready supply of marginal, borderline or (for them) problematical instances. What if Otto's notebook were replaced by a silicon brain implant programmed with the details of his best route to MOMA, along with any amount of other information as and when required? Or again, what if the device had wireless access to a data-bank reliably and regularly primed with just the sorts of details that enable Otto to find his way around and generally manage his life? And what if that provision were further enhanced at some future yet presently conceivable stage of advance by a highly sophisticated feedback system which could detect and respond to Otto's informational needs through its capacity to 'read his mind', i.e. pick up and suitably interpret certain recognisable kinds of neural activity? Such scenarios are thought to create a large problem for internalism since they force the question of exactly where – at what point on the scale of deepening physical as well as psycho-cognitive integration with Otto's life-world – the device in question might properly count as a fully fledged extension of his mind. Clark's wager is that the internalists will be stuck for an answer, or at least for any answer that doesn't beg the question against the EM hypothesis. They will either resort to some shifty fallback position with distinct though disavowed Cartesian implications or else bite the bullet, deny that slippery-slope arguments of this sort possess any genuine force, and continue to maintain – as Fodor does – that underived content is the mark of the mental and that minds just ain't outside the head.

This seems to me a striking example – one of many to be found in philosophy, perhaps for reasons endemic to that discipline – of a debate carried on with great intelligence, wit and resourcefulness by both parties and yet without reasonable hope of a decisive outcome or, to adapt Dr Johnson's mordant phrase, a conclusion in which something is concluded. Thus it exemplifies the way in which advocates of two flatly opposed positions can each bring up a range of strong and, on their own terms, convincing arguments while curiously failing to engage each other except at a level where every last move in the debate seems to be programmed in advance. Of course it might be said that this is only to be expected since, after all, the quarrel between EM advocates and intra-cranialists is just another version – a techno-savvy update – of old controversies like those around Cartesian dualism or, what is usually somewhere in the offing, free will versus determinism. Hence no doubt the depth of commitment on both sides but also, perhaps in consequence of that, the lack of any real prospect that either party will achieve some decisive advantage or come up with some knock-down rejoinder. Chalmers and Clark have no end of slippery-slope instances by which, as they think, to create new problems for the internalist while s/he in turn has arguments in plenty (usually involving an appeal to some aspect or analogue of intentionality) whereby, as s/he thinks, to refute the proponents of strong EM. The latter then respond that Fodor and his allies are merely betraying their residual Cartesianism by attaching such an undue weight of significance to the (supposedly) issue-settling witness of conscious, reflective or deliberative thought.

Slippery-slope instances include the use of fingers for counting or multiplication vis-à-vis the use of electronic calculators; the Filofax vis-à-vis the iPhone; diagrams and tables of various kinds; the popular (if old-fashioned) image of the engineer always with a slide-rule attached to his (*sic*) belt; the scrabble player shifting letters around in an offline trial of word-constructing possibilities; and any number of kindred cases where an 'old' appliance finds its equivalent – at whatever technologically geared-up remove – in some present-day invention. Also very apt to their purpose is the computer game Tetris where players have to rapidly perceive various objects of this or that geometric shape as they descend from the top of the screen and build a wall at the bottom by intercepting and rotating them so as to fit the available slots or sockets.[14] Here the slippery-slope runs: (1) the game-player does all this 'in her head', i.e. by rotating the shapes in her mind's eye and relying on her unaided sense of visual-spatial orientation; (2) she can either choose to proceed as in (1) or else press a button to rotate the objects on screen (with some advantage in terms of speed); and (3), looking forward to a plausibly not-so-far-off future, the player has been fitted with a brain implant – a silicon-based neural chip – which allows her to perform the action just as quickly as did the computer in situation (2) but without pressing the button since now the operation is carried out through an act of the conjoint mind/brain along with its integral (or 'internally' hard-wired) shape-shifting device. Clark and Chalmers present this particular case with very little in the way of commentary or analysis, clearly regarding it as something of a clincher or knock-down argument on their side of the debate.

The second (anti-Cartesian) line of attack relates closely to this because, as Chalmers and Clark see it, the upshot of all those slippery-slope instances if pressed right through is to leave no room – no philosophically habitable space – for the appeal to conscious mind-states as a demarcation criterion. A whole range of basic mental activities, including some (like language use) of a highly complex and sophisticated kind, are such as not only to proceed for the most part without conscious or deliberative thought but actually to require – for their normal functioning – that this should be the case. So when opponents claim that another salient difference between Otto and Inga is the liability of Otto's notebook – like all such prostheses – to loss, damage or sabotage the EM party promptly rejoins that Inga's brain is liable to the same sorts of accident and, besides that, subject to episodes of distraction, drowsiness or sleep. The intended effect of all this is to soften up opponents by steadily removing any rational ground they might have (or purport to have) for maintaining the idea of a qualitative difference between mind, intentionality or natural memory and various mind-extending devices like those instanced above. Indeed that effect is clearly visible in the writing of EM theorists where already there has developed a regular tendency to use the language of computing, networks, feedback loops, etc., when describing what would normally – folk-psychologically – dictate the choice of a mentalist or intentionalist idiom. So when Chalmers and Clark rehearse the various standard objections to the EM hypothesis they go so far as to concede the possibility that 'Inga's "central" processes and her memory probably have a relatively high-bandwidth link between them, compared to the low-grade connection between Otto and his notebook.'[15]

However, this is a concession in which nothing much is conceded since the difference concerned – when phrased and conceived in this manner – is one that works out entirely in favour of their own central proposition. That is to say, their talk of high versus low bandwidths joins onto the nowadays familiar analogy between mind and the central processing unit of a computer so as to suggest that this whole way of thinking has a more than analogical force. What it helps to drive home is the message that memory, along with other aspects of human mental life, should be thought of in resolutely physicalist terms and hence as including any and all of those physical devices that serve to extend its cognitive powers.

III

Another main area of debate in this context is the distinction between standing and occurrent beliefs, the latter defined as conscious or present-to-mind at some given point in time and the former – by contrast – as those of which we are not conscious or presently aware although we would acknowledge them if asked or act upon them if prompted. This distinction is seen as crucial by the anti-EM party since it arguably falls in with their case for consciousness as the source of 'underived content', and hence with their claim that extra-cranial devices simply cannot be integral constituents of mind unless one adopts the pan-psychist idea that everything partakes of consciousness in some, however slight, degree. One can therefore understand why Chalmers should profess a certain sympathy with such ideas since the case for pan-psychism can readily be stated in terms that fit in well enough with the EM hypothesis, i.e. through its likewise seeking to remove the mind/world barrier, albeit in a more far-reaching way and on no such basically physicalist grounds.[16] From the pro-EM standpoint it is just as crucial to deny that occurrent thoughts, beliefs or memories have any kind of privileged status vis-à-vis standing or dispositional mind-states. After all, the former seem maximally unlikely candidates for replacement or replication by devices outside the skull while the latter are much more readily conceived – though not by Fodor and company – as subject to this or that form of prosthetic extension. So EM advocates typically take the line that since no beliefs are wholly or purely occurrent – since they are all reliant for their power to guide or influence behaviour on a background of standing belief-dispositions – that distinction cannot serve as a basis for rejecting the EM claim.

Here again they deploy a version of the slippery-slope argument, in this case reasoning from the fact that possessors of a normally functioning Inga-type 'internal' memory must all the same have recourse, at whatever unconscious or preconscious level, to stored information that cannot plausibly be thought of as punctually present to mind. In short, if the mark of the mental is underived content and if underived content is possessed by occurrent but not by standing beliefs then Inga's situation in this regard is no different from Otto's. Or rather, their situations differ in a relative but not in a decisive way since although Inga is no doubt better placed for quick and ready access to her memories without having to consult a notebook she still has the need – conscious or not – to check out the reliability of any knowledge or guidance thus obtained against the stock of information laid down in her standing memory. Of course the opponents of EM will be routinely unimpressed by this argument, on the one hand because (according to them) it once again begs the question by denying, rather than disproving, the existence of underived content, and on the other because they (Fodor at least) reject the validity of slippery-slope arguments in general. Besides, they may respond, the point about Inga's having (like Otto) to 'consult' her memory is far less telling than the point that Otto has to *believe* in the accuracy of his notebook – has to invest it, so to speak, with a quality of creditworthiness – in a way that necessarily involves the exercise of underived intentional or sense-bestowing powers. To which of course the EM-advocates predictably come back with the further iteration of their basic case: that quite simply there is no such thing as 'underived content', and hence that there is no difference – in principle if not for certain practical purposes – between Inga's and Otto's situations.

It should be clear by now that this dispute is of the kind – the peculiarly philosophical kind – that is very likely to run and run until boredom sets in, or until there is a switch of interest among members of the relevant (largely academic) community. This is not to conclude that it is a 'merely' academic dispute, in the sense of having nothing important or relevant to say to anyone outside the community of those with the time and incentive to pursue such matters. On the contrary: it has some large ethical and socio-political implications, as Chalmers makes clear when he remarks that if the EM hypothesis achieves wide acceptance then 'in some cases interfering with someone's environment will have the same moral significance as interfering with their person'.[17] Moreover, if physical devices like notebooks and iPhones can qualify as genuinely mind-extending in the strong sense proposed then all the more must this apply to those 'significant others' – persons with whom the individual concerned is regularly, closely or intimately in contact – who serve not only as sources of information but (at least under normal circumstances) as active and cooperative members of his or her life-world. Clark and Chalmers acknowledge this, sure enough, but tend to underplay the significance of it or treat it as a non-essential aspect of their case. They prefer to offer instances like that of one's financial accountant or trusted waiter at a favourite restaurant rather than partners, relatives or people more personally close to home. The reason for this preference is not far to seek since the EM hypothesis is primarily one having to do with processes of information-uptake and information-transfer occurring in a depersonalised context, whether that of Otto's consulting his notebook or somebody's consulting their accountant. Even the favourite-waiter example seems to be chosen – fully in line with standard priorities – so as to place greatest emphasis on considerations such as special expertise, reliability, habitual contact, ease of communication and so forth.

Thus the idea of socially (as opposed to physically or artefactually) extended cognition is one that Clark is willing to endorse – 'no reason why not' – but without anything like the partisan vigour that he brings to his argument for the mind-expanding power of note-books and iPhones. Of course this is hardly surprising given his and Chalmers' primary emphasis on the ways in which material imple-ments and devices, rather than other minds, have a role in extending our cognitive powers. However, it does tend to bias their approach in favour of that physical or techno-prosthetic dimension and thus prevent them from fully acknowledging the depth and extent of those human, social or intersubjective dimensions that shape so much of our mental lives. The resultant philosophy of mind is one that inclines not so much toward naturalism as understood by most of its present-day advocates but rather toward a mechanistic conception that so emphatically repudiates one aspect of Cartesian dualism, i.e. that of *res cogitans* or the mentalist 'ghost in the machine', that it ends up by granting pride of place to an all-encompassing *res extensa* or inertly physical realm.

Of course the phrase 'inertly physical' is one that the EM theorists would reject out of hand, implying as it does the existence of an altogether distinct 'mental', 'subjective', 'intentional', 'phenomeno-logical' or 'underived-content' domain where physicalism meets its ultimate limit in that which transcends any possible physicalist speci-fication. By taking that line – so the charge sheet runs – the anti-EM brigade are merely buying into the same old vitalist delusion, the idea of some mysterious life-force beyond reach of scientific or rational explanation, that has typified so many reactive movements of thought over the past two centuries and more. However, this would be to misidentify the main point at issue in the EM debate, as distinct from the point endlessly belaboured – and to no great avail, on the evidence presented here – by parties on both sides. What really matters, I am suggesting, is not so much the question as normally posed, that is to say, internalism = mentalism + individualism versus extended mind = individual mind/brain + various physical prosthe-ses. Rather it is a different, more searching and relevant question of the form: cognitive individualism = this or that solitary brain + various, chiefly physical prostheses versus the socially extended mind = everything belonging to the human sphere wherein there can be no more sense to the distinction between minds and brains than there is to the distinction between 'individual' minds/brains and their range of intersubjectively salient inputs, contacts or relationships. That this is not – or not primarily – the kind of question raised by EM theorists should at least give pause to anyone assessing their proposal on grounds of intuitive acceptability.

Of course intuition need not have the last word in these matters and should probably not be allowed too prominent a voice at any stage in the debate. After all, the progress of scientific knowledge has come about very largely despite and against the weight of (supposed) self-evidence attaching to common-sense-intuitive ideas and beliefs. That history runs from Galileo's heliocentric hypothesis to the advent of non-Euclidean geometries (with their shock to the Kantian a priori system) and – in consequence – the relativistic conception of space and time. All the same it is far from clear that intuition should always take a back seat when it comes to philosophy of mind or to issues in epistemology which concern that very question of just how far we can or should rely on such apodictic sources. Here at least there is a case – one urged by thinkers in the phenomenological line of descent from Husserl, a tradition oddly conspicuous by its absence from EM debate – that understanding might yet be advanced by a suitably disciplined and rigorous approach to certain intuitions concerning the scope and limits of the properly (non-analogically) mental.[18]

This is not to say – far from it – that any claims in that regard should be subject to assessment on terms laid down by the Cartesian tribunal of conscious awareness or reflective self-knowledge. Indeed few ruling ideas have led to greater wastage of time, effort and ingenuity than the deep-laid philosophical conviction that knowledge must involve a conscious mind-state or some kind of privileged first-person epistemic access. Thus it will count among the most useful services rendered by advocates of strong EM if they manage to shift attention away from the 'hard problem' in philosophy of mind, i.e. the famously intractable but (as I have argued elsewhere) much hyped and in the end not very interesting problem of consciousness.[19] On the other hand their way of setting about that worthy task is one that raises some equally intractable problems, among them – as critics like Fodor remark – that of drawing a non-arbitrary line between what properly belongs to mind on this expansive account and what must be considered extra-mental since lacking the requisite degree of informational richness, relevance, complexity or readiness to hand. This difficulty might best be got over, and without serious detriment to their own case, were the EM theorists a bit more receptive – or a bit less prickly – in their response to the above-cited range of counter-arguments from a broadly phenomenological standpoint. Clark and Chalmers may be right that some of those objections issue from misconceived ideas about the existence of human free-will as dependent on the absolute autonomy of mind, or from a strain of shamefaced Cartesianism that has found another refuge under cover of which to continue the campaign. Thus it now takes the form of a strain of individualism seemingly purged of such dualist residues but squarely opposed to any idea that mind might extend beyond the boundaries of this or that isolated brain, skull or skin sack. Such is the diagnosis routinely offered by EM theorists whenever confronted with some argument involving the phenomenological appeal to given aspects of our experiential being-in-the-world, or our place-ment as so many spatio-temporally located human agents with a certain, albeit at times highly qualified sense of existing within those boundaries.

Indeed his keenness to have done with such arguments leads Clark to suggest that this whole debate might be seen as evidence that 'the mind is itself too disunified to count as a scientific kind', and hence to ask: 'might the EM debate form part of a reductio of the very notion of mind in Cognitive Science?'[20] In other words, might we not be better off abandoning not only dualism, mentalism and skin-sack individualism but also – for this would seem to be Clark's proposal – all those branches of cognitive science and cognitive psychology that find any room for mental or phenomenological predicates? At this stage it strikes me that the only appropriate rejoinder is one that involves babies washed away with the bathwater or noses cut off to spite faces. Where the EM theorists go wrong is by too readily saddling (perceived) opponents with a view of these issues that equates the mental with the conscious, or thought and belief with their surrogate forms – their phantom delegates – in the 'Cartesian theatre' of dualist imagining. Otherwise they would have less trouble in conceding that those opponents do have a point, and moreover an EM-compatible point, when they resist going so far as Chalmers and Clark with the project of barrier-dismantling, or with decon-structing categorical distinctions such as that between the mental and the mechanical. More precisely, these objectors – or the cannier among them – think it is worth hanging onto the intuitive distinction between (1) that which is most aptly characterised as belonging to the broadly intentional (i.e. belief-related, thought-involving, cogni-tive, rational, purposive or generally mindful) realm and (2) that which it makes better sense to think of as belonging to a different (i.e. physical and extra-cranial) domain, at least when considered under its normal or primary range of descriptions.[21]

IV

It is here – in contesting the mechanistic bias of much EM argument – that Fodor is able to mount his two strongest lines of attack. First, he rejects the kinds of slippery-slope reasoning often used by EM theorists since he considers them to be no more cogent or decisive when deployed in this context than in other set-piece instances like the classical sorites-type (pseudo-)dilemmas. Second, he makes the cardinal point about underived content – or intentionality – as 'the mark of the mental' and hence as pertaining to notebooks, maps, GPS units, iPhones, etc., only in a strictly derivative sense or else by the loosest of analogies. As we have seen, Clark and Chalmers are inclined to treat this sort of argument as yet further evidence of backsliding into thoroughly discredited Cartesian ways of thought. Yet the charge clearly lacks force if one construes 'underived' not in terms of individual mentality or first-person privileged epistemic access but rather with reference to that wider transpersonal or intersubjective context in the absence of which human beings would be unable to mean, intend or signify anything whatsoever. This is not to deny the EM thesis in its other, wholly defensible form, namely that those various extra-cranial devices are indeed mind-extending, mind-expanding and mind-enhancing in a way that changes and might potentially transform the range and scope of our mental capacities. What it does call into doubt is the far-out version of that thesis according to which the history of those developments is sufficient to obliterate the boundary between mind and the various ancillary (no matter how useful, reliable or even indispensable) devices that have come to play a major role in the lives of many human beings.

That supplements have an odd habit of reversing the normal order of priorities – shifting the emphasis from 'supplement = mere (strictly unnecessary) add-on or optional extra' to 'supplement = that which is needed in order to repair or make good some existing shortfall or deficit' – is a point that Jacques Derrida demonstrates to brilliant effect in his book *Of Grammatology*.[22] However, it also emerges very strikingly through straightforward reflection on the complex of meanings or logico-semantic implications inherent in these two, on the face of it downright contradictory yet closely entangled senses of the word. It seems to me that this debate around the EM hypothesis has a lot to do with what Derrida calls the 'logic of supplementarity' and the kinds of joint reversal-and-displacement to which certain binary distinctions may be subject through a critical account that no longer takes for granted the supposedly self-evident, logical, rational or 'natural' order of priority between them. On the other hand Derrida is equally insistent – as against some other, less canny or cautious exponents of the deconstructive turn – that there is no point in carrying out this inversion of priorities unless it meets the twofold strict requirement exemplified by his own critical practice. That is to say, it must (1) be shown to follow from a rigorous analysis of the terms in question along with the complex, paradoxical or contradic-tory relationship between them, and (2) succeed in revealing the strictly unwarranted (i.e. the arbitrary or ideologically motivated) ascription of superiority or dominance to one term over the other.

I cannot see that the strong-EM case meets those requirements or convincingly demands so radical an overhaul of our basic conception of mind vis-à-vis the non-mental or – as the debate is currently played out – the intra- vis-à-vis the extra-cranial. Like Chalmers I do all sorts of things with my iPhone, among them downloading and listen-ing to music, watching films, reading books and journals, accessing the Internet, finding my way on bike-rides via GPS (shades of Otto and his notebook), making phone calls once in a while, taking photos or videos, setting myself maths and logic puzzles, doing sound-recordings (of myself and others) and looking up a whole vast range of otherwise elusive information. Also like Chalmers I am sometimes tempted to think of it as something more literally mind-integral – more closely or intimately bound up with my meanings, intentions or thought processes – than could ever be allowed by the more moder-ate construal of the EM thesis here proposed. This is especially the case when it offers me some otherwise unavailable and life-enriching musical experience or provides ready access to some otherwise inac-cessible information source combined with a capacity for searching out relevant passages and self-addressed memos across all the other devices (desktop, laptop, Kindle, etc.) to which my iPhone is linked. However, I normally set that temptation aside by reflecting that there is still a great difference between what goes on in my head and what goes on outside it, no matter how much those various externalities may affect, extend, augment or refine my unaided powers of calculation, recollection, logical reasoning or even – where many would surely dissent – inventive though disciplined hypothesis construction.

Indeed there is a sense in which the slippery-slope argument beloved of EM enthusiasts can be turned right around and used to challenge their standard line of reasoning. I have been the grateful beneficiary of various electronic music media from LP to CD, mini-disc, MP3 and now iTunes and should acknowledge that they have contributed greatly to my mental and physical (not to say spiritual) well-being over the years. Still I would be confusing the issue and committing a fairly gross kind of category mistake if I claimed that the devices in question were literally a part of my musical experience or were bound up with it in some intrinsic and response-constitutive way rather than serving as handy – marvellously handy – technological resources for delivering that experience. The same applies to the distinction between intra-cranial (mental-intentional) and extra-cranial (prosthetic) dimensions of information-processing or whatever goes into the business of cognitive uptake. If that distinction can be made to look delusory or merely naive then this is no doubt due to the present-day dominance of naturalistic approaches in epistemology and philosophy of mind, and the consequent suspicion that any attempt to draw such a line must be in hock to residual Cartesian ways of thought.

That this objection misfires, since intentionality (or Fodor's 'underived content') can perfectly well go along with a naturalised epistemology, is a case that I have presented in detail elsewhere and which finds support in a good deal of recent work in those same disciplines.[23] What emerges is something more in line with that moderate version of the EM thesis which treats extra-cranial prosthetic devices as no doubt playing all manner of informative, restorative, memory-boosting, intelligence-stretching, creativity-provoking or other such mentally enhancing roles without for that reason demanding recognition as integral components of mind. Rejecting the lessons of phenomenology or viewing it as merely a species of 'psychologism' (for which read: subjectivism/relativism run amok) is one of those deep-laid articles of faith or largely unquestioned imperatives handed down by the founding fathers – Frege in particular – that typify the discourse of mainstream analytic philosophy.[24] Even thinkers who have lately questioned that imperative or sought to negotiate a renewal of ties between the two traditions – an increasing number of late – still tend to assume that Frege got it pretty much right with regard to the irrelevance of phenomenological considerations when it comes to logic and the formal sciences.[25]

It seems to me that this assumption, whether or not valid in that particular context, has exerted a distorting effect when carried over into different areas of debate like those surrounding the strong EM hypothesis. It has led philosophers like Chalmers and Clark to treat any resistance to their case in its full-strength or uncompromising form as just a throwback to quaintly subjectivist or 'psychologistic' modes of thought. However, this is a flat misunderstanding of the opposition case and one that badly distorts the issue between these contending parties. In short, there is no reason – partisanship or prejudice aside – to suppose that a belief in the distinctness of mind from its various ancillary, prosthetic or supplementary aids is necessarily a sign of Cartesian leanings. Nor is it to go along with those thinkers – among them followers of Wittgenstein and subscribers to Donald Davidson's idea of 'anomalous monism' – who regard mind-talk and physicalist talk as each making sense in its own proper (topic-relative) sphere, and hence as incapable of coming into conflict except through some categorical confusion or failure to respect their respective scope and limits.[26] Rather it is to recognise that phenomenology can and should have its say in any discussion of these issues, and moreover that this can and should go along with the commitment to a thoroughly naturalised conception of mind and its various attributes. However – crucially – this is a phenomenology of the extended mind where that extension is primarily social or inter-subjective in character, i.e. no longer restricted to the realm of first-person apodictic thought, judgement and experience that occupied the main focus of Husserlian phenomenological enquiry.

Here it joins with other anti-individualist or transpersonal conceptions, many of which trace their lineage back to Spinoza's radically heterodox thesis – developed very much in opposition to Descartes – that mind is a properly collective (or multitudinous) phenomenon which gains its power and capacity for action precisely through achieving the maximal extent of interactive communal exchange.[27] This is why recent intellectual historians have identified Spinozism as the leading force in that largely underground 'radical enlightenment' that pressed its social-transformative claims far beyond anything countenanced by the purveyors of 'official' enlightenment values and beliefs, Kant chief among them.[28] Thus the idea of 'multitude' has nowadays been taken up by a number of thinkers who seek to develop a social-political ontology that would break altogether with the individualist and epistemologically oriented modes of philosophising bequeathed by Descartes and Kant.[29] One feature of that tradition has been its periodic tendency – above all in Descartes – to combine a subjectivist-idealist appeal to the supposed self-evident and privileged status of first-person epistemic warrant with an otherwise thoroughly mechanistic worldview, thus squeezing out any notion of mind as manifest through modes of intersubjective, interpersonal, or 'multitudinous' assemblage. It seems to me that the 'strong' EM thesis shows a similar penchant for all things physical-mechanical and a similar tendency to downplay the role of those other, more than supplementary resources which pertain to mind in its trans-individual dimension.

One need not be a Marxist – though probably it helps – to detect here a telltale symptom of the process (call it reification or commodi-fication) that converts the products of human labour, invention or creative ingenuity into so many items of inertly physical matter. Of course the advocates of strong EM will again protest that this charge is grossly misconceived since what they are proposing is a radical shift in just the opposite direction, that is, from conceiving note-books, iPhones and so forth as physical artefacts and nothing more to conceiving them as animated (so to speak) by human intentionality. Yet it is precisely Marx's point in his writing on the uncanny 'logic' of commodity fetishism that this is indeed a two-way exchange of properties or attributes although one that has the predominant effect of rendering the animate inert rather than vice versa.[30] Thus, in EM terms, the mind-extending powers of extra-cranial devices are rou-tinely extolled without taking adequate account of their dependence on the mind-expanding power of communal or collective human intelligence. This produces a reified, commodified or fetishised conception of technology which in turn leads us to think of human beings as creatures of the various (whether lo-tech or hi-tech) gizmos that are taken to constitute a large and increasingly pervasive aspect of their life-worlds. So there is, I suggest, good reason to resist the more hard-line versions of the EM thesis, or those that take literally its claim that notebooks and iPhones are integral parts of – rather than highly useful, versatile and often much relied upon additions to – our core repertory of cognitive powers. Otherwise it is likely to result not so much in a newly expansive conception of the mental that embraces all sorts of items hitherto deemed inertly physical but rather, despite what its advocates may claim, in a shift of perception that works to precisely opposite effect.

This likelihood increases as the EM case is pushed beyond examples having to do with memory, knowledge, reasoning, logic, calculation and the more algorithmic or formal-procedural aspects of human intelligence. After all, the whole approach finds its best, most convincing set-piece instances in technologies – whether notebooks or iPhones – that have as their primary function the more efficient marshalling of information or the better working of our rational thought-procedures. As I have said, Chalmers and Clark are by no means unaware of this challenge and indeed make a point of confronting it head on. Thus to the questions 'what about socially extended cognition?' and 'could my mental states be partly constituted by the states of other thinkers?' they respond that 'in an unusually interdependent couple, it is entirely possible that one partner's beliefs will play the same sort of role for the other as the notebook plays for Otto'.[31] This does at least take us further into the realm of significant intersubjective or interpersonal exchange than their allusion to the kind of relationship that people have with their financially trusted accountant or the favourite waiter in their favourite restaurant. Still it doesn't take us that much further since the interdependent-couple case is one that confines the range of relevant examples to relationships of the most intimate (hence socially exclusive) kind and thereby works to debar any reference to the collective – i.e. the socio-political or 'multitudinous' – dimension of human interdependent activity.

V

Chalmers and Clark go on to raise the question as to what consequences flow from an acceptance of the strong EM thesis for our conception of 'that most problematic entity, the self'.[32] The passage needs quoting at length because it brings out very clearly the effect of such thinking in terms of that wider, i.e. not only trans-individual but also properly public or non-intimate since transpersonal sphere. 'Does the spread of cognitive processes out into the world imply some correlative leakage of the self into local surroundings?', they ask. Yes indeed, since it is only the diehard (or shamefaced) Cartesians who would seek to shore up the citadel of the self – or personal identity – against all encroachments from 'outside'. Thus:

> Most of us already accept that the boundaries of the self outstrip the boundaries of consciousness: my dispositional beliefs, for example, constitute in some deep sense part of who I am. If so, then our previous discussion implies that these boundaries may also fall beyond the skin. The information in Otto's notebook, for example, is a central part of his identity as a cognitive agent. What this comes to is that Otto *himself* is best regarded as an extended system, a coupling of biological organism and external resources. To consistently resist this conclusion, we should have to shrink the self into a mere bundle of occurrent states, severely threatening the

> psychological continuity of the self. Far better to take the broader view, and see agents themselves as spread-out into the world.[33]

This passage perfectly exemplifies the way that strong EM uses the bugbear of Cartesian dualism – with all its well-known problems concerning selfhood or personal identity vis-à-vis the 'external world' – in order to prop up its case. There are three main issues that it raises with particular force so I shall end this discussion by focusing on them and drawing the relevant conclusions with regard to the EM programme in its currently most visible and vigorous guise.

First: if the boundaries need pushing back then it is far from clear – indeed highly doubtful – that they need pushing so as to include an ever-increasing range of technological appliances, accessories or gadgets that cannot (except on a thoroughly mechanistic worldview) lay claim to a constitutive role in the shaping of human identity. Second: if it is true that mind–world boundaries must be thought of as falling 'outside the skin' then getting inside other people's skins (and allowing them to get inside ours) is more important – more crucial to overcoming that Cartesian legacy – than extending our nominal definition of 'mind' to include this or that item of physical paraphernalia. And third: if Otto's notebook is deemed 'a central part of his identity as a cognitive agent' then this claim needs some very careful unpacking. Maybe it qualifies for such a role only in so far as we are considering his 'identity' in strictly 'cognitive' terms, that is in line with the bias typically displayed by the advocates of strong EM. But in that case one should surely be given pause by the emphatic claim that 'Otto *himself* is best regarded as an extended system, a coupling of biological organism and external resources.' For then it is hard to avoid the conclusion that selfhood and identity must be a matter of states that pertain very largely – perhaps entirely – at an infra-personal, pre-volitional or sub-doxastic level.

So far from preserving the 'psychological continuity of the self' this idea of agents as 'spread-out into the world' is much likelier to induce a generalised scepticism with regard to any claim for the self as playing an other than notional or place-filler role. In effect it is squeezed out – reduced to insignificance – by that direct 'coupling of biological organism and external resources' that Chalmers and Clark envisage as providing all that's required in the way of explanatory content. Indeed, the very fact of their resorting to talk of 'external' versus 'internal' is enough to suggest that the 'shrinkage' of the self here imputed to internalists is perhaps more a feature of the EM approach and its reduction of mind to a 'mere bundle' of dispositional (rather than occurrent) states. At any rate if there is a genuine threat to the 'psychological continuity of the self' then it looms much larger from the EM direction than from any overemphasis on phenomeno-logical aspects of human thought and experience. Acceptance of the thesis in its strong or literal form is apt to produce an increasingly mechanised image of the mind that ignores or discounts those prop-erties of it – chief among them its distinctive intentionality – which stand in the way of such acceptance. What most needs stressing is the basic point that a theory of mind duly heedful of the relevant distinc-tions need not (indeed should not for its own philosophical good) get into conflict with a naturalised conception of mind vis-à-vis brain and its ambient physical and social world. However, if attention is focused solely on physical aspects of the extended mind – thus ignor-ing its social or interpersonal aspects – then this is sure to produce a distorted perspective and a tendency to replicate those same vexing dualisms that the EM proponents hope to have resolved once and for all.

At any rate there is room to doubt Clark's and Chalmers' claim – or to find in it a certain revealing ambiguity – when they confidently state that 'once the hegemony of skin and skull is usurped, we may be able to see ourselves more truly as creatures of the world'.[34] In the strong version it is a thesis with some fairly discomforting overtones for those whose relationship with various items of not so peripheral technology may involve a mixture of dependence, fascination and a sense that we are indeed becoming 'creatures' of a world – a world of all-embracing informatics – with designs on the scope and limits of our selfhood.

Notes

1. David J. Chalmers and Andy Clark, 'The extended mind', in Richard Menary (ed.), *The Extended Mind* (Cambridge, MA: MIT Press, 2010), pp. 27–42. For further discussions pro and contra the EM thesis, see especially Frederick Adams and Kenneth Aizawa, *The Bounds of Cognition* (Oxford: Blackwell, 2008); Lynne Rudder Baker, 'Persons and the extended mind thesis', *Zygon*, 44: 3 (2009), pp. 642–58; Andy Clark, *Natural-Born Cyborgs: Minds, Technologies and the Future of Human Intelligence* (Oxford: Oxford University Press, 2003), 'Curing cognitive hiccups: a defence of the extended mind', *Journal of Philosophy*, 104: 4 (2007), pp. 163–92, and 'Intrinsic content,

active memory, and the extended mind', *Analysis*, 65: 285 (2005), pp. 1–11; Brie Gertler and Lawrence Shapiro (eds), *Arguing About the Mind* (London: Routledge, 2007); Susan Hurley (ed.), *Consciousness in Action* (Cambridge, MA: Harvard University Press, 1998) and 'Vehicles, contents, conceptual structure and externalism', *Analysis*, 58: 1 (1998), pp. 1–6; Richard Menary, *Cognitive Integration: Mind and Cognition Unbounded* (London: Palgrave, 2007); Mark Rowlands, 'Extended cognition and the mark of the cognitive', *Philosophical Psychology*, 22: 1 (2009), pp. 1–19 and 'The extended mind', *Zygon*, 44: 3 (2009), pp. 628–41.

2. Jerry Fodor, 'Where is my mind?', *London Review of Books*, 31: 3 (2009), pp. 13–15.

3. See also Fodor, *Psychosemantics* (Cambridge, MA: MIT Press, 1987) and *The Elm and the Expert* (Cambridge, MA: MIT Press, 1994).

4. Fodor, 'Where is my mind?', op. cit., p. 15.

5. John R. Searle, *Intentionality: An Essay in the Philosophy of Mind* (Cambridge: Cambridge University Press, 1983).

6. For a vigorously argued presentation of the eliminativist or central-state materialist case, see Paul M. Churchland, *Scientific Realism and the Plasticity of Mind* (Cambridge: Cambridge University Press, 1979).

7. For further discussion of this possible convergence between phenomenological and naturalistic conceptions of mind, see Christopher Norris, *Re-Thinking the Cogito: Naturalism, Reason and the Venture of Thought* (London: Continuum, 2010).

8. Chalmers and Clark, 'The extended mind' (note 1, above), p. 29.

9. Andy Clark, *Supersizing the Mind: Embodiment, Action and Cognitive Extension* (Oxford: Oxford University Press, 2008).

10. Fodor, 'Where is my mind?', op. cit., p. 13.

11. Ibid.

12. Clark, *Supersizing the Mind*, op. cit., p. 96.

13. David Chalmers, 'Fodor on the extended mind', at http://fragments. consc.net/djc/2009/202/fodor-on-the-extended-mind.html (accessed 15 April 2011).

14. Chalmers and Clark, 'The extended mind', op. cit., pp. 27 ff.

15. Ibid., p. 44.

16. See especially Chalmers, *The Conscious Mind: In Search of a Fundamental Theory* (Oxford: Oxford University Press, 1996).

17. Chalmers and Clark, 'The extended mind', op. cit., p. 45.

18. See, for instance, Shaun Gallagher and Dan Zahavi, *The Phenomenological Mind: An Introduction to Philosophy of Mind and Cognitive Science* (London: Routledge, 2008); Barry Smith and David Woodruff Smith (eds), *The Cambridge Companion to Husserl* (Cambridge: Cambridge University Press, 1995); David Woodruff Smith, *Husserl* (London: Routledge, 2007); Dan Zahavi, *Subjectivity*

and Selfhood: Investigating the First-Person Perspective (Cambridge, MA: MIT Press, 2008).

19. Norris, *Re-Thinking the Cogito*, op. cit.

20. Clark, 'Memento's revenge: the extended mind, extended', in Menary (ed.), *The Extended Mind* (note 1, above), pp. 43–66, at p. 65.

21. See, for instance, Adams and Aizawa, *The Bounds of Cognition* (note 1, above); also various contributors to Gertler and Shapiro (eds), *Arguing About the Mind* and Menary (ed.), *The Extended Mind* (note 1, above). Among others resistant to the EM proposal, at least in its full-strength form, see also Gary Bartlett, 'Whither internalism? How internalists should respond to the extended-mind hypothesis', *Metaphilosophy*, 39 (2008), pp. 163–84, and Robert D. Rupert, 'Challenges to the hypothesis of extended mentation', *Journal of Philosophy*, 101: 8 (2004), pp. 389–428. For some wider though highly relevant contexts of debate, see P. Robbins and M. Aydede (eds), *The Cambridge Handbook of Situated Cognition* (Cambridge: Cambridge University Press, 2009).

22. Jacques Derrida, *Of Grammatology*, trans. G. C. Spivak (Baltimore: Johns Hopkins University Press, 1976).

23. Norris, *Re-Thinking the Cogito*, op. cit.

24. For a more detailed account, see Norris, 'Who's afraid of psychologism? Normativity, truth, and epistemic warrant', in *On Truth and Meaning: Language, Logic and the Grounds of Belief* (London: Continuum, 2006), pp. 12–40.

25. See especially Michael Dummett, *Origins of Analytical Philosophy* (Cambridge, MA: Harvard University Press, 1993).

26. See, for instance, Severin Schroeder (ed.), *Wittgenstein and Contemporary Philosophy of Mind* (Basingstoke: Palgrave-Macmillan, 2001); also Donald Davidson, *Essays on Actions and Events*, 2nd edn (Oxford: Oxford University Press, 2001).

27. See especially Antonio Negri, *The Savage Anomaly: The Power of Spinoza's Metaphysics and Politics*, trans. Michael Hardt (Minneapolis: University of Minnesota Press, 1991); also Gilles Deleuze, *Spinoza: Practical Philosophy*, trans. Robert Hurley (San Francisco: City Lights Books, 1988) and *Expressionism in Philosophy: Spinoza*, trans. Martin Joughin (New York: Zone Books, 1992).

28. Jonathan Israel, *Radical Enlightenment: Philosophy and the Making of Modernity, 1650–1750* (Oxford: Oxford University Press, 2002); see also Christopher Norris, *Spinoza and the Origins of Modern Critical Theory* (Oxford: Blackwell, 1991); Paul Wienpahl, *The Radical Spinoza* (New York: New York University Press, 1979); Yirmiyahu Yovel, *Spinoza and Other Heretics*, Vol. One: *The Marrano of Reason*, and Vol. 2: *The Adventures of Immanence* (Princeton: Princeton University Press, 1989).

29. See especially Michael Hardt and Antonio Negri, *Empire* (Cambridge, MA: Harvard University Press, 2000) and *Multitude: War and Democracy in the Age of Empire* (New York: Penguin, 2004).
30. Karl Marx, *Capital*, Vol. One, *A Critique of Political Economy* (Harmondsworth: Penguin, 1992), Chapter One, Section Four.
31. Chalmers and Clark, 'The extended mind', op. cit., p. 41.
32. Ibid., p. 42.
33. Ibid.
34. Ibid.

CHAPTER 5

Inaesthetics and Transitory Ontology: The Case of Political Song

I

My thinking for this chapter involved a progressive narrowing of focus from ontology of art to ontology of music and thence, via ontology of song, to that even more specific or pared-down object domain that I have dubbed (in what is probably a nonce usage of the phrase) 'the ontology of political song'. Why should anyone propose so curious a topic or so strange a conjunction of three distinct topics – ontology, politics and song – which could be conjoined only through some perverse desire, as Dr Johnson somewhat unfairly remarked of the metaphysical poets, to yoke incompatibles by violence together? If ontological considerations have any place in the discussion of music then that place needs earning by some hard argument since music is surely, of all the arts, the hardest to pin down, define or characterise in terms of its ontological status. As regards particular musical works this has to do chiefly with their distinctive and perduring mode of existence quite apart from their more or less extensive history of variant performances or interpretations.[1] Such problems become all the more daunting when politics enters the picture with its effect of creating a highly localised or context-specific link between 'work' (if that concept has any purchase here), performance history and particular socially mediated instances of production/reception. Thus it might well be argued that the term 'ontology' is subject to abuse – wrenched away from its proper usage – when applied to a genre like political song whose very nature it is to exist, so to speak, on the wing and to resist treatment (heavy-handed philosophical treatment) in terms of its ontology or quasi-objective mode of being.

Such is at any rate likely to be the reaction even among those who would in principle acknowledge the case for addressing the ontology of art, of music and (however grudgingly) of song. Still, they might say, does there not come a point on the scale of diminishing returns where the domain in question is so markedly bereft of distinguishing *ontological* features – so much a product of circumstance, occasion, context, impulse, passing inspiration, adaptive ingenuity, etc. – that the term 'ontological' seems utterly out of place? After all, philosophers have difficulty enough with the ontology of musical works on account of their inhabiting an indistinct zone between this or that performance, history of performances, ideal performance, work qua score, work qua composer's intent and (maybe) a realm of Platonic forms that is somehow accessed by all musical works or at any rate those that achieve classic status.[2] The range of possibilities is such that every attempt at a solution in line with any of these alternatives seems to generate insoluble problems. These problems are multiplied and deepened when the genre in question is that of song with its typical brevity, economy of utterance, lack of (at any rate long-range or formally imposing) structural markers, and – most often – extreme reliance on subtleties and nuances of performance as well as closeness of rapport between singer and other musicians. All the more must this apply in the case of political song where these context-dependent features are yet further relativised by their insertion into a socio-cultural context or a highly specific situation which – it might be thought – removes any possible justification for affording them the dubious honour of a place in the ontological scheme of things. Such a claim is misconceived by reason of its failure to respect the proper scope of ontology as a highly developed discipline of thought yet one that has certain limits of proper or legitimate applicability. It also goes wrong by erroneously seeking to dignify a genre such as political song by subjecting it to just the kind of discriminative process – the application of high-art derived and philosophically elaborated concepts and categories – which are wholly off the point in a context like this. Moreover, so the argument goes, it is liable to have just the opposite of its intended effect in so far as it risks devaluing that genre by holding it accountable to alien standards or criteria.

Such objections are apt to press pretty hard in a nominalist or anti-essentialist direction and deploy some version of the argument that political song is really not a 'genre' in any reputable sense of that term. This is because – on a certain understanding of musical ontology or ontology in general – it fails to meet the baseline generic requirement of possessing at least certain specifiable features, traits or distinctive marks that are not wholly or exhaustively context-relative. That is, it falls short of fully fledged generic belonging precisely in so far as its defining characteristic is that which marks it as a product of the strictly contingent or generically non-subsumable encounter between some particular set of socio-cultural-political circumstances and some particular, politically inspired or ethically motivated musical response. Yet this is none the less a generic description and one that has a fair claim to capture what is distinctive – even generically salient – about political song as performed in the kinds of situation (for instance on picket lines, at protest meetings or in response to state-sponsored injustice or violence) that most aptly qualify for that description. Here we are on familiar ground for anyone who has read Jacques Derrida's essays, such as 'The Law of Genre' and 'Before the Law', concerning the curious twists of logic – the paradoxes of inclusion and non-inclusion – that tend to crop up as soon as one asks what it means for a work to belong to some existing genre, or what properly counts as a mark of generic membership.[3] At their least challenging these paradoxes have to do with the point made by T. S. Eliot, again with the metaphysical poets in mind, namely that our reading of past writers must be very different from any reading that they might themselves have produced quite simply because our awareness of them includes many things that they could not have known, including (crucially) the subsequent impact or reception history of their own work.[4] More tellingly, the paradoxes take us into regions of logic, mathematics or meta-mathematics where thinking comes up against Russell's famous problem about self-predication, i.e. 'the set of all sets that are not members of themselves', or 'the barber who shaves everyone in town except those who shave themselves' (in which case who shaves the barber?).[5]

This is not the place for a lengthy exposition of that problem or its various attempted solutions, among them Russell's stopgap remedy – his so-called Theory of Types – vetoing any formula that mixed first-order (object-language) expressions with second-order (meta-linguistic) levels of analysis, and so on up through the hierarchy of levels with a similar injunction at every stage so as to prevent such problems from arising in the first place. Sufficient to say – with an eye to our present topic – that although its home-ground is in logic, mathematics and the formal sciences this issue has a significant bearing on that of generic membership or affiliation as raised by Derrida's deconstructive quizzing of the boundaries between work and world, text and context, or art and its socio-politico-cultural-material environment. Thus any issue concerning the 'law of genre' and its constant liability to raids and incursions from across the generic border is closely bound up with the issue of aesthetic autonomy. Both questions are raised with peculiar force by works, performances or events – such as political songs – which would seem to be tokens maximally open to change or transformation from one context to the next, and hence minimally open to subsumption under this or that context-transcendent generic type. That is, they are peculiarly ill suited to treatment under the usual range of descriptive, prescriptive or evaluative predicates based on the presumed autonomy of the musical work as a self-sufficient type with the ontological wherewithal to hold its identity conditions firm across manifold shifting contexts of performance.

Hence, according to autonomists, the need to distinguish that work from the various factors – historical, political, socio-cultural, psycho-biographical and so forth – that make up its background history.[6] These latter kinds of circumstance may well have played some role in the music's genesis and perhaps in its reception history but cannot – or should not, to this way of thinking – be allowed to affect our 'purely' musical response, itself arrived at through a cultivated grasp of all and only those formal structures intrinsic to the work itself. Nothing could be further from the mode of existence enjoyed by most political songs, composed as they are very often on the hoof, under threat, against the clock or out of some urgent communicative need and therefore with little regard to such high-cultural notions of musical autonomy. Indeed it is very clearly a part of their purpose – almost a defining feature of political song – to invite the kind of *engagé* (or *enragé*) listener response that has no truck with that aestheticist creed or that appeal to timeless values beyond the time-bound contexts of production and reception. Such an auditor hears in the punctual coupling of words, music and event a call to action all the more effective for involving precisely those 'extraneous' elements that the formalist seeks to preclude.

So one main reason for my odd choice of topic, 'the ontology of political song', is that it offers a particularly strong challenge to certain deep-laid assumptions concerning the status or mode of existence proper to musical works. Those assumptions have primarily to do with their formal autonomy and hence their capacity to transcend the order of merely contingent events, whether singing events (e.g. street performances) or events of a more directly political character. Of course that distinction is one that any writer or performer of political songs would reject straight off as failing to recognise that certain songs in certain contexts have a singular capacity to mobilise protest and strengthen resistance to various forms of social injustice that is 'directly political' in every sense of the phrase. Still there is a question as to whether such songs, or the best of them, may be said to possess that galvanising power not only in virtue of their timeliness and their happening to ride some wave of popular discontent but also on account of certain musical attributes – melodic, harmonic, rhythmic, structural – which place them in a class apart, or which define them as veritable classics of the genre. The problem for anyone who makes this claim is that the notion of 'the classic' comes laden with a weight of inherited ideas concerning the markers of canonical status – of literary or musical greatness – and their timeless, transcendent character. It is this way of thinking that political song most pointedly calls into question since its very existence as a popular alternative to high-cultural art forms is premised on its audibly not going along with the various ideologies (of genius, transcendence, organic form, structural complexity, etc.) promoted by the guardians of musical good taste. Yet there are other, less ideologically compromised ways of thinking about 'the classic' – among them Frank Kermode's marvellously subtle and nuanced reflections on the topic – that entail no such commitment.[7] For Kermode, the classic is most typically a work 'patient of interpretation', or apt to reveal new possibilities of meaning in response to shifting historical-cultural circumstances. On his account it is still a work – not just a 'text' dissolved into its context or reception history – but a work whose very capacity to survive those changes should be taken as evidence of its openness to a range of alternative readings.

II

I should not wish to say that 'classic' political or protest songs should be thought of in exactly those terms, i.e. as sharing with Kermode's prime examples (from Homer and Virgil to Dante and Shakespeare) this quality of holding senses in reserve, or this capacity for endless self-renewal in the face of unending historical change. To make such a claim would be doubly mistaken, on the one hand by ignoring Kermode's emphasis on the subtle, oblique or roundabout ways in which the classic text succeeds in holding out against the tides of historical mutability, and on the other by ignoring the very different range of musical, verbal, social and communal factors that make for the survival of political or protest songs from one specific context to another. What ultimately underwrites Kermode's idea of the classic is the notion that there must be some structural feature or set of features by which to explain this inexhaustibility of sense, this joint resistance and responsiveness to pressures of time and change that would otherwise have long since consigned the work to oblivion. If he doesn't go far toward saying just where those structures might be located then this is no doubt because Kermode had by this stage travelled his own long path from an openness to certain structuralist ways of thinking about narrative and language to a more hermeneutically oriented sense of everything – all those subtleties of meaning and oblique implication – that the text withholds from any too direct or overly technical approach.[8] Indeed the greatest virtue of Kermode's criticism is the way that it managed, over five decades, to occupy that difficult middle ground between 'theory' in its various high-powered manifestations and a mode of reflective, meditative brooding on what he knew to lie beyond the limits of critical system or method. Still there is clearly a sense in which this space for manoeuvre between theory and that which theory occludes or fails to acknowledge is itself a high-cultural or intensely theoretical space which finds no room for genres (or anti-genres) such as political song. For it is precisely their distinctive mark – their claim to an ontological niche quite apart from other, more familiar or tractable genres – that they occupy a different space and one that is more radically open to the reception-changing impact of historical, social and political events.

Of course my approach is itself open to the charge of manifest inconsistency since it has already brought a whole battery of heavy-weight theory and theorists to bear on what it asserts to be a mode of politically motivated music-making which intrinsically eludes specification in terms of any preconceived theory. It seems to me that this charge sticks – constitutes a powerful objection to what I have said so far and will go on to say – only if there is something fundamentally wrong or misconceived about the whole business of theorising in relation to music, literature and the arts. Otherwise the main lesson is that enquiry into ontological issues in the broadly aesthetic sphere had better be ready to adjust its critical focus so as to accommodate the range of cases – including some on the outermost fringes of that sphere, conventionally speaking – which should properly be taken into account by any such enquiry. My point is that conventions often run very deep and that it actually requires an effort of thought with strong theoretical back-up if we are ever to succeed in breaking or at any rate loosening their hold. Thus it may take something like Derrida's complex modal-logical reflections on the deviant logics of supplementarity, iterability or parergonality – along with his intricate drawing-out of those aporias intrinsic to the 'law of genre' – in order to shift some of our basic assumptions concerning the scope and limits of aesthetic response.[9] Such thinking against the orthodox (canonically invested) grain is strictly prerequisite if any serious question is to be raised with respect to what should or should not qualify as a musical work or an instance of art as distinct from an instance of music put to political or other such supposedly non-artistic ends. At any rate we won't get far in any discussion of ontological issues vis-à-vis musical works (or performances) unless, like Derrida, we make a regular practice of challenging those otherwise largely unspoken assumptions that underlie our routine habits of judgement and response.

It might even be said that political song is itself such a practice – or exerts such a deconstructive force – by dint of very pointedly calling into question certain deep-laid values and beliefs concerning the autonomy of musical form, its transcendence of the merely contingent or temporal, and the inviolable unity of words and music as a touchstone of aesthetic worth. Moreover, those values are further contested by the very existence of a genre (or anti-genre) that so conspicuously flouts the Kantian veto on artworks that have some palpable design on the listener/viewer/reader – some purpose to persuade, arouse or convert – and which therefore conspicuously fail to meet Kant's requirement of aesthetic disinterest.[10] After all it might seem self-evident that any item of purported 'political song' that did manage to satisfy this criterion would *ipso facto* be a bad or ineffectual instance of the kind since incapable of stirring anyone to action or decisively changing their minds. Here again we might usefully recall Derrida's deconstructive reading of Austinian speech-act theory and his convincing demonstration – *pace* opponents like John Searle – that Austin's distinctions, like Kant's before him, are a deal more complex and problematical than his orthodox commentators wish to allow.[11] Just as Kant ends up by unwittingly subverting his own elaborate system of binary pairs – among them 'free' and 'adherent' beauty, aesthetic form and instrumental function, or the artwork itself and its various framing, ornamental or extraneous features – so Austin ends up by providing all manner of problematic instances and arguments that cast doubt on whether he can really hold the line between constative and performative modes of utterance.[12] Where the cases differ is in Kant's deep attachment to the virtues of large-scale system and method – requiring that his doctrine of the faculties be deconstructed in a likewise systematic way – as compared with Austin's gamy readiness to junk the system (or his current version of the system) if it looks like getting in the way of some particularly choice example. It is just such instances of speech-act anomaly ('misfires', as Austin called them) that Searle considers marginal *by very definition* since they fall short of straightforward performative success while Derrida counts them especially revealing since they demonstrate the inbuilt possibility that speech-acts might always turn out to function or signify in various non-standard, unpredictable or non-speaker-intended ways.

As hardly needs saying this is also the predicament of political songs, destined as they are – if they succeed in 'catching on' – to undergo a history of changing contexts and varied applications which may result in their becoming very largely detached from any meaning or motive plausibly imputed to the original writer, singer or group of performers. In this respect our thinking about political song – especially with regard to its elusive ontological status – can profit from Derrida's meticulous tracing of the fault lines that run through Kant's various attempted demarcations between art and non-art or pure and impure modes of aesthetic response, as likewise through the various terms and distinctions by which Austin seeks to hold a normative line between proper and improper, valid and invalid, or 'felicitous' and 'infelicitous' modes of speech-act utterance.[13] Indeed there is something markedly anomalous about the very genre of song, existing as it does across such a range of forms, types, musical-verbal structures, cultural traditions, social contexts, communicative roles, performance locales and so forth, as almost to constitute an anti-genre or a nominal kind identified only by its meeting certain far from precise or exacting criteria. Thus the minimal requirements would be roughly (1) its being sung or involving the combination of words and music; (2) its relative brevity compared with other, more extended or structurally complex genres such as those of the cantata, oratorio or opera; (3) its predominantly lyrical nature, that is, the emphasis on expressive elements – again jointly verbal and musical – that give particular songs their distinctive character; and (4) the way that it tends to focus attention on the singer, who is often the songwriter, as source and in some sense subjective guarantor of the feelings thereby expressed. Yet of course one could take each of the above desiderata and come up with a song, or several, that failed to satisfy the supposed requirement and thus raised doubts as to whether this is really a genre even in the proposed minimalist sense. (Consider point for point Mendelssohn's 'Songs Without Words', Mahler's symphonic *Song of the Earth*, didactic or primarily political songs (like those of

Hanns Eisler or Kurt Weill), or the numerous songs – often parts of some larger dramatic or narrative work – that crucially depend for their meaning and effect on our grasping the disparity between what's expressed and what we are intended to make of it.) And if song in general exhibits such a highly elusive ontological character – such extreme resistance to categorisation in clear-cut generic terms – then this is even more strikingly the case with regard to political song. For we are here confronted with a genre (or quasi-genre) that goes yet further toward raising large questions with regard to its own status as a verbal-musical kind or as a token of anything – any definite or trans-context specifiable type – that could serve to fix its generic identity.

This is not to suggest that in switching focus from 'classical' song (i.e. concert-hall *Lieder* of whatever period or style) to instances of political street-song we are lowering our sights in musical-evaluative terms or electing to consider a sub-genre with no pretensions to high artistic, cultural or aesthetic worth. Hanns Eisler's songs, in particular his settings of Brecht, are equal to the finest of the twentieth or any century if heard without prejudice regarding their strongly marked didactic intent and with an ear to those features typically prized by devotees of the high *Lieder* tradition. They are no less accomplished – dramatically powerful, melodically striking, harmonically resourceful and structurally complex – for the fact of their overt political content or, on occasion, their activist concern to discourage the listener from taking refuge in a purely aesthetic or contemplative mode of response. All the same their very success in so doing comes about through their constant supply of reminders, musical and verbal, that there is a world beyond the concert hall and that events in that world – like those that befell the twice-over émigré Eisler, driven out first by the Nazis and then by the watchdogs of US anti-communism – cannot be kept at bay by any amount of artistic creativity or degree of formal inventiveness. Indeed it is one of the most distinctive things about Eisler's music, not only his songs but also his larger-scale choral and orchestral works, that it maintains this perpetual sense of a nervous sensitivity to 'outside' events or the impact of 'extra-musical' promptings. This is probably why he seems most at ease, even in large-scale compositions like his epic yet intensely personal *Deutsche Sinfonie*, when writing in a long-breathed melodic style with song-like contours and a strong sense that only by such means can he combine the pressure of subjective feelings with an adequate response to the pressure of (mostly dire) historical or political occurrences.

Political song is the genre that most effectively unites these otherwise conflicting imperatives and which makes it possible for music
to express both the passionate force of individual commitment and
the historical or socio-political context within which it finds a larger
significance. Ontologically speaking, it is that which (in certain cases)
has the capacity to maintain its distinctive character while undergoing sometimes drastic changes of context, motivating purpose or
performative intent. Songs that started life as protests against British
government policy during the miners' strike of 1983 have since done
service in a great many other campaigns, sometimes very largely
unaltered (except in so far as the shift of context changed their perceived character) and sometimes with verbal modification so as to
update their content or enhance their specific relevance. On a larger
time-scale, songs that had their origin in the suffering or revolt of
black slaves in the American Deep South are nowadays revived – not
just recycled – in the name of anti-poverty campaigns, anti-war protests and calls for the rescheduling or outright cancellation of third-
world debt. What gives the songs in question this remarkable staying
power – beyond some vague appeal to 'the test of time' – is a complex
amalgam of musical and verbal features that is likely to elude the
best efforts of formal analysis but which is recognisable to anyone
who has sung them and registered their continuing impact when
performed on any such politically charged occasion. Here again one
might aptly recall what Derrida has to say about that minimal trait
of 'iterability' that enables speech-acts to function, i.e. to retain a
certain recognisable (ethically and socially requisite) performative
force despite their occurring across a potentially limitless range of
contexts and their involving the ever-present possibility of deviant
(or devious) motives on the utterer's part.[14] Just as this 'iterable'
property of speech-acts is such as to resist any systematic formalisation of the kind attempted by theorists like Searle so likewise the
'classic' quality of certain political songs – those that have retained
their radical force – is none the less real for its holding out against
methods and techniques of analysis trained up on masterworks of the
mainstream classical repertoire.

If I placed some queasy scare quotes around the word 'classic'
in that last sentence then it is no doubt a sign of my unease about
dragging these songs into the orbit of a high-cultural or academic
discourse where they are likely to suffer a gross misprision of their
musical, verbal and political character. All the same, as Terry Eagleton
has argued, it is just as mistaken for left cultural theorists to let go the

whole kit and caboodle of 'bourgeois' aesthetics – especially its talk of arch-bourgeois values such as beauty, sublimity or aesthetic disinterest – on account of its being so deeply bound up with the hegemonic interests of a once dominant though now declining cultural and socio-political class.[15] The fact that those values have largely been monopolised by that particular power bloc doesn't mean that they cannot or should not be recovered – won back through a concerted effort – by those among the marginalised and dispossessed who have most to gain from their redefinition in left-activist terms. This is why the label 'classic' may justifiably be used to describe those songs that have shown a special capacity to renew their impact from one situation to the next and have thus come to manifest a singular strength of jointly musical, political and socio-cultural appeal. Indeed, as Kermode very deftly brings out, if there is one perennial feature of the classic then it is the absence of just those reference-fixing indices that would otherwise place certain clearly marked limits on the range of options for anyone seeking authenticity or wishing to remain true to the song's original context and motivation.

Of course 'authenticity' is a notion widely challenged among left cultural theorists – often taking their lead from Adorno – since it is thought to harbour an appeal to supposedly 'timeless' or 'transcendent' values such as those invested in the high tradition of accredited musical or literary masterworks.[16] However, so it is argued, values of this kind even when adduced as the upshot of a lengthy and detailed formal analysis always have a local habitation in the time and place (that is to say the formative ideological conditions) of their particular socio-politico-cultural setting. Such criticism of the Western musical and literary canons has been carried to a high point of technical refinement by various schools of thought – New Musicologists, New Historicists, deconstructionists, cultural materialists, feminists, the more analytically minded postmodernists – well practised in revealing the various sleights of hand by which promoters of a high formalist doctrine manage to occlude what is in fact a highly specific set of class-based or gender-related ideological commitments.[17] From their point of view Kermode could only be selling out when he argues for a stance of mitigated scepticism vis-à-vis the classic, that is, an approach that would balance the claims of intrinsic literary (or musical) worth against the claims of an anti-canonical case for regarding 'the classic' as one of those ideas that have served as a useful means of upholding the cultural and socio-political status quo. If anyone thought to extend Kermode's argument to the case of political song then they would surely invite the charge of misrepresenting what is by its very nature a context-specific, historically located, resolutely non-transcendent mode of expression. That is to say, they would be seen as deludedly seeking to boost its status by hooking it up to an aesthetic ideology that no longer possesses the least credibility even when applied to works in the mainstream classical repertoire.[18]

Such is at any rate the sort of claim nowadays put forward by zealous deconstructors of the Western musical canon. This project they pursue partly by engaging those works in a heterodox or counter-canonical way and partly by challenging the discourse of post-Schenkerian music analysis with its deep attachment to (supposedly) conservative notions like organic form, thematic development, harmonic complexity, structural integration, progressive tonality, voice-leading, long-range reconciliation of conflicting key centres and so forth.[19] To think (and to listen) in accordance with these notions is to signal one's complicity – so the argument goes – with a formalist mystique of the unified artwork which mistakes the culturally constructed character of all such aesthetic notions for natural properties somehow inherent in 'the work itself', or else in the musical language (most often that of the high Austro-German line of descent from Bach to Brahms or Wagner) that made such achievements possible.[20] And if this line of thought has a certain plausibility with regard to the dominant values of 'high' musical culture and their modes of propagation through the arcane discourse of academic musicology then it seems even nearer the mark when applied to any claim for this or that political song as a veritable 'classic' of its kind. After all, what could be plainer as a matter of straightforward response to words and music alike than the fact that such 'works' constitute a standing affront to that whole classical-romantic aesthetic of timeless, transcendent, ahistorical and hence apolitical values?

It is the latter idea – along with its rootedly nationalist or chauvinist overtones – that finds oblique yet highly effective since technically geared-up expression in the various methods of formal analysis bequeathed by German music theorists of the nineteenth century to their present-day academic heirs. Such a notion is maximally remote from the ethos of direct activist engagement that typifies the best, most powerful instances of political song like those that have emerged from various situations of racial oppression, social injustice and class or gender inequality. To this extent the methods of musical analysis as widely practised nowadays are the result of combining a Kantian emphasis on the formal or structural features of the artwork with a marked devaluation of anything describable as programmatic content. Hence the formalist veto on any music that has some palpable design on the listener, or that seeks to put its message across to best advantage by exerting the maximum persuasive or exhortatory force. It is here that political songs are most likely to offend the arbiters of good taste, or those who equate any admixture of 'extraneous' (i.e. non-formal) elements – such as, most egregiously, political propaganda – with a failure to respect the cardinal requirement of aesthetic disinterest. However, there is no reason to accept this purist attitude, or to go along with the decidedly conservative outlook in philosophical aesthetics which aims to drive a wedge between works of art and the contexts – including the socio-political contexts – of their production and reception.

III

Again it is Kermode, in his book *History and Value*, who has given us by far the most subtle and perceptive treatment of this issue by examining the mainly left-wing English poetry and fiction of the 1930s and tracing the complex patterns of relationship between value as a matter of historical-political 'relevance' and value as a matter of critical esteem or canonical status.[21] What emerges from Kermode's scrupulously nuanced yet far from apolitical reflections is the sheer impossibility of imposing any such divorce, or coming up with a plausible account of literary value that would somehow exclude any reference to the way that literary (or musical) works have fared under certain specific yet historically changing conditions. It is here – at the elusive point of intersection between aesthetic, hermeneutic and socio-political modes of response – that Kermode locates his idea of 'the classic' and along with it his answer, albeit couched in suitably qualified and tentative terms, to the ancient question of just what enables some and not other works to enjoy a long, culturally varied and sometimes unpredictable afterlife. This is an approach that on the one hand keeps its distance from old-style notions of the artwork as possessed of a timeless and altogether context-transcendent value while on the other hand rejecting the opposite (reactive) tendency to find nothing more in literature or music than an ideological sounding-board or a means of imposing this or that set of hegemonic beliefs. It is also, I would argue, a conception well suited to explain why it is that political songs – a few of them – have precisely this phoenix-like capacity to renew their force or to acquire new dimensions of relevance and motivational power from one protest movement to the next. That is to say, their longevity is not so much a matter of some deep-laid, essential or intrinsic quality of words and music that preserves them intact against the ravages of time and chance but rather a matter of their exceptional adaptability to changes of social and political circumstance.

It is perhaps now time to recapitulate the main points of my argument so far in order to firm up the basis for what I have to say in the rest of this chapter. Thus: (1) if the term 'ontology' makes any kind of sense as applied to works of art then it had better be applicable to musical works, in which case (2) it had better be applicable to those works falling under the generic description 'song', and moreover (3) it had best apply convincingly to political song as a litmus-test since this places the maximal strain on received notions of generic character or identity. Hence the particular problem it poses for any formal ontology of art based on the presumed existence of certain distinctive traits by which to recognise and specify what counts as a genuine instance of the kind. After all, 'political song' is a pretty elastic label and one that is apt to find itself stretched around some dubious candidate items if taken to denote any relatively short and self-contained vocal work with a text that makes either overt or covert reference to certain themes of a political character. Thus the British national anthem would have to qualify under this definition although there seems good reason to withhold the title on account of its patently belonging to a genre that endorses rather than challenges the institutional status quo, and whose stolid combination of flag-waving words and foursquare music is very much deployed to that end. Yet there are other national anthems – most strikingly those, like 'Amhrán na bhFiann' (Irish Republic) or 'Nkosi Sikelel' iAfrika' (post-Apartheid South Africa, originally ANC) – which, although in very different ways, continue to communicate something of the oppositional spirit or the strength of concerted popular resistance that went into their making and the often strife-torn history of their early performances. Indeed the very fact of this (so to speak) stress-induced and to that extent historically indexed character has a lot to do with their staying-power as classics of the genre.

This helps to explain why a classic of the 1983 British miners' strike like 'We Are Women, We Are Strong' should thereafter have turned up as a highly effective rallying call at numerous sites and in numerous seemingly disparate socio-political contexts over the past quarter-century of popular anti-government protest.[22] It can best be put down to that song's having so perfectly captured the quiet determination, resilience and unselfconscious heroism not only of the miners' wives and partners but of a great many others whose livelihoods and lives were under threat from government economic and social policy. The case is rather different with those hardy perennials like 'We Shall Not Be Moved' where the sentiments expressed, like the melody and harmonies, are so broadly generic – so capable of being adapted to just about any political context – as to offer a kind of Rorschach blot for those in search of all-purpose emotional uplift. It seems to me that, in order to count as a genuine classic of political song, the piece in question must exhibit something more than this smoothly accommodating power to absorb a great range of otherwise diverse feelings, values, beliefs and commitments. This 'something more' can I think best be specified in ontological terms, even though the terms involved are sure to be somewhat fugitive given that political songs exist very largely in and through their reception-history and thus exhibit a peculiar degree of dependence on contextual cues and the vagaries of historically situated listener-response. All the same, as I have said, it would be wrong to conclude from this that they fall short of classic status in so far as they fail to meet certain formal standards – at any rate certain widely agreed-upon and clearly specifiable criteria – that alone make it possible for judgement to transcend the shifting tides of social change or cultural fashion.

One might take a lead in thinking about this question from the title of Alain Badiou's essay *Briefings on Existence: A Short Treatise on Transitory Ontology*, as indeed from Badiou's entire project to date.[23] That project has to do with the relationship between being and event, or the way that certain unpredictable and yet (as it turns out) epochal or world-changing events – certain breakthrough discoveries whether in mathematics, science, the arts or politics – can lead to a radical transformation in our powers of ontological grasp and hence to a shift in the relationship between currently existing knowledge and objective (recognition-transcendent) truth.[24] What is most remarkable about Badiou's work is its emphasis on truth as always exceeding our utmost powers of cognitive, epistemic or rational grasp and yet as that which constantly exerts a truth-conducive pressure through its absence – its way of creating problems, lacunae, unresolved dilemmas – in our present-best state of understanding. This is not the place for a detailed exposition of Badiou's masterwork *Being and Event*.[25] Sufficient to say that he makes this case not only in relation to mathematics (very much Badiou's disciplinary home-ground) but also to the physical sciences, politics and art. More specifically: in each case it is a matter of truths that are opened up for discovery at a certain stage in the process of knowledge acquisition or cultural-political advance yet which may require a more or less extended process of further working-out at the hands of those faithful exponents – 'militants of truth' – whose office it is to explore their as yet obscure or unrecognisable implications.

However, the main point I wish to make for present purposes is that Badiou offers a distinctive, and distinctly promising, line of enquiry for anyone pondering the ontology of political song and its status vis-à-vis conceptions of art or aesthetic value on the one hand and conceptions of politics or political engagement on the other. Thus on his account there is no choice to be made, as orthodox (e.g. Kantian) approaches would have it, between the value-sphere of artistic creativity or inventiveness and the action-oriented practical sphere of incentives to political change. In each case it is a matter of truth-claims – whether claims in respect of an as yet unachieved state of political justice or claims for the integrity of certain as yet unrecognised artistic practices – that exert a potentially transformative pressure on current ideas but which cannot be realised (carried into practice or brought to the point of adequate conceptualisation) under presently existing conditions. Moreover, it is with respect to ontology – to the question 'What exists?' as distinct from 'What counts as existing within some given mathematical, scientific, artistic or political conception?' – that those conditions are brought into question or subject to standards of truth that transcend the criteria of presently existing knowledge. Above all, this enables an extension of truth-values beyond the realms of mathematics, science and the factual (e.g. historical) disciplines to other areas – such as politics and art – where they have rarely if ever been invoked in so emphatic and rigorously argued a manner.

Thus it is worth thinking some more about Badiou's seemingly oxymoronic or at any rate odd conjunction of terms in the phrase 'transitory ontology'. What it signifies – in short – is a conception of ontological enquiry as none the less objective, rigorous or truth-oriented for the fact that its scope and limits are subject to a constant process of transformation through advances in the range of available forms, techniques, investigative methods, hypotheses, theorems or proof-procedures. Badiou's paradigm case is that of mathematics and, more specifically, post-Cantorian set theory since it is here that thinking can be seen to engage with an order of truths that always necessarily exceeds or transcends any given state of knowledge.[26] It is in consequence of the 'count-as-one' – that is to say, through some schema or selective device for including certain multiples and excluding certain others – that thought is enabled to establish a range of operational concepts and categories within the otherwise featureless domain of 'inconsistent multiplicity'. Most important is Cantor's famous demonstration that there exist manifold 'sizes' or orders of infinity, such as those of the integers and the even numbers, and moreover – contrary to the verdict of most philosophers and many mathematicians from the ancient Greeks down – that thought is quite capable of working productively (framing hypotheses for proof or refutation) in this paradox-prone region of transfinite set theory.[27] Indeed, it is through the process of 'turning paradox into concept' – a process most strikingly exemplified by Cantor's conceptual breakthrough – that intellectual advances typically come about, whether in mathematics, the physical sciences, politics or art. Hence the main thesis of Badiou's work: that in each case the truth of any given situation (scientific paradigm, political order, artistic stage of advance) will exceed any current state of knowledge even among specialists or expert practitioners and yet be contained within that situation in the form of so far unrecognised problems, dilemmas, paradoxes or elements (multiples) that lack any means of representation in the currently accredited count-as-one.

Politically speaking, this claim works out in a strikingly literal way since it applies to those marginal, stateless or disenfranchised minorities – prototypically, for Badiou, the *sans-papiers* or migrant workers of mainly North African origin – who find themselves excluded from the count-as-one since their lack of official documentation effectively deprives them of civic status or acknowledged social identity.[28] All the same the very fact of their ignored or largely invisible existence on the fringes of a *soi-disant* 'democratic' social order is such as potentially to call that order into question or constitute a challenge to the self-image projected by its state-sponsored apologists. At certain times – during periods of crisis or rising communal tension – those minorities may well turn out to occupy an 'evental site' which then becomes the focus of wider social unrest and potentially the flashpoint for some larger-scale challenge to the dominant structures of socio-political power. In the physical sciences revolutions come about most often at a stage of conceptual crisis in this or that particular region when the anomalies, failed predictions or conflicts of evidence with theory have become simply unignorable and when something – some crucial load-bearing part of the old paradigm – collapses under the strain. In the arts likewise such transformations typically occur at times of imminent breakdown: in music, say, with the stretching of resources and extreme intensification of affect that overtook the tonal system in the late nineteenth century, or in literature with the advent of modernist poetic and fictional genres that signalled a decisive rupture with previous (realist or naturalistic) modes of representation.

For Badiou it is not, most emphatically, a question of following thinkers like Quine and Kuhn – or for that matter Wittgenstein and Foucault – by adopting a full-blown ontological-relativist approach that would, in effect, sink the difference between ontology and epistemology, along with that between epistemology and the history of shifting paradigms, discourses, conceptual schemes, belief systems, language games, cultural 'forms of life' or whatever.[29] Indeed he never misses a chance to denounce the linguistic-cultural turn across a wide range of twentieth-century philosophical movements, 'analytic' and 'continental' alike, as merely an update of the age-old sophistical device that evades any challenge on grounds of knowledge or truth by resorting to language, or the suasive arts of rhetoric, as a substitute for reasoned argument. Rather it is a question, as with the set-theoretical (Cantor) event, of real advances – not merely shifts – in the scope of human cognitive, epistemic or intellectual grasp that involve the discovery of hitherto unknown truths located in hitherto unexplored reaches of the ontological terrain even though those truths and that terrain pre-exist the fact and the means of their discovery. They are properly to be understood in objectivist terms, i.e. as 'recognition-transcendent' or 'epistemically unconstrained' despite their belonging to a history of investigative thought wherein the various operative notions of ontology – of what is objectively there to be discovered – have undergone manifold and sometimes drastic transformations.[30] Thus Badiou very pointedly avoids the blatant normative deficit, or the problem of rational underdetermination, that afflicts ontological-relativist accounts according to which (as in Quine) to exist *just is* to be the value of a bound variable, or (as in Kuhn) scientists living before and after some major paradigm-change *just do* in a literal sense of the phrase inhabit 'different worlds'.[31]

IV

Clearly there is much more needed by way of close engagement with Badiou's work if the reader is to be in any strong position to assess these claims. However, my purpose here is to suggest that his thinking offers some useful guidance for our enquiry into the ontology of political song. More specifically, it may bring us closer to defining the mode of existence of songs whose comparative longevity and power to energise protest across a great range of political movements and causes is such as to merit their being accorded 'classic' status even though – for reasons that I have essayed above – that term seems rather out of place in this context. Badiou's idea of 'transitory ontology' best catches what I have in mind, namely the elusive combination of extreme adaptability or context-sensitivity with the singular power to retain a distinctive musical and verbal-ideational character throughout those (seemingly) protean guises. On his account the marks of a genuine event, as distinct from an episode falsely so deemed, are first that it make room for the discovery of a truth beyond any present-best state of knowledge, and second that it henceforth demand the allegiance – the intellectual, scientific or political fidelity – of those committed to its working out or the following through of its implications. False claimants may fill up the history books and make the headlines on a regular basis but are none the less false for that since their occurrence, although unforeseen at the time, is retrospectively explainable as the outcome of various anterior happenings and in-place or ongoing developments.[32] Genuine events may pass largely unnoticed at the time or, like abortive revolutions, go down only in the annals of failure and yet linger on in the memories of those attuned to their so-far unrealised potential and thereby hold in reserve the potential to spark some future transformation.

Badiou offers many such examples, chief among them the Paris Commune of 1871 and Cantor's radical rethinking of mathematics on the basis of set theory as applied to the multiple orders of infinity.[33] Thus despite the strong resistance to Cantor's ideas put up by many well-placed mathematicians at the time, and despite the Commune's having been suppressed in the most brutal and (apparently) decisive way, both can now be seen as events of the first order since set theory went on to revolutionise mathematical thought while the Commune continues to inspire and motivate successive generations of political activists. This is why I have made the case – an improbable case, so it might be thought – for understanding the ontology of political

song in light of Badiou's writings on mathematics and his extension of set-theoretical concepts to other, seemingly remote contexts
of discussion. That case rests partly on the way that he establishes
a more than analogical relation, via set theory, between the three
principal areas – politics, music and poetry – which must enter into
any adequate account of what makes a classic instance of the kind.
Also it helps to explain how one can speak in ontological terms of
an art form – again, if that is the right term – that depends so much
on its contexts or occasions of performance and which therefore
seems to elude all the terms and conditions typically proposed by
critics and philosophers seeking to define what constitutes a veritable
classic. Thus a really effective political song is one that catches the
counter-hegemonic spirit of its time and succeeds in communicat-
ing that force of resistance to activists in later, politically changed
circumstances. By the same token it is one that not only responds to
the potential for some future transformative event – whether in the
short or the long term – but can itself be heard to constitute such an
event on account of its power to express and articulate those pressures of unrest in response to forms of economic, political and social
injustice that are building toward a structural crisis point. It is here
that Badiou's radical rethinking of the relationship between art, politics and truth (in his own heterodox yet clearly defined sense of that
term) has the greatest power to illuminate our present enquiry into
the ontology of political song. At any rate it goes some way toward
explaining the anomalous status of a genre that somehow combines
an extreme responsiveness to changes in its historically emergent
contexts and conditions of existence with a striking capacity to retain
its political as well as its musical-expressive charge despite and across
those changes.

The issue is broached most directly in Badiou's *Handbook of
Inaesthetics* where he examines the various kinds of relationship
that have characterised art in its dealing with philosophy and politics.[34] Among them may be counted its Brechtian 'didactic' role as
a more or less compliant vehicle for conveying some preconceived
political content (even if with the aid of certain formal innovations),
its 'classical' role as a well-crafted product that satisfies purely aesthetic criteria and lays no claim to any truth beyond that of its own
artefactual contriving, and the romantic role in which it aspires to a
creative autonomy or self-sufficient power of world-transformative
vision that would free art from all such prosaic or quotidian ties.
As scarcely needs saying Badiou has little sympathy with the latter

conception, denying as it does his cardinal thesis that philosophy has its own special role in providing a more perspicuous account – a conceptual articulation – of truths that must remain implicit in the artwork. That is, they exist in the 'subtractive' mode of that which cannot find direct expression but can none the less be shown to haunt the work as a structural absence or symptomatic silence and thereby to indicate the future possibility of some as yet unknown further stage of advance. Romanticism, with its Shelleyan idea of the artist as unacknowledged legislator, effectively sells art short by ignoring its kinship with the likewise subtractive procedures through which mathematicians 'turn paradox into concept', or physics undergoes periodic revolutions through coming up against recalcitrant data, or political transformations are seen – albeit after the event – to have been brought about through the existence of 'uncounted' or unrecognised multiples at evental sites on the margins of the instituted body politic. Classicism fails yet more grievously since it makes a full-scale aesthetic creed of severing any link between art and truth, or any pretension on the artist's part to express, convey or communicate truths beyond the technical aspects of their craft.

Then there is the fourth, distinctively modernist conception of art whereby it breaks with all three of those previous modes – didactic, classic and romantic – and devotes itself in stead to a self-reflexive dealing with issues of language, discourse or representation that constantly call its own status into question. It is clear from his writings on (for instance) Mallarmé and Beckett that Badiou is strongly drawn to many works of this kind since for him they constitute one of the ways in which art can create or discover its equivalent to the breakthrough achievements of a formal discipline like set theory. However, he also has strong reservations about the tendency of other such works to become overly hermetic, self-absorbed or preoccupied with linguistic or formal-technical devices and developments at the cost of renouncing any involvement with 'extraneous', i.e. political or socio-historical conditions. After all, this brings them within close range of the turn toward various language-based schools of thought – Wittgensteinian, hermeneutic, poststructuralist or neo-pragmatist – that Badiou regards as a betrayal of philosophy and moreover as lending support to the status quo by reducing all issues of reason and truth to the question of what makes sense by the lights of this or that discourse, language game, signifying system or horizon of intelligibility.[35] Thus art, like philosophy, had best avoid being too closely linked – 'sutured', in the idiom that Badiou derives from Lacanian psychoanalysis – to any of those conditions (politics among them, but also prevailing ideas of aesthetic value or form) whose function is artistically enabling up to a point but whose effect if taken beyond that point is to deprive art of its particular role as an oblique though potentially powerful means of access to truth.

This is one sense of the term 'inaesthetics' as deployed in the title of Badiou's book: the capacity of certain (rather rare and often under-recognised) artistic practices to question or challenge accepted notions of what properly constitutes art or what counts as aesthetically valid. Another is the sense in which it denotes a strong and principled opposition to any idea that art should occupy a realm of distinctively aesthetic experience removed from all commerce with 'extra-artistic' interests or imperatives. Badiou's great aim is to specify how art can express or give form to truths that 'inexist' – that lack as yet any adequate means of conceptual articulation – yet which may none the less be signified obliquely by those gaps, anomalies or absences of formal closure that art is best able to reveal through its inventive capacity for testing the limits of established (e.g. realist, figurative or conventional) languages and genres.[36] To this extent art has a purchase on truth that may require the mediating offices of philosophy to spell out its implications but which could not possibly have been achieved except by means of its artistic presentation. I have argued here that political song is a test-case for this thesis since it is a genre (or anti-genre) that confronts the existing political order with a downright challenge to all those values political, social, ethical and musical which serve to maintain the preferential self-image of a stable and properly functioning liberal democracy.

The starting-point of set-theoretical reasoning is the null set – in Badiou's terminology the 'void' – which, despite its foundational character, eludes any ascription of properties or determinate membership conditions. That is to say, it is included in every multiple as a constituent part or strictly indispensable element yet cannot be reckoned as properly belonging to the count-as-one by any of the usual admission criteria.[37] So it is, by far from fanciful analogy, that socially excluded or victimised minorities continue to exist at the margins of the body politic and, through the very fact of this marginal status, to exert a potentially transformative pressure on the forms of state-administered surveillance and control. Nor are the arts by any means excluded from this critical role since they also have the capacity to function as reminders of that which cannot be expressed or represented in any language, form or genre available to artists working within the dominant socio-cultural conditions of their own time and place. If the phrase 'ontology of political song' makes any kind of sense – if is not just a bad case of semantic inflation applied to a wholly inappropriate since temporally fleeting and insubstantial (quasi-)artistic cultural phenomenon – then the best means of defending its entitlement to treatment on these terms is by conjoining Badiou's idea of 'inaesthetics' with his notion of 'transitory ontology'. What we are enabled to think without conceptual embarrassment is the standing possibility of artworks (nothing less) that are very much products of their own historical and cultural-political context yet which also have the power to live on – like the 'classic' in other, more elevated terms of address – and renew their inspirational charge across a wide range of historical, geographical and socio-political situations.

This is mainly in virtue of Badiou's deploying a 'subtractive' conception of truth whereby, as in the history of set-theoretical advances, progress comes about through locating those absences, lacunae, stress-points, anomalies, dilemmas, paradoxes and so forth, that signal the need for some as yet unknown but obscurely prefigured advance. In set theory there is a known method by which such advances can best be explained, i.e. how it is that mathematical truth can run ahead of present-best mathematical knowledge and yet exert a knowledge-transformative power on those who are still operating with the old concepts yet who find themselves uneasily responsive to that which finds no place in current understanding. Such is the procedure of 'forcing', devised (or discovered) by the mathematician Paul Cohen who managed to explain its operative conditions in formal, i.e. set-theoretical, terms.[38] This has been the topic of some highly pertinent commentary by Badiou who takes it to have decisive implications for our grasp of how epochal changes come about in disciplines, fields or histories of thought far afield from mathematics, at least on the commonplace understanding of what mathematics is or does. Whenever there occurs the kind of major transformation that is loosely described, after Kuhn, as a wholesale 'paradigm-shift' then this is sure to involve another instance of the process whereby thought becomes alert to the existence of certain hitherto unrecognised problems, paradoxes or truth-value gaps.

At these points it is only by way of a 'generic' procedure, in Cohen's mathematically defined sense of that term, that knowledge is enabled to transcend its previous limits and achieve a new stage of conceptual advance. Then it becomes possible to explain – always after the truth-event – how and why those limits had remained in place despite their having always *potentially* been subject to the forcing effect of such unresolved issues at (or beyond) the margins of intelligibility. My main point here has been to argue that political song occupies that same, intrinsically hard to specify since at present not fully realised or recognised ontological domain. That is to say, it gives verbal-musical voice to the standing possibility of a mismatch between that which we are able to know or cognise under currently existing historical, political or socio-cultural conditions and that which may none the less be prefigured – obliquely expressed or latently contained – within those very conditions. Just as knowledge always falls short of truth in mathematics or the physical sciences so likewise our grasp of what can be achieved in the way of political progress falls short of what *might* counterfactually be achieved if only thought were able to grasp the possibilities for radical change held out by the failings (e.g. the democratic deficit) that characterise some given social order. Or again, for those who come later and keep faith with the inaugural truth-event, these may be possibilities that they are able to imagine or conceive yet unable to realise – fully comprehend and carry into practice – by any means presently at their disposal.

If I were writing primarily for a readership of musicologists then I should feel obliged to press further toward an account of just what it is – what specific combination of features melodic, harmonic, rhythmic and of course conjointly musical-verbal – that constitutes the classic status or character of some political songs. My own best guess is one that I would advance with a measure of confidence after singing in a socialist street-choir for many years and in support of many political causes from the 1983 miners' strike and the anti-apartheid campaign to protests in connection with sundry events in Northern Ireland, Chile, Columbia, Guatemala, Nicaragua, Iraq and (more recently) Libya. It has to do with a certain quality, analogous to 'forcing' in the set-theoretical domain, whereby such songs are able to communicate – 'connote' would be too weak a term – the idea of an as yet unachieved but achievable state of justice that finds voice in their words and their music, and which thereby exerts a potentially transformative pressure on existing (conventionally inculcated) notions of the social good. Musically speaking this involves certain distinctive melodic, harmonic and rhythmic patterns that manage to combine a vigorous sense of shared opposition to regnant structures of authority and power with a contrasting sense of the forces currently ranged against them and the outside chance of those structures giving way in response to any such challenge. I say 'contrasting' rather than 'countervailing' because protest songs draw much of their expressive and performative power from this readiness to face the possibility or likelihood of imminent defeat, but also this strong intimation of a will to hold out for the long term despite the current odds. Indeed I would suggest that the crucial difference between 'political song' in the authentic sense of that phrase and 'political song' in the broader, non-qualitative sense that would include, say, 'Rule Britannia' or 'God Save the Queen' has precisely to do with whether or not some particular song is able to express so complex a range of highly charged and powerfully motivating sentiments.

V

To explain in detail how these feelings are combined in the best, most potent and moving political songs is no doubt a task for literary criticism and music analysis rather than for someone, like myself, making forays into that region where aesthetics overlaps with politics and where both intersect with the elusive domain of musical ontology. We can take a lead from Badiou's conception of being and event as forever bound up in an asymptotic process of discovery – an open-ended dialectic of 'infinite truth' and approximative states of knowledge – that is driven on from one landmark stage to the next by the powers of creative, inventive, paradigm-transformative or progressively oriented thought. This conception in its detailed working out by Badiou is one that very aptly captures the 'transitory ontology' of political song. It does so through a bringing-together of art, politics and – improbably enough – those formal procedures that he finds most strongly represented in the history of set-theoretical advances from Cantor to the present day. What this enables us to think is a conception of art that would endorse none of those received ideas – least of all Kantian ideas about aesthetic disinterest or beauty as the product of an ideal harmony between the faculties in a state of perfect disengagement from all aesthetically extraneous matters – that have left such a deep imprint even on philosophies of art which expressly disavow them.[39] On the other hand Badiou can be seen to offer equally powerful arguments against the radically nominalist or conventionalist approach of a thinker like Nelson Goodman who would press just as far in the opposite direction, i.e. toward a wholesale dissolution of art into the various 'art'-constitutive languages or modes of representation that properly (that is, by agreed-upon criteria) serve to define it.[40] Nothing could be further from Badiou's passionate defence of the truth-telling power vested in art, along with his justified suspicion of those – especially followers of Kant – who consign artistic truth to a realm of autonomous or 'purely' aesthetic values wherein that power would languish unexercised. If any meaning attaches to the phrase 'ontology of political song' then Badiou's is the approach that can best accommodate so potent, resilient and endlessly renewable and yet so protean or context-dependent a genre.

Of course this leaves room for the sceptic to respond by batting my claim right back and asserting that the phrase is indeed meaningless since even granting that such talk makes sense when applied to objects falling under various regional ontologies – such as those of the physical sciences or Austin's 'medium-sized dry goods' – it doesn't when applied to the kind of ersatz or pseudo-entity in question here. However, if this argument goes through, then the sceptic's case would extend well beyond items like political song to songs in general, musical works at large, artworks of whatever description (as distinct from their physical tokens or modes of instantiation) and beyond that to abstract entities such as those of mathematics and the formal sciences. Again, the sceptic or the Quinean lover of austere desert landscapes may grasp this nettle without the least compunction and declare – albeit without Quine's blessing, since oddly enough he counted himself a Platonist in matters mathematical – that we are better off dumping all such commitments beyond the ontological-relativist idea that to be *just is* to be the value of a variable which in turn should be deemed nothing more than a matter of what happens to play a certain role in this or that going 'ontological scheme'.[41] Badiou's is an ontology which, when applied to political song, holds out against any such wholesale relativist slide while none the less making allowance for the way that its identity conditions change under shifts in some existing (dominant or emergent) set of socio-political circumstances. In this way it may help us to rethink the character of such works in relation to some of the more restrictive categories of high-cultural or canon-preserving aesthetic discourse. Moreover, it offers a litmus test for issues in musical aesthetics generally since political song is the most extreme instance of that highly elusive ontological status that characterises all musical works.

Notes

1. See for instance – from a range of positions – Ben Caplan and Carl Matheson, 'Can a musical work be created?', *British Journal of Aesthetics*, 44 (2004), pp. 113–34; Gregory Currie, *An Ontology of Art* (New York: St. Martin's Press, 1989); Julian Dodd, 'Musical works as eternal types', *British Journal of Aesthetics*, 40 (2000), pp. 242–40, 'Defending musical Platonism', *British Journal of Aesthetics*, 42 (2002), pp. 380–402, 'Types, continuants, and the ontology of music', *British Journal of Aesthetics*, 44 (2004), pp. 342–60, *Works of Art: An Essay in Ontology* (Oxford: Oxford University Press, 2007); Peter Kivy, 'Platonism in music', *Grazer Philosophische Studien*, 19 (1983), pp. 109–29, and 'Platonism in music: another kind of defence', *American Philosophical Quarterly*, 24 (1987), pp. 245–52; Jerrold Levinson, *Music, Art and Metaphysics* (Ithaca, NY: Cornell University Press, 1990); Christopher Norris, *Platonism, Music and the Listener's Share* (London: Continuum, 2006); Stefano Predelli, 'Against musical Platonism', *British Journal of Aesthetics*, 35 (1995), pp. 338–50, 'Musical ontology and the argument from creation', *British Journal of Aesthetics*, 41 (2001), pp. 279–92, 'Platonism in music: a kind of refutation', *Revue Internationale de Philosophie*, 238 (2006), pp. 401–14; Robert A. Sharpe, 'Music, Platonism and performance: some ontological strains', *British Journal of Aesthetics*, 35 (1995), pp. 38–48; Nicholas Wolterstorff, 'Toward an ontology of art works', *Nous*, 9 (1975), pp. 115–42, and *Works and Worlds of Art* (Oxford: Clarendon Press, 1980).
2. See especially Sharpe, 'Music, Platonism and performance', op. cit.
3. Jacques Derrida, 'The law of genre', trans. Avital Ronell, *Critical Inquiry*, 7 (Fall 1980), pp. 55–81, and 'Before the law', trans. Ronell, in Derrida, *Acts of Literature*, ed. Derek Attridge (London: Routledge, 1992), pp. 181–220.
4. T. S. Eliot, 'Tradition and the individual talent', in *Selected Essays* (London: Faber, 1964), pp. 3–11.
5. See Bertrand Russell *Introduction to Mathematical Philosophy* (London: Allen & Unwin, 1930); also Michael Potter, *Set Theory and Its Philosophy: A Critical Introduction* (Oxford: Oxford University Press, 2004).
6. See various entries under note 1 (above); also, for some marvellously deft and subtle meditations on this topic, Geoffrey Hartman, *Beyond Formalism: Literary Essays 1958–1970* (New Haven, CT: Yale University Press, 1970).
7. See especially Frank Kermode, *The Classic* (London: Faber, 1975), and *History and Value* (Oxford: Clarendon Press, 1988). I discuss this and other aspects of his work in Norris, 'Remembering Frank Kermode', *Textual Practice*, 25: 1 (February 2011), pp. 1–13.

8. See, for instance, Kermode, *Not Entitled: A Memoir* (New York: Farrar, Straus & Giroux, 1991), and *Pieces of My Mind: Writings 1958–2002* (London: Allen Lane, 2003); also Michael Payne and John Schad (eds), *life.after.theory: Interviews with Jacques Derrida, Frank Kermode, Christopher Norris, and Toril Moi* (London: Continuum, 2003).

9. See entries under note 3, above; also Norris, 'Supplementarity and deviant logics: Derrida *versus* Quine', *Philosophical Forum*, XXIX (1998), pp. 1–27, and 'Deconstruction, analysis, and deviant logic: Derrida at the limits of thought', *Harvard Review of Philosophy*, 14 (Fall 2006), pp. 36–61.

10. Immanuel Kant, *Critique of Judgement*, trans. J. C. Meredith (Oxford: Clarendon Press, 1978).

11. See J. L. Austin, *How to Do Things with Words* (Oxford: Oxford University Press, 1963); Derrida, 'Signature event context', *Glyph*, Vol. I (Baltimore: Johns Hopkins University Press, 1977), pp. 172–97, 'Limited Inc a b c', *Glyph*, Vol. II (Baltimore: Johns Hopkins University Press, 1977), pp. 162–254, and 'Afterword: toward an ethic of conversation', in *Limited Inc*, ed. Gerald Graff (Evanston: Northwestern University Press, 1979), pp. 111–60; also John R. Searle, 'Reiterating the differences: a reply to Derrida', *Glyph*, Vol. I (Baltimore: Johns Hopkins University Press, 1977), pp. 198–208.

12. For Derrida's deconstructive reading of Kant see 'The parergon', in *The Truth in Painting*, trans. Geoff Bennington and Ian McLeod (Chicago: University of Chicago Press), pp. 15–147.

13. Austin, *How to Do Things with Words*, op. cit. For some further brilliant arabesques around these Austinian/Derridean themes, see Shoshana Felman, *The Literary Speech-Act: Don Juan with J. L. Austin, or Seduction in Two Languages*, trans. Catherine Porter (Ithaca, NY: Cornell University Press, 1983).

14. Derrida, 'Signature event context', op. cit.

15. Terry Eagleton, *The Ideology of the Aesthetic* (Oxford: Blackwell, 1990).

16. T. W. Adorno, *The Jargon of Authenticity* (London: Routledge & Kegan Paul, 1973); Lydia Goehr, *The Imaginary Museum of Musical Works: An Essay in the Philosophy of Music*, revised edn (Oxford: Oxford University Press, 2007); Susan McClary, *The Content of Musical Form* (Berkeley and Los Angeles: University of California Press, 2001).

17. Katherine Bergeron and Philip V. Bohlman (eds), *Disciplining Music: Musicology and Its Canons* (Chicago: University of Chicago Press, 1992); Scott Burnham, 'A. B. Marx and the gendering of sonata form', in Ian Bent (ed.), *Music Theory in the Age of Romanticism* (Cambridge: Cambridge University Press, 1996), pp. 163–86; Nicholas Cook and

Mark Everist (eds), *Re-Thinking Music* (Oxford: Oxford University Press, 1999); Joseph Kerman, 'How we got into analysis, and how to get out', *Critical Inquiry*, 7 (1980), pp. 311–31, 'A few canonic variations', *Critical Inquiry*, 10 (1983), pp. 107–25, *Musicology* (London: Fontana, 1985); Kevin Korsyn, 'Brahms research and aesthetic ideology', *Music Analysis*, 12 (1993), pp. 89–103; Lawrence Kramer, *Classical Music and Postmodern Knowledge* (Berkeley and Los Angeles: University of California Press, 1995); Judy Lochhead and Joseph Auner (eds), *Postmodern Music/Postmodern Thought* (New York: Garland, 2002); Ruth A. Solie (ed.), *Musicology and Difference* (Berkeley and Los Angeles: University of California Press, 1993); Leo Treitler, 'Music analysis in a historical context', in *Music and the Historical Imagination* (Cambridge, MA: Harvard University Press, 1989), pp. 67–78.

18. See, for instance, Paul de Man, *Aesthetic Ideology*, ed. Andrzej Warminski (Minneapolis: University of Minnesota Press, 1996); Philippe Lacoue-Labarthe and Jean-Luc Nancy, *The Literary Absolute: The Theory of Literature in German Romanticism*, trans. Philip Barnard and Cheryl Lester (Albany, NY: State University of New York Press, 1988); Christopher Norris, *Paul de Man: Deconstruction and the Critique of Aesthetic Ideology* (New York: Routledge, 1988).

19. Heinrich Schenker, *Free Composition*, trans. and ed. Ernst Oster (New York: Longman, 1979). For some representative critiques and revaluations, see Leslie D. Blasius, *Schenker's Argument and the Claims of Music Theory* (Cambridge: Cambridge University Press, 1996); E. Narmour, *Beyond Schenkerism: The Need for Alternatives in Music Analysis* (Chicago: University of Chicago Press, 1977); Hedi Siegel (ed.), *Schenker Studies* (Cambridge University Press, 1990); Leo Treitler, 'Music analysis in a historical context', op. cit.; Maury Yeston (ed.), *Readings in Schenker Analysis and Other Approaches* (New Haven, CT: Yale University Press, 1977).

20. See notes 16, 17 and 18, above.

21. See note 7, above.

22. For some highly relevant (and in many ways heartening) social-historical-political background, see *We Are Women, We Are Strong* . . . (Sheffield: Sheffield Women Against Pit Closures, 1987). A lot of the same social and political history is covered, though with more of an international dimension, in Beatrice Smith's well-documented book about my own Welsh socialist choir, *Stand Up and Sing: A Pictorial History of Cor Cochion Caerdydd, 1983–2003* (Aberystwyth: Y Lolfa, 2003).

23. Alain Badiou, *Briefings on Existence: A Short Treatise on Transitory Ontology* (Albany, NY: State University of New York Press, 2006).

24. See especially Badiou, *Being and Event*, trans. Oliver Feltham (London: Continuum, 2005); also *Infinite Thought: Truth and the Return to Philosophy*, trans. Oliver Feltham and Justin Clemens (London: Continuum, 2003) and *Theoretical Writings*, ed. and trans. Ray Brassier and Alberto Toscano (London: Continuum, 2004).

25. For a detailed introduction, see Christopher Norris, *Badiou's* Being and Event: *A Reader's Guide* (London: Continuum, 2009).

26. See entries under notes 24 and 25, above; also Badiou, 'Being: multiple and void. Plato/Cantor' and 'Theory of the pure multiple: paradoxes and critical decision', in *Being and Event*, op. cit., pp. 21–77 and 38–48; also 'Ontology is mathematics' and 'The subtraction of truth', in *Theoretical Writings*, op. cit., pp. 1–93 and 95–160.

27. For a highly accessible introduction to these and other relevant chapters in the history of modern mathematics, see Badiou, *Number and Numbers*, trans. Robin MacKay (Cambridge: Polity, 2008); also Michael Potter, *Set Theory and Its Philosophy: A Critical Introduction* (Oxford: Oxford University Press, 2004).

28. See, for instance, Badiou, *Metapolitics*, trans. Jason Barker (London: Verso, 2005), *Polemics*, trans. Steve Corcoran (London: Verso, 2006), *Century*, trans. Alberto Toscano (Cambridge: Polity Press, 2007).

29. See in particular W. V. Quine, 'Two dogmas of empiricism', in *From a Logical Point of View*, 2nd edn (Cambridge, MA: Harvard University Press, 1961); Thomas S. Kuhn, *The Structure of Scientific Revolutions*, 2nd edn (Chicago: Chicago University Press, 1970); Ludwig Wittgenstein, *Philosophical Investigations*, trans. G. E. M. Anscombe (Oxford: Blackwell, 1953); Michel Foucault, *The Order of Things*, trans. A. Sheridan (London: Tavistock, 1973).

30. For further discussion of this issue and its associated terminology, see Norris, *Truth Matters: Realism, Anti-realism and Response-dependence* (Edinburgh: Edinburgh University Press, 2002).

31. See note 29, above.

32. See note 28, above.

33. See notes 24 and 28, above.

34. Badiou, *Handbook of Inaesthetics*, trans. Alberto Toscano (Stanford: Stanford University Press, 2005).

35. Badiou, *Manifesto for Philosophy*, trans. Norman Madarasz (Albany, NY: State University of New York Press, 1999).

36. For a full-scale elaboration of these themes across a wide range of subject areas, see Badiou, *Logics of Worlds* (*Being and Event*, Vol. 2), trans. Alberto Toscano (London: Continuum, 2009).

37. See notes 24 and 26, above.

38. Paul J. Cohen, *Set Theory and the Continuum Hypothesis* (New York: W. A. Benjamin, 1966).

39. Kant, *Critique of Judgement* (note 10, above).

40. Nelson Goodman, *Languages of Art: An Approach to a Theory of Symbols* (Indianapolis: Hackett, 1976).
41. Quine, 'Two dogmas of empiricism', op. cit.; also *Ontological Relativity and Other Essays* (New York: Columbia University Press, 1969).

CHAPTER 6

Speculative Realism: An Interim Report

I

Like a good many others I was greatly impressed when I first read Quentin Meillassoux's *After Finitude* – at any rate its opening section – and even more so to witness its extraordinary impact among the livelier sections of the continental philosophy community over the next few years.[1] What the book clearly marked was a full-scale retreat (for which read 'advance') from the kinds of far-out anti-realist, constructivist or socio-linguistic-relativist position that had captured the high ground across large swathes of the post-1970 continentally influenced humanities, philosophy included. In its place there now emerged a hard-line objectivist realism which defined itself squarely against that whole theoretical-cultural mindset. Moreover it did so with primary reference to just those disputed zones, like epistemology and philosophy of science, where anti-realism had pressed its case with maximum vehemence and rhetorical if not argumentative force.

Hence the effect of high drama that Meillassoux achieved with now his famous opening passage concerning the 'arche-fossil' and its erstwhile habitat, the 'ancestral realm'. He takes these to offer a standing refutation of the basic anti-realist idea that truth is coextensive with the scope and limits of attainable human knowledge, or that it cannot exceed the bounds of cognitive-linguistic representation.[2] This doctrine is simply not capable of accommodating truths, such as that embodied in the fossil, which confront it with the sheer impossibility of thinking that the truth of their having existed pre-historically could be somehow ruled out by the fact that there were no human beings (or other sentient life-forms) around at the time. If such is indeed the logical upshot, whatever the various attempts to avoid it by producing some compromise formula, then better give up that whole misconceived project and accept that truth and reality are in no way dependent on human perceptual, cognitive or linguistic-representational capacities.[3] Thus speculative realism, on Meillassoux's account, constitutes a really decisive break with those sundry movements of thought – from hermeneutics, structuralism, poststructuralism, postmodernism, Foucauldian discourse theory, and Rortian neo-pragmatism to social constructivism and the strong sociology of knowledge – which had made it a high point of radical doctrine to assert just the opposite case.[4] This is no doubt why his book became first a debating point and then, very soon, something of a cult object among the swelling company of those – mostly younger philosophers with an existing interest in one or other of those movements – who signed up as speculative realists. Indeed there soon emerged the first signs of that fissile tendency or proneness to generate internal rifts, groupings and (in this case fairly amicable) differences of view that have often gone along with such collective shifts of allegiance.[5]

Still there is a good measure of agreement as to what marks out speculative realism (henceforth SR) from the major currencies of postwar continental thought, or – to be precise – those mainly French-influenced movements that have achieved greatest visibility as cultural exports. One claim that emphatically unites the SR clan is that the linguistic turn in its structuralist and poststructuralist manifestations, as well as its sundry analytic forms, stands in a direct line of descent from German idealism. On their diagnosis things went grossly awry when Kant, having been roused from his dogmatic slumbers by the challenge of Humean scepticism, responded by announcing his 'Copernican revolution' in epistemology.[6] Earlier philosophers, from Descartes down, had treated the problem of knowledge as a problem about somehow proving that our cognitive faculties were reliably in touch with an external, objective, mind-independent reality. Since Kant considered Hume to have shown once and for all that this was an impossible project – since human knowers had absolutely no means of access to reality except through the various concepts, categories and sensuous intuitions that alone afforded such access – therefore philosophy must now renounce its old, self-deluding quest and instead seek to limn the scope and the limits of that same cognitive apparatus. Hence the whole immensely complicated business of Kantian epistemological critique, designed to beat the bounds of human cognition and preclude any speculative overreaching whether by knowledge in its vain attempt to scale the metaphysical heights or by metaphysics in its equally vain pretension to offer itself as a source of probative knowledge.

It is chiefly these negative or cautionary aspects of Kant's philosophy – its constant placing of limits, restrictions or *ne plus ultra* conditions on the enterprise of human enquiry – that Meillassoux, like his mentor Alain Badiou, finds so very irksome.[7] More specifically, it is the twofold dogmatic requirement first that philosophy not bother its head with those old, strictly unanswerable questions concerning the existence, nature and properties of objective, mind-independent reality, and second that it not indulge itself in metaphysical speculations that transgress the limits of human sensory or perceptual grasp yet none the less see fit to claim some kind of cognitive warrant. Thus the twin terms 'speculative' and 'realism' both have a strong anti-Kantian charge closely linked to the central claims and motivation of the SR project. 'Speculation' is what its proponents rely on to carry them past the limits of phenomenal cognition or beyond any epistemology, like Kant's, for which phenomenal cognition provides both a model and a strict boundary-marker. It is also, and for just that reason, what enables thought to make strong argumentative use of certain instances, like the arche-fossil, that are taken to confront the idealist, constructivist or anti-realist with the fact of an objective reality that far antedated the emergence of human sentience. Such strictly pre-historical objects bear witness to the basic realist claim that human beings and their particular (as it happens highly limited) powers of sensory, perceptual or cognitive grasp are by no means prerequisite to the existence or indeed the nature, structure or properties of what those beings sometimes manage to cognise. Of course anti-realism comes in various strengths and kinds, some of them seeking to head off the standard range of counter-arguments by giving themselves suitably emollient names like 'internal realism', 'framework-relative realism' or 'quasi-realism'.[8] However, these compromise theories invariably work out as a more or less fig-leaf version of 'realism' which in the end yields so much ground to anti-realism (and relativism) that the fig-leaf might as well be discarded.

This is why any properly realist philosophy of science has to adopt an objectivist ontology – that is to say, one that allows the truth-value of our various statements, theories and predictions to be fixed by the way things stand in reality whatever our present-best belief concerning them – as well as a workable epistemology that convincingly explains our knowledge of the growth of knowledge.[9] Anything less – any concession to the idea of truth as epistemically constrained – can easily be used as the thin end of an anti-realist or ontological-relativist wedge. One may even end up in the absurd position of a

'constructive empiricist' like Bas van Fraassen according to whom
we should not ascribe reality to anything that exceeds the powers
of technologically unaided human perception through its being too
small, too large, too fast, too remote or too complex to be registered
clearly by creatures with our kind of sensory-physical constitution.[10]
Or rather, those items have a decent claim to reality when perceived
with the aid of relatively simple pieces of apparatus (such as optical
telescopes or microscopes) but not if they require more advanced
and sophisticated, hence less 'direct', means of observation. Thus,
on his account, we are better off trusting to our eyesight and peering
at the moons of Jupiter through a spaceship window than deploying
the latest radio telescope with superlative powers of resolution and
based on design and construction principles that are well understood.[11] Such are the warpings of critical intelligence brought about
by a commitment to the perverse logic of anti-realism conjoined with
a basically Lockean empiricist epistemology and a deep scepticism
regarding the scope and truth-indicative power of rational inference
to the best explanation. Hence the countervailing SR emphasis on the
verification-transcendent character of truth or the fact – albeit knowable only through an exercise of speculative reason – that human
knowledge may always fall short of objectivity and truth. From this
objectivist standpoint reality must be thought to extend unknow-
ably far beyond the confines of human perceptual-conceptual grasp
and its spatio-temporally indexed character. Thus the arche-fossil is
(or should be) enough to convince us of the extreme parochialism
entailed by any version of the anti-realist doctrine which supposes
that truth or knowledge are epistemically constrained, i.e. that they
are ineluctably subject to the scope and limits of human knowledge.

This latter notion is one that Meillassoux deems to have taken
hold with Kant, and thereafter – very largely through Kant's ubiquitous and diverse influence – to have exerted something like a
stranglehold on philosophy right down to the currently prevailing
strains of continental and analytic thought. His watchword for it is
'correlationism', a term that is nowadays bandied about by speculative realists with the toning of mixed pity and contempt that once, in
the heyday of poststructuralism and postmodernism, attached to the
term 'realism'. It connotes the idea – basic to the 'old' correspondence theory of truth – that knowledge consists in a correlation or
matching-up between on the one hand perceptions, observations,
mind-states, beliefs, propositions, statements, theories, hypotheses,
predictions, etc., and on the other hand various real-world existent

or physically instantiated states of affairs. Of course, when expressed in these terms, the idea might seem perfectly consistent with a realist outlook according to which truth consists precisely in the correlation, correspondence or matching-up between the way things stand in reality and the way that they are represented by this or that aspirant truth-claim or candidate theory. However, as is clear from large swathes of post-Kantian intellectual history, this understanding of the doctrine has very often come under sceptical strain or pressure when it is asked – in familiar anti-realist fashion – what could possibly constitute or serve to legitimise the kind of 'correspondence' here in question. Or again: how can those putative 'facts' to which our statements, beliefs, descriptions, theories and so forth, are supposed to correspond be taken as themselves anything other than linguistic (or at any rate conceptually articulated) entities? After all, if truth is humanly (epistemically) accessible then it must come in forms adapted to the intelligence of human knowers. And if this is the case – if all known or knowable truths are in some sense pre-adapted to human cognition – then correspondence theorists who suppose the contrary (who take it that truth, objectively conceived, dictates what shall count as veridical knowledge) are *ex hypothesi* barking up the wrong tree.[12]

On this view the realist conception with respect to every branch of human enquiry is in the same dead-end predicament as that supposedly identified by Paul Benacerraf in a well-known essay on philosophy of mathematics.[13] That is, it runs up against the dilemma that if truth is objective then it might always exceed, surpass or transcend the powers of present-best (or even best-humanly-attainable) knowledge while if truth is redefined (in constructivist, anti-realist, or other such non-objectivist terms) then it is no longer truth as the realist would have it but something more like '"truth" to the best of our always fallible, error-prone, or corrigible best belief'. Although the issue is posed most strikingly with respect to mathematics and the formal sciences it is one that has been raised to broadly similar effect across a wide range of subject areas including philosophy of science and epistemology.[14] In each case the argument standardly proceeds from correlationist premises – or some version of truth-as-correspondence – to the claim that this realist order of priorities needs to be reversed since truth can only be a matter of attainable human knowledge and human knowledge only a matter of optimised epistemic warrant. It is here – in its steadfast opposition to precisely this sceptical twist on the correspondence theory – that speculative realism stakes out its distinctive philosophical ground. 'Correlationism' is thus held to signify the fateful inversion of priorities that philosophy suffered when it followed Kant in his 'Copernican revolution' – falsely so called – and henceforth took epistemology, rather than ontology, as its primary concern. Indeed, as Meillassoux says, it is ironic that Kant should advance that immodest comparison since the effect of his revolution in thought, so far from conceptually displacing humanity from the centre of the cosmos, has rather been to confirm human beings in the presumption that they (or their particular species-relative range of cognitive powers) are the final arbiters of reality and truth.

II

If Meillassoux deploys his arche-fossil as a standing rebuke to anti-realist pretensions at one end of the historical timescale then Ray Brassier mounts the same sort of challenge from the opposite end.[15] For him, the great fault of mainstream epistemology and philosophy of science is that they buy into an agenda where the terms of debate, whatever their professed stance on this issue, are always at some point subject to assessment with reference to an ultimately anthropocentric framework of beliefs. According to Brassier, this is most apparent in their striking failure – or plain incapacity – to reckon not only with the fact of human mortal finitude but also with the prospect, brought home very forcibly by present-day physics, that human beings and all other sentient (including extra-terrestrial) life-forms will be subject to total extinction with the heat-death and final dissolution of the universe. Thus he takes a decidedly sceptical view – in common with other SR thinkers – of Kant's claim (like Husserl's after him) to be reasoning in a transcendental rather than a merely empirical mode, that is, to be talking about the a priori conditions of possibility for thought, knowledge, judgement and experience in general rather than about some given psychological, dispositional, cultural or more broadly anthropological mindset.[16] For it is a basic part of the SR project to insist that nothing short of objectivist realism – certainly no Kantian attempt to make up for the loss of it by the appeal to some supposedly invariant set of a priori conditions on the scope and limits of human knowledge – can account for what science tells us concerning the mind-independence of reality and truth.

Moreover, that project has ambitions beyond what might, as I have presented it so far, strike many analytic philosophers of science as a fairly familiar (if dramatically worked up) rendition of the standard case against anti-realism in its relativist, constructivist, instrumentalist, pragmatist, conventionalist or framework-internalist forms. Those ambitions take it into speculative territory where analytic philosophers would fear (or disdain) to tread, although – to be fair – the SR community would hardly take this as reason for grave concern. Brassier's above-mentioned animadversions on the heat-death of the universe and what it means for our conduct of epistemological debate are one fairly obvious instance of this step beyond anything that those in the analytic mainstream would count as philosophically valid. Another is the line of speculative reasoning that Meillassoux broaches in the second part of *After Finitude*, having devoted the first part to putting the realist-objectivist case in a way that is perhaps more striking and forceful than genuinely radical or original. Indeed I shall argue that the somewhat disjointed or broken-backed character of his book is symptomatic of certain deep-laid strains and tensions not only within Meillassoux's project but within the SR project as a whole. Other commentators – notably Perry Anderson – have remarked upon something similar in relation to earlier efflorescences of theory in times of real-world political setback or retreat.[17] Thus it is often the case with self-consciously radical movements of thought which emerge despite (or perhaps in response to) adverse political circumstances that they exhibit a kind of structural ambivalence or chronic oscillation between overt radicalism and something that is ultimately far less challenging to received ways of thought. In the SR case this duality – or conceptual fault-line – runs between a scientific-realist outlook which, although expressed with dramatic flair, is distinctly under-theorised or lacking in philosophical substance and, on the other hand, a speculative bent that leans so far in a 'radical' (self-consciously heterodox) direction as to lose touch with any workable variety of scientific realism.

In other words there comes a tipping point where certain kinds or degrees of speculative licence, conjoined with a certain fondness for extravagant (not always very pertinent) cosmic scenarios, tend to weaken a thinker's critical purchase on the issues under review. This is especially the case when, as here, the variety of realism in question is one that has emerged in reactive opposition to a regnant anti-realism and which – perhaps for that reason – tends to adopt a hard-line contrary stance without having yet developed the resources (in particular the modal and logico-semantic resources) to fully support its claims.[18] Hence, I suggest, the marked SR inclination toward

lines of (strictly speaking) metaphysical speculation that rather too
often pass themselves off as having some direct or decisive import
for science and philosophy of science. Of course there is no thinking
about philosophy of science – or indeed about science – without a
whole range of metaphysical commitments, whether of a Kuhnian
'normal' or 'revolutionary' kind. One common error of sundry,
otherwise highly diverse movements of twentieth-century thought,
from logical positivism/empiricism to structuralism and poststructuralism, was to ignore this simple truth and habitually invest their
usage of the term 'metaphysics' with a routine pejorative force. Yet
if philosophy of science has worked its way clear of this massively
disabling prejudice then it has done so by dint of much hard critical
and clarificatory work at the interstices of logic, metaphysics and
epistemology.[19] For all the reasons cited above this has not – or not
yet – been the case with SR, despite nascent signs that some of its
exponents are moving in that direction.[20]

Briefly summarised, Meillassoux's claim in the second part of
After Finitude is that the best way to break with Kant's malign influence is to go back to Hume, but to a thinker who bears absolutely no
resemblance either to the Hume that Kant acknowledges as having
delivered his wake-up call or to the Hume who very often figures as a
football in current analytic debate. This has to do with the question
whether Hume was indeed, as widely thought, a deep-dyed sceptic
about the existence of causal laws and (by implication) physical
reality along with all its imputed structures, properties, dispositions,
etc., or whether on the contrary he espoused an outlook of epistemological (rather than ontological) scepticism and merely doubted
our capacity ever to achieve certain knowledge of them.[21] But if the
'new Hume' is deemed a radical departure from orthodoxy by the
standards laid down for interpreting classical thinkers among mainstream analytic types it is tame stuff when compared with the reading
of Hume that Meillassoux comes up with. His Hume is a realist in
the sense that Humean scepticism about laws of nature is taken as a
downright disbelief that such laws really, truly exist – or a belief that
they really, truly don't – rather than a mere disbelief in our capacity
(as epistemically restricted human knowers) to find them out. More
than that: Meillassoux's Hume is one who thinks – who argues with
impeccable logic and consistency – that if there exist 'laws of nature'
or physical ground-rules of any sort then they are utterly contingent,
momentarily changeable, subject to random fluctuation or apt to
transmute into something radically different without any underly-

ing cause or reason explaining why this should have occurred. For Meillassoux the only real necessity is the necessity of contingency, or the rational requirement – in a shrewdly aimed *bouleversement* of Leibniz – that we should reason from the infinite multiplicity of possible worlds to the necessarily possible existence of innumerable worlds in which the 'basic' or 'fundamental' laws of physics in our particular world no longer apply. The Leibnizian principle of reason is thereby turned back against itself and becomes, in effect, a principle declaring the rationally demonstrable non-existence of any reasons (or causal explanations) for anything that would hold good beyond the solitary moment of their happening to state some (necessarily transient) necessary truth.

Thus Meillassoux proposes a flat-out reversal of Leibniz's argument from God's omniscience to the idea that all truths are necessary although many will appear contingent through our creaturely lack of such divine knowledge. On the contrary: what reason does (or should) tell us is that any intelligence with the power to see beyond those human cognitive limits would be prey to no such high-rationalist illusion. It would then reveal that in truth the very canons of rationality, logic, evidential warrant, abductive inference to the best explanation and so forth are (for all that we can know) epistemically valid – if at all – only for some limited time and thereafter quite possibly subject to radical change. One might expect Meillassoux to argue for this extraordinary thesis partly through an appeal to the 'evidence' of various physical-scientific developments (especially the many-worlds interpretation of quantum mechanics) and partly through modal-logical considerations having to do with the supposedly 'real' existence of possible though non-actual worlds.[22] However, more crucial to his thinking is the argument from post-Cantorian set theory – as developed in Badiou's *Being and Event* – to the effect that 'inconsistent multiplicity' will always and necessarily exceed any limiting order of consistency imposed upon it.[23] That is to say, the history of set-theoretical methods, concepts and techniques has been one of constantly pushing back the borders of that new-found 'mathematicians' paradise' that David Hilbert acclaimed in 1900.[24] It started out with Cantor's breakthrough discovery, contrary to the teaching of philosophers from Plato and Aristotle down, that there existed a real or actual (as distinct from merely virtual) order of infinity, defined as applying to any set whose members could be placed in a one-to-one relation with one of its proper sub-sets. (Consider the infinity of natural numbers, or integers, vis-à-vis the infinities of even or odd numbers.) That discovery led on to Cantor's epochal proof – an affront to common-sense intuition as well as to many eminent mathematicians at the time – that the infinity of integers was only the first in a series of larger orders of infinity, such as that of the real numbers.

This is not the place for any lengthier treatment of the ontological, political, scientific and other far-reaching consequences that Badiou draws from his intensive engagement with set theory and its philosophy. My point is that Meillassoux takes its lessons very much to heart in constructing his radically heterodox reading of Hume and his argument for the absolute contingency of anything that might count as a 'law' of nature. The result is to make of Hume both the ultimate epistemological sceptic (in so far as he takes any such 'laws' to be radically contingent and hence beyond our best powers of rational grasp) and the ultimate ontological realist (in so far as he takes this to be an objective truth about the physical world and not just a way of acknowledging our own strictly limited or temporally indexed epistemic powers). Hence the crucial significance, for Meillassoux, of Badiou's claim that 'mathematics is ontology' and his exposition of post-Cantorian set theory – especially in so far as it reveals the existence of multiple orders of infinity – as our best (indeed our sole adequate) guide in ontological matters. What this enables (Meillassoux would say: absolutely requires) us to think is that there is – must be – an infinite number of ways in which the 'laws of physics' might lie, or an infinite range of possible transformations from moment to moment in the radically contingent or underdetermined structure of physical reality. No doubt the objection could be raised that this makes it hard, or downright impossible, to explain how techno-science has achieved such an impressive record of achievements to date. Such arguments are something of a realist stock-in-trade, especially in response to sceptical or relativist claims that since scientists are now known to have got so many things wrong in the past then surely it is hubris to suppose that their present-day efforts are at last managing to cut nature at the joints.[25] To which realists just as often respond with a version of the 'no miracles' case, i.e. that if science hadn't got most things right with regard to the nature and structure of physical reality then the fact that our technologies work so well could only be due to some massive cosmic coincidence.[26]

Meillassoux again has a novel twist on this familiar topic of debate. If his 'necessity of contingency' thesis holds good – if any presently existing 'laws of nature' are merely an infinitesimal subset of the infinitely many such laws that could come into force from one millisecond to the next – this must surely be thought to throw a huge paradox into any argument on either side of the realism/anti-realism issue. Thus it allows, even strictly requires, that there will sometimes be intervals – of which the present might just be one – when they keep falling out the same way over a long enough period for scientific knowledge (and human enquiry generally) to get up and running. These intervals will in effect be 'singularities' by suggestive analogy with the current mathematical-physical sense of that term, but subject to the fairly mind-boggling difference that what here renders them so massively improbable, hence infrequent, is precisely the reverse of that standard usage. It is not the fact of their constituting a singular exception to the fundamental constants or the baseline physical laws – since these are (for all that we can know) changing momentarily for no assignable reason – but rather their happening (against all the odds) to remain in place or in force throughout some appreciable timespan. It is only by the sheerest of flukes that the conditions could exist whereby those laws might come to provide a basis for any physical science meriting the name. In which case the old debates over scientific realism must seem hopelessly naive or off-the-point, as must the closely related dispute between 'old' and 'new' Humeans over whether Hume was a full-strength or only half-strength sceptic. What all those parties fail to grasp – on Meillassoux's submission – is that Hume got it right about the problem of knowledge but got it right in a way that he himself failed to grasp and moreover, paradoxically, could not have taken on board without undermining his professed sceptical outlook. For if this outlook finds its justification in the inconstancy of nature itself rather than the uncertain or error-prone character of human knowledge, then of course that truth about the world – along with our capacity, as speculative realists, to grasp it – is sufficient to refute the sceptic's claim, albeit while raising other problems that might make the traditional problem of knowledge appear philosophical child's play.

III

Clearly for Meillassoux there is no discrepancy between the first and second portions of *After Finitude*, or no good reason to suppose that a strong ontological-realist approach of the sort that his book propounds with such eloquence might come into conflict with his doctrine of absolute contingency. Yet if the latter is taken at anything

like face value – as it certainly asks to be taken – then it is certainly
not realism-compatible in any sense of 'realism' that will hold
up against various well-honed lines of attack from the sceptical-
relativist, constructivist, conventionalist or anti-realist quarter. More
specifically, it blocks the appeal to abduction – or the argument from
inference to the best explanation – which has long been a staple of
the realist case against Humean and other forms of sceptical doubt.[27]
For, as I have said, that argument gains its strength from a version of
the no-miracles (or cosmic-coincidence) rejoinder whereby the realist
requires of the sceptic that he explain the various notable achievements of science by some means other than the well-supported
rational inference that it has managed to accumulate a fair stock of
knowledge concerning a good range of really existent objects along
with their properties, structures, dispositions, causal powers and so
forth.[28] No doubt the previous sentence contains a good many terms
and associated concepts – including 'rational inference' – that will
strike the sceptic as flagrantly begging all the main points at issue.
Still the realist's challenge retains its force since the sceptic has yet
to meet it by doing what the realist quite reasonably requires, i.e.
providing that non-miraculist alternative, rather than retreating, as
so often happens, into a somewhat childish 'who says?' posture of
reiterated flat denial.

At this stage the realist is right to claim, on the basis of inference to the best explanation, that scepticism of this all-purpose or
indiscriminate variety – as distinct from the scepticism that comes
of a critical and questioning attitude to received ideas – is nothing
more than a tedious irrelevance or product of hyper-cultivated
doubt. However, the speculative realist who follows Meillassoux
to the point of endorsing his 'necessity of contingency' argument
along with his extraordinary reading of Hume will in consequence
be deprived of any such resource in battling the diehard sceptic.
That resource is available only on condition that one not deny, as a
matter of a priori commitment, that there exists sufficient continuity,
stability or permanence about the basic laws of nature to ensure that
knowledge has something determinate to be knowledge about, or
that the truth (or falsehood) of our scientific theories, hypotheses and
predictions has to do with the way things stand in objective reality.
After all, if Meillassoux is right – and (*concesso non dato*) if this
could ever be established by any means at our scientific, theoretical
or speculative disposal – then for that very reason it is impossible to
conceive what might properly count as confirming or falsifying any

such claim. Quite simply, and again for all that we could know, the truth-conditions would be in such a state of undetectably rapid and discontinuous change that the realist – at any rate the champion of realism in a genuine and substantive rather than a purely notional sense – would be played off the field for lack of any means to specify, define or apply them.

No doubt it could be argued, in support of Meillassoux's position, that ontological realism of his uncompromising kind is sure to involve the always possible coming apart of present-best knowledge (or optimal belief by the lights of this or that expert community) from truth objectively conceived. However, as shown by the recent history of analytic debate on this topic, any statement of the strong ontological case had better go along with a convincingly worked out epistemology – an adequate account of how such truths might come within range of human apprehension or cognitive grasp – if it is not to court the standard range of sceptical responses. Otherwise it will invite some version of the Benacerraf-type argument (first proposed with reference to philosophy of mathematics but capable of extension across other domains of scientific knowledge) that one can either have truth objectively conceived or truth within the limits of human epistemic capacity but surely not both on pain of self-contradiction.[29] What the realist above all needs to demonstrate is the falsity of this *tertium non datur* line of argument since it ignores – or perforce has to reject in keeping with its own fixed anti-realist agenda – the possibility that truth is both objective (i.e. epistemically unconstrained) and nevertheless sometimes capable, under benign epistemic conditions, of falling within human cognitive ken. There are quite a few Anglophone philosophers of science and epistemologists (myself included) who have for some time now been pursuing this project of supplying the *tertium* or arguing against that drastic and misconceived pseudo-dilemma.[30] However, such arguments require a lot more than the kind of wire-drawn dialectic that Meillassoux – to this extent in company with the sceptics and anti-realists – deploys in his heterodox reading of Hume and his equally heterodox (since scepticism-inducing) conception of a realism based on or conducive to the doctrine of absolute contingency. Thus any readers who endorse the arguments to be found in the first part of *After Finitude* should find themselves at odds with, or utterly perplexed by, the arguments put forward in its second part.

I think there are several reasons for what I have called this curiously broken-backed character of Meillassoux's book. One is the multiform fixation of postwar French philosophy – starting out with the existentialist Sartre's *pour soi/en soi* dichotomy and continued in his later Marxist-inflected distinction between praxis and the practico-inert – on resistance to what is perceived as the threatening encroachment of scientistic or 'positivist' methodologies into the space of human autonomy and freedom.[31] This is still very evident, albeit in a heavily repressed and displaced guise, even after the late-1960s structuralist/poststructuralist turn against existentialism, humanist Marxism and all such subject-centred philosophies. Thus it typically issues in an emphasis on infinitised textual polysemy as opposed to the methodological ambitions of classic high structuralism, on the 'molecular' flows of desiring-production as opposed to the 'molar' forms of self-authorised rational discourse, on the criss-crossing patterns of 'rhyzomatic' coupling as opposed to all tree-like (hierarchical) structures, and on that whole nexus of radically antinomian ideas that goes under the name 'French Nietzsche'.[32] To which might be added the way that Meillassoux blithely swings across, in the course of one short book, from a hard-line objectivist or ontological realism that takes absolutely no hostages from that Janus-faced adversary camp to a far-out speculative (quasi-)ontology of Heraclitean flux that offers no hold for any but a notional and explanatorily vacuous realism. One doesn't need to be a card-carrying Freudian in order to remark how SR manages to combine a conscious – indeed programmatic – reaction against these old anti-*chosiste* obsessions with a lingering attraction to them, or a residual (unacknowledged) desire to debunk any ontology that would find room for realism in any guise.

Another reason, I suggest, is the fact that SR has emerged on the 'continental' scene as a kind of hothouse plant that appears all the more strange and exotic for its having taken root and actually blossomed in that improbable locale. Thus the very idea that large numbers of younger philosophers and theorists with a background (mostly) in continental thought and with distinctly 'radical' leanings should now be flocking to the banner of objectivist realism is one that is still apt to raise eyebrows among those who belatedly stumble across it. However, this situation has also brought certain disadvantages, among them the marked SR tendency to ignore a whole range of significant ideas and developments within analytic philosophy of science. I have already mentioned one aspect of this, namely the absence of any adequate engagement with the debates around causal realism and inference to the best explanation, debates which are – or should be – central to its own interests. Again, there is the so-far missed opportunity of a sustained and productive encounter with the advocates of critical realism, an intellectually mature and broad-based movement which might supply – among other things – a more nuanced and substantive account of the complex or variously 'strati-fied' relationship between ontology and epistemology.[33] Without such active exposure to currents of thought beyond its own, rather self-enclosed domain SR runs the risk not only of neglecting impor-tant developments elsewhere but also of becoming overly attached to a set of ideas – or a canon of texts and thinkers – that are thereby exempted from adequately critical treatment.

One sign that SR has grown up in a somewhat hermetic research environment is precisely the above-noted tendency, most visible in the writings of Graham Harman, to substitute the word for the deed – or the slogan for the detailed investigative work – when it comes to that real-world object domain that supposedly occupies its main focus of enquiry. After all, there is not much point in continu-ally reeling off great lists of wildly assorted objects if the upshot is merely to remark on their extreme diversity, or irreducible thinginess, without (as it seems) much interest in just what makes them the way they are.[34] Thus one looks in vain for any serious attempt to link up the abstract realist-objectivist commitment with a depth-ontological or causal-explanatory account of the structures, properties or dispo-sitions that – according to our present-best physical theories – play that constitutive role. To some extent this can be put down to the strong Heideggerian influence on SR, and on Harman's work in particular. After all it is a high point of principle for Heidegger, in his joint meditation on thing-hood and the 'question of technology', to discount such science-led concerns as merely ontic and a product of the age-old Western metaphysical will-to-power over subject and object alike.[35] To be sure, Harman has a novel take on these themes and certainly shares nothing of that downright anti-scientific preju-dice. Much better his light-touch way with these topics – his breezy (if somewhat routine) celebration of the sheer multiplicity of objects each flaunting its strictly irreducible *haeccitas* – than Heidegger's solemn lucubrations. Nevertheless, Harman's thinking has this much in common with depth-ontology in the *echt*-Heideggerian mode: that it finds no room for anything like what a scientist (or science-led phi-losopher of science) would count as a contribution to knowledge or a claim worth serious evaluation in point of truth-content or validity.

For Heidegger, of course, such objections are completely off the track and a sure sign that the objector is still in the grip of that same vulgar misconception that substitutes the ontic for the ontological, or confuses physical beings – including their scientifically determinable properties – with the issues they raise for a thinking attuned to the primordial question of Being. Although Harman eschews this heavyweight rhetoric of authenticity he does carry over from it the idea that the thingness of things – or the objectivity of objects – is best conserved by simply letting them be in their own, uniquely individual character rather than seeking to analyse, conceptualise or explain their constitutive properties by subjecting them to the investigative methods developed by the physical sciences. Another likely source of problems here is Harman's devotion to the work of Bruno Latour, whom he follows in striving to efface the distinction between subjects and objects, persons and things, or human agents (e.g. scientists, engineers and technologists) and those various items, whether 'natural kinds' or humanly created/devised/invented 'artefacts', to which their efforts are applied.[36] In Latour this approach – 'actor-network theory' – goes along with a well-informed interest not only in the complex passages and reversals of agency-passivity between human beings and (so-called) inanimate objects but also in the detailed character of scientific theories, even if these are treated to a hefty dose of relativisation in the strong-sociological mode.[37] However, what Harman takes from Latour is not so much the studious involvement with intra-scientific episodes and developments but rather, by selective reading, the desire to grant objects an agentive power or a quasi-animate (even animist) efficacy far beyond anything remotely conceivable on scientific causal-explanatory terms.

The trouble is that this leaves him with a wildly promiscuous or undifferentiated notion of objecthood and an idea of agency – of what makes the difference when push comes to shove – that simply ducks rather than addresses or much less resolves the old Kantian correlationist issue. That is to say, it does what no realist should ever want to do and takes the word (i.e. the actor-network theoretical word) for the practical deed of having actually achieved, in theory and in practice, that wished-for overcoming of all the troublesome dualisms that Kant's project left in its wake and that philosophers, 'analytic' and 'continental' alike, have ever since been struggling to escape. But this is not a problem that can find its solution in any amount of strategically soft-focused object-celebratory talk or any vague invocation of powers exerted in who-knows-what physical way by who-knows-what kinds of interactive or mysteriously propa-

gated influence. This is no doubt why Harman gets into problems –
having to press speculation to the limit and beyond – when it comes
to the issue of causality or the question as to how all those diverse
and utterly singular objects could possibly enter into causal relationship. Hence his somewhat desperate recourse to a version of the old
occasionalist doctrine – recast as a notion of 'vicarious causation' –
by way of explaining how, despite their impregnably isolated status,
they can none the less be observed to act upon each other, or at least
be observed to behave somehow in concert.[38] After all this was a
theologically inspired and motivated doctrine which, in keeping with
its provenance, presumed the incapacity of mere inert matter to exert
causal powers or possess any kind of active causal efficacy were it not
for God's presidential role in first setting the entire machinery to work
and then ensuring its coordinated operation across and between all
resultant sequences of observed cause and effect.[39] If later advocates
sometimes tried to reduce that divine role or make the process more
immanently self-sustaining, as seems to be Harman's idea, then their
attempts typically ran aground on the scholastic version of a well-
known problem. Thus it failed to explain precisely how – in God's
absence – the realia in question came to affect one another in ways
both regular and, unless on a 'straight' Humean view, having every
appearance of being grounded in certain causal powers, structural
attributes, dispositional properties and so forth.

IV

Indeed the shadow of Hume's much-debated occasionalism looms
large over many aspects of the SR project. Chief among them is its
strongly marked reactive tendency to swing right across from the
sceptical upshot that it sees as lying in wait for all forms of correlationist doctrine to a notionally object-centred or *chosiste* way of
thinking that lacks any adequate ontological, inferential or causal-
explanatory backup. More than that, it shows signs – most overtly in
the second part of *After Finitude* and in what has appeared in print
or by report of Meillassoux's later work – that this can perfectly well
go along with a taste for certain again fairly outré kinds of far-out
speculative theology. These are based in part on his 'necessity of
contingency' argument, i.e. the ultra-Humean claim that causality is
not just epistemologically but ontologically contingent, and in part
on the set-theoretically derived idea that God, even if he doesn't exist
now, might all the same quite conceivably come to exist in one of

those infinite alternative realities that could always spring into being from one moment to the next.[40] It thus runs the risk – one apparently welcomed by some (though emphatically not all) of its current devotees – that SR will be seen to fall in with the nowadays widespread tendency among certain philosophically clued-up theologians to recruit various forms of scientific realism for their own very different though ostensibly compatible purposes.[41] This risk is considerably heightened by its tendency – rooted in a deeply ambivalent relationship to various episodes in the wake of Kant's critical philosophy – to oscillate between polarities bequeathed by its complex and inherently destabilising range of contributory sources and influences. Among them, most problematically, are the twin extremes of a purebred rationalism boldly daring to push speculation into realms forever closed to our senses five and a radical empiricism itself often pressed to the point where it runs into all the same problems (chiefly that of a chronic normative deficit) as afflicted the more bullish battalions of analytic philosophy a quarter-century back.

All this – along with its proximate background in debates around the waning hegemony of earlier radical (e.g. poststructuralist) movements in continental thought – has left SR with a marked liability to adopt hard-line doctrinal positions that soon turn out highly fissile and prone to flip over into something that appears flatly at odds with its primary commitment. No doubt it may be said that any readers impressed by the arguments for a science-led outlook of robust ontological realism put forward in the first part of Meillassoux's book are under no obligation to endorse, or take seriously, the sorts of wire-drawn speculative thinking pursued (or indulged) in its sequel. After all there is often room, even with the most designedly systematic thinkers, to adopt a selective approach and value (say) Aquinas's particular variant of Aristotelian realism while rejecting some of its scholastic and all of its theological scaffolding, or to criticise Kantian ethics with Hegel as an ally while roundly rejecting just about everything else in Hegel's philosophy. However, this pick-and-mix approach has its limits, especially in a case – like SR – where the doctrine has been arrived at through a knock-down thought experiment (the arche-fossil) which, apart from the somewhat routine appeal to carbon dating, is clearly presumed to require nothing further in the way of more detailed evidential, inferential, causal-explanatory, abductive or other such justificatory reasoning. It is this distinct underprovision of resources for strengthening its realist credentials, scientific as well as philosophical, that leaves SR distinctly overexposed to the siren call of a theology that has always had plenty of tricks up its sleeve (*vide* Aquinas again) for co-opting the likely opposition.

Nor does it help very much to be told, as by Harman, that causation comes about through a kind of diffuse intentionality, or an agentive power whose ill-defined locus seems to involve a panpsychist appeal to quasi-mental forces somehow vested in the objects themselves. Here one really wants to say: yes, speculate all you like when you reach the limits of present-best science – and present-best philosophy of science – but do (for realism's sake) first test its limits and see what's available in the way of other, less whacky or credibility-stretching resources. Among the latter, as I have said, is a good amount of broadly analytic work that engages with the closely related topics of causality, rational inference and scientific theory-selection. That SR has mostly ignored that work, or noticed it only in cursory fashion, is especially unfortunate given the vital role it might play in strengthening the realist component of the SR project and somewhat curbing the tendency to various forms of speculative excess. This might go some way toward providing a robust and reliable bridge between the continental-rationalist tradition (which SR inherits, albeit in significantly modified form) and those elements in the mainly British empiricist tradition that have striven to overcome what was, until recently, its pronounced Humean-sceptical bias. It is primarily the lack of such a bridge – the disconnect between speculative thought and that real-world object domain to which it pays fulsome but notional tribute – that constitutes the main unresolved difficulty with the SR project as presently conceived. Very probably this is attributable in part to the influence of Badiou's set-theoretically based ontology, one which (a point often raised by commentators on *Being and Event*) operates at a fairly abstract or generalised level and leaves a good deal of work to be done by way of linkage to specific situations or real-world states of affairs.[42]

More recently, in its sequel *Logics of Worlds*, Badiou has set out to answer this objection by providing a more grounded ontology where situations are indexed according to the degree of 'appearance' or perceptible/intelligible salience in them of various participant (or relatively non-participant) objects, properties, persons, groups, etc.[43] However, compared with *Being and Event*, this is a somewhat discursive and roundabout – even, at times, self-indulgent – work which has some passages of extraordinary brilliance but which doesn't have anything like the sustained argumentative power of that earlier text. Besides, it is still pitched at a pretty high level of abstraction if one takes the scientific-realist view (as endorsed by Meillassoux and, with varying degrees of conviction, by other SR theorists) that science – and physics in particular – should serve as the primary reference point for assignments of reality and truth. My point, to repeat, is that SR has grown up in a context where the fact of its being a distinctly 'continental' and markedly Francophile movement has brought certain disadvantages in terms of its genesis and reception history. On the one hand this has tended to exaggerate its intellectual novelty – since realism has generally had a poor press among recent French philosophers – and on the other to cut it off from those developments in analytic ontology, epistemology and philosophy of science that might have helped strengthen its realist credentials. Ironically enough, given its anti-Kantian stance, there is a sense in which these problems are reminiscent of those that Kant identified in the rationalist metaphysicians of his day whose attempts to derive substantive or real-world-applicable truths by the exercise of pure (speculative) reason miscarried and thereby reopened the door to Humean scepticism.[44]

Such is the danger with any new movement of thought that stakes its claim against a ruling doxology and tends to take this squarely oppositional stance as sufficient guarantee of its own doctrinal rectitude. This one has inherited a range of ideas, sources and allegiances that can be seen to have left it with more than its share of unresolved tensions and conflicts. In particular it has had to cope with the fall-out not just from one but from two sizable bodies of thought – continental and analytic – that have both, in their different ways, tended strongly over the past three decades toward various types of constructivism, conventionalism, instrumentalism, linguistified (Rortyan) pragmatism or fully fledged anti-realism that make it hard for any emergent opposition to avoid adopting an embattled and, at times, a philosophically under-elaborated stance. But of course SR is a young and vigorous movement, and moreover one with sufficient diversity within its own ranks to resist the lure of any single orthodox creed.

Notes

1. Quentin Meillassoux, *After Finitude: An Essay on the Necessity of Contingency*, trans. Ray Brassier (London: Continuum, 2008).
2. For further discussion see Christopher Norris, *Truth Matters: Realism,*

Anti-realism and Response-dependence (Edinburgh: Edinburgh University Press, 2002), and *Philosophy of Language and the Challenge to Scientific Realism* (London: Routledge, 2004).

3. In this moderating vein, see especially Crispin Wright, *Truth and Objectivity* (Cambridge, MA: Harvard University Press, 1992), and *Realism, Meaning, and Truth*, 2nd edn (Oxford: Blackwell, 1993); also – for a range of critical views – John Haldane and Crispin Wright (eds), *Reality, Representation, and Projection* (New York: Oxford University Press, 1993).

4. I offer a highly critical survey of these various movements of thought in Norris, *Against Relativism: Philosophy of Science, Deconstruction and Critical Theory* (Oxford: Blackwell, 1997).

5. For a representative sampling, see *The Speculative Turn: Essays in Continental Materialism and Realism*, ed. Levi Bryant, Nick Srnicek and Graham Harman (Melbourne: re.press, 2011).

6. Immanuel Kant, *Critique of Pure Reason*, trans. N. Kemp Smith (London: Macmillan, 1964).

7. For a particularly waspish passage on Kant, see Alain Badiou, *Logics of Worlds*, trans. Alberto Toscano (London: Continuum, 2006), pp. 535–6.

8. See especially Hilary Putnam, *Reason, Truth and History* (Cambridge: Cambridge University Press, 1981), and Simon Blackburn, *Essays in Quasi-Realism* (Oxford: Oxford University Press, 1993); also Norris, *Hilary Putnam: Realism, Reason, and the Uses of Uncertainty* (Manchester: Manchester University Press, 2002).

9. For statements of the realist-objectivist position, see Norris, *On Truth and Meaning: Language, Logic and the Grounds of Belief* (London: Continuum, 2006); also William P. Alston, *A Realist Conception of Truth* (Ithaca, NY: Cornell University Press, 1996); Michael Devitt, *Realism and Truth*, 2nd edn (Princeton: Princeton University Press, 1997); Jerrold J. Katz, *Realistic Rationalism* (Cambridge, MA: MIT Press, 1996).

10. See Bas van Fraassen, *The Scientific Image* (Oxford: Oxford University Press, 1980); also – for an extended critique of van Fraassen's approach – Norris, 'Anti-realism and constructive empiricism: is there a (real) difference?' and 'Ontology according to van Fraassen: some problems with constructive empiricism', in *Against Relativism*, op. cit., pp. 166–95 and 196–217.

11. Van Fraassen's views on this topic are strongly contested in Ian Hacking, 'Do we see through a microscope?', *Pacific Philosophical Quarterly*, 62 (1981), pp. 305–22, and *Representing and Intervening: Introductory Topics in Philosophy of Science* (Cambridge: Cambridge University Press, 1983). Other relevant sources include G. Maxwell, 'The ontological status of theoretical entities', in H. Feigl and G. Maxwell (eds),

Minnesota Studies in the Philosophy of Science, 3 (1962), pp. 3–27; C. J. Misak, *Verificationism: Its History and Prospects* (London: Routledge, 1995); Paul M. Churchland and C. M. Hooker (eds), *Images of Science: Essays on Realism and Empiricism, with a Reply from Bas C. van Fraassen* (Chicago: University of Chicago Press, 1985).

12. On the issue of truth and epistemic constraint, see especially Michael Dummett, *Truth and Other Enigmas* (London: Duckworth, 1978), and *The Logical Basis of Metaphysics* (London: Duckworth, 1991); Michael Luntley, *Language, Logic and Experience: The Case for Anti-realism* (London: Duckworth, 1988); Gerald Vision, *Modern Anti-Realism and Manufactured Truth* (London: Routledge, 1988); Neil Tennant, *The Taming of the True* (Oxford: Clarendon Press, 2002).

13. Paul Benacerraf, 'What numbers could not be', *Philosophical Review*, 74 (1965), pp. 47–73. For further discussion see Norris, *Truth Matters*, op. cit. and Benacerraf and Hilary Putnam (eds), *Philosophy of Mathematics: Selected Readings*, 2nd edn (Cambridge: Cambridge University Press, 1983).

14. See notes 3, 8, 12 and 13, above.

15. Ray Brassier, *Nihil Unbound: Enlightenment and Extinction* (London: Palgrave-Macmillan, 2010).

16. Kant, *Critique of Pure Reason*, op. cit.; Edmund Husserl, *Formal and Transcendental Logic*, trans. Dorion Cairns (The Hague: Martinus Nijhoff, 1969), and *Experience and Judgment: Investigations in a Genealogy of Logic*, trans. James S. Churchill and Karl Ameriks (Evanston: Northwestern University Press, 1973).

17. Perry Anderson, *Considerations on Western Marxism* (London: New Left Books, 1976); also Norris, *Reclaiming Truth: Contribution to a Critique of Cultural Relativism* (London: Lawrence & Wishart, 1996).

18. On the crucial relevance of this sort of work, see Norris, *Philosophy of Language and the Challenge to Scientific Realism* and *Hilary Putnam* (notes 2 and 8 above); also – for the classic texts on this topic – Saul Kripke, *Naming and Necessity* (Oxford: Blackwell, 1980) and Hilary Putnam, 'Is semantics possible?', 'The meaning of "meaning"', and 'Language and reality', in *Mind, Language and Reality* (Cambridge: Cambridge University Press, 1975), pp. 139–52, 215–71 and 272–90. For further discussion from a range of viewpoints see Leonard Linsky (ed.), *Reference and Modality* (Oxford: Oxford University Press, 1971), and Stephen Schwartz (ed.), *Naming, Necessity, and Natural Kinds* (Ithaca, NY: Cornell University Press, 1977).

19. See entries under note 18, above.

20. See note 5, above.

21. See especially Rupert Read and Kenneth A. Richman (eds), *The New Hume Debate* (London: Routledge, 2000); Galen Strawson, *The Secret*

Connexion: Causation, Realism, and David Hume (Oxford: Clarendon Press, 1989).

22. For a detailed treatment of these topics, see Norris, *Quantum Theory and the Flight from Realism: Philosophical Perspectives on Quantum Mechanics* (London: Routledge, 2000).

23. Alain Badiou, *Being and Event*, trans. Oliver Feltham (London: Continuum, 2005).

24. For an illuminating survey of these developments, see Michael Potter, *Set Theory and Its Philosophy* (Oxford: Oxford University Press, 2004); also Badiou, *Being and Event*, op. cit.

25. See, for instance, Larry Laudan, 'A confutation of convergent realism', *Philosophy of Science*, 48 (1981), pp. 19–49.

26. On this side of the debate, see J. Aronson, R. Harré and E. Way, *Realism Rescued: How Scientific Progress Is Possible* (London: Duckworth, 1994); Roy Bhaskar, *A Realist Theory of Science* (Leeds: Leeds Books, 1975); Michael Devitt, *Realism and Truth*, 2nd edn, op. cit.; Jarrett Leplin (ed.), *Scientific Realism* (Berkeley: University of California Press, 1984), especially Richard Boyd, 'The current status of scientific realism', pp. 41–82; Stathis Psillos, *Scientific Realism: How Science Tracks Truth* (London: Routledge, 1999); Wesley C. Salmon, *Scientific Realism and the Causal Structure of the World* (Princeton: Princeton University Press, 1984).

27. Gilbert Harman, 'Inference to the best explanation', *Philosophical Review*, 74 (1965), pp. 88–95; Peter Lipton, *Inference to the Best Explanation*, 2nd edn (London: Routledge, 2004).

28. See entries under note 26, above.

29. See note 13, above.

30. See notes 2, 18, 26 and 27, above.

31. Jean-Paul Sartre, *Being and Nothingness: An Essay on Phenomenological Ontology*, trans. Hazel Barnes (London: Routledge, 2003); *Critique of Dialectical Reason*, Vol. 1: *Theory of Practical Ensembles*, trans. A. Sheridan-Smith (London: New Left Books, 1976) and Vol. 2, *The Intelligibility of History*, trans. Quintin Hoare (London: Verso, 1991).

32. For representative surveys, see Etienne Balibar and John Rajchman (eds), *French Philosophy since 1945: Problems, Concepts, Inventions* (New York: New Press, 2011); Garry Gutting, *Thinking the Impossible: French Philosophy since 1960* (Oxford: Oxford University Press, 2011); John McCumber, *Time and Philosophy: A History of Continental Thought* (Durham: Acumen, 2011).

33. See, for instance, Roy Bhaskar, *Scientific Realism and Human Emancipation* (London: New Left Books, 1986); Roy Bhaskar et al. (eds), *Critical Realism: Essential Readings* (London: Routledge, 1998); Andrew Collier, *Critical Realism: An Introduction to Roy Bhaskar's Philosophy* (London: Verso, 1994); José Lopez and Garry Potter (eds),

After Postmodernism: An Introduction to Critical Realism (London: Athlone, 2001); William Outhewaite, *New Philosophies of Social Science: Realism, Hermeneutics and Critical Theory* (Basingstoke: Macmillan, 1987).

34. See, for instance, Graham Harman, *Tool-Being: Heidegger and the Metaphysics of Objects* (New York: Open Court, 2002); *Guerrilla Metaphysics: Phenomenology and the Carpentry of Things* (New York: Open Court, 2005); *Prince of Networks: Bruno Latour and metaphysics* (Melbourne: re.press, 2009).

35. See Martin Heidegger, *The Question Concerning Technology and Other Essays*, trans. William Lovitt (New York: Harper & Row, 1977).

36. See, for instance, Bruno Latour, *Science in Action: How to Follow Scientists and Engineers Through Society* (Cambridge, MA: Harvard University Press, 1987); *Pandora's Hope: Essays in the Reality of Science Studies* (Cambridge, MA: Harvard University Press, 1999); also Latour and Graham Harman, *The Prince and the Wolf: Latour and Harman at the LSE* (Winchester: Zero Books, 2011). In a related vein, see Jane Bennett, *Vibrant Matter: A Political Ecology of Things* (Durham, NC: Duke University Press, 2010).

37. Latour, *Reassembling the Social: An Introduction to Actor-Network Theory* (Oxford: Oxford University Press, 2005).

38. See entries under note 34, above.

39. For further discussion see Steven Nadler (ed.), *Causation in Early Modern Philosophy* (University Park: Penn State University Press, 1993), and Nadler (ed.), *The Cambridge Companion to Malebranche* (Cambridge: Cambridge University Press, 2000).

40. See Graham Harman, *Quentin Meillassoux: Philosophy in the Making* (Edinburgh: Edinburgh University Press, 2011).

41. See, for instance, Alister T. McGrath, *A Scientific Theology*, Vols 1–3 (London: T. & T. Clark, 2001, 2002 and 2003); also – for a vigorous and pointed critique of this and similar arguments – Fabio Gironi, 'The theological hijacking of realism: critical realism in "science and religion"', *Journal of Critical Realism*, 11: 1 (2012), pp. 40–75.

42. See especially Peter Hallward, *Badiou: A Subject to Truth* (Minneapolis: University of Minnesota Press, 2003).

43. See note 7, above.

44. Kant, *Critique of Pure Reason*, op. cit.

CHAPTER 7

Provoking Philosophy:
Shakespeare, Johnson, Wittgenstein, Derrida

I

When Keats famously remarked of Shakespeare that he possessed the attribute of 'negative capability' – as opposed to the *echt-*Wordsworthian 'egotistical sublime' – he very clearly meant it as a compliment (to Shakespeare, not Wordsworth) and also perhaps, in mock-modest style, as a piece of implicit self-description.[1] There has been a good deal of critical debate as to just what he might have meant by that cryptic phrase and I shall draw on it here by way of suggesting that the description applies just as well, albeit in a somewhat different way, to certain prominent features of Jacques Derrida's writing. Another way of approaching this topic is the *via negativa* of asking what it might be that Shakespeare and Derrida have in common and that some philosophers find unsettling, offensive or downright rebarbative.[2] In fact Keats's reasons for admiring Shakespeare's peculiarly 'negative' genius each have a counterpart in one or other of the arguments advanced (whether by philosophers or a minority of literary critics) for thinking Shakespeare to be grossly overrated. Moreover, they each find a near equivalent in one or other of the reasons often put forward by those in the mainly analytic camp for treating Derrida as a latter-day sophist – or mere charlatan – whose admirers (wouldn't you know?) hail mostly from departments of literature or, just as bad, from departments of philosophy bitten by the dread 'continental' bug. So what I aim to do here is take the negative route by way of these familiar objections and use them as a kind of litmus-test for those shared Shakespearean-Derridean traits that have tended to create such an adverse response among readers wedded to a certain conception of linguistic, conceptual and ethical propriety.

Of course Shakespeare has had plenty of admirers in the broadly philosophical community, past and present, and so few detractors as to make my case seem flimsy at best and at worst just an instance of that typically Derridean desire to subvert all the standards of rational debate. Thus it might well be said that the only noted philosopher of recent times who has registered genuine doubts on this score – who indeed seems utterly baffled by the fact that Shakespeare has enjoyed such widespread acclaim – is Ludwig Wittgenstein in the various wondering, incredulous or downright scandalised *obiter dicta* published or reported by friends and disciples after his death.[3] And again, in more positive terms, there are some who have expressed not only a keen admiration for Shakespeare as poet and dramatist but also a conviction that one – perhaps the best – way of raising central issues about language, ethics and human relationships (or the sometimes tragic failures thereof) is through a close and sensitive reading of Shakespeare. Such reading may be part of a larger project, like that of Martha Nussbaum, to wean philosophy away from its attachment to overly abstract or generalised (e.g. Kantian) conceptions of ethics and bring it down to earth – to the messy contingencies of situated human conduct and choice – through immersion in the kinds of moral dilemma most vividly enacted in literary works.[4] Or it may take the form, as with Stanley Cavell, of a sustained and intensive brooding on certain key Shakespearean themes – in particular themes of solitude, doubt, mistrust, self-deception and the craving for a perfect (impossible) union of minds – which can be seen to dramatise various issues in current philosophical thought.[5] At any rate there is little enough in common – or so it might appear – between the high esteem in which Shakespeare is held by those who have written about him from a broadly philosophic standpoint and the sorts of attack launched against Derrida by mainstream analytic philosophers in whom the fierceness of denunciatory zeal very often seems to vary inversely with the depth or extent of their acquaintance with his work.[6]

Thus it is fair to say that Wittgenstein is out on a limb among his fellow philosophers when he expresses a strongly negative view of Shakespeare's plays on account of what he thinks their verbal self-indulgence, their formal shortcomings, their frequent lapses of motivational or psychological plausibility, and – above all – their lack of a firm moral compass that would properly apportion weal or woe to the kinds and degrees of human virtue or vice. The following passage from *Culture and Value* catches precisely the curious mixture of puzzlement, misgiving, renewed confidence in his own judgement and sheer exasperation with the judgement of others that typifies Wittgenstein's remarks.

When, for instance, I hear the expression of admiration for Shakespeare by distinguished men in the course of several centuries, I can never rid myself of the suspicion that praising him has been the conventional thing to do; though I have to tell myself that this is not how it is. It takes the authority of a Milton really to convince me. I take it for granted that he was incorruptible. – But I don't of course mean by this that I don't believe an enormous amount of praise to have been, and still to be, lavished on Shakespeare without understanding and for the wrong reasons by a thousand professors of literature.[7]

To this extent he comes out pretty much in agreement with those well-known critics of Shakespeare such as Dr Johnson, Tolstoy and Shaw who have drawn up a strikingly similar charge sheet but done so from the standpoint of creative/imaginative writers with their own very definite axes to grind.[8] They were either (like Johnson) measuring their distance from Shakespeare in historical-political and cultural-ideological terms, or setting up as self-declared rivals to him like Shaw, or else – like the aging Tolstoy with his aspirations to sainthood – writing from a standpoint that required Shakespeare as a suitable foil to his own grand gesture of ascetic renunciation.

That is to say, Shakespeare figured for Shaw as a brilliantly gifted but ultimately trifling dramatist who had squandered his talent on plays which, unlike Shaw's, had nothing of a serious, morally improving or politically progressive nature to impart. For Johnson, Tolstoy and Wittgenstein, on the other hand, he figured as the powerful disturbing embodiment of various possibilities – political and social as well as creative or linguistic – which for various reasons these thinkers had come to mistrust, disown or reject. In Johnson's case, as emerges very clearly in his writing on other early (i.e. pre-Civil War) seventeenth-century poets such as Donne, what triggered this response was a dread of some further such outbreak of political and religious strife, along with a sense of that conflict's having been prefigured, even somehow brought about, by the kinds of verbal licence – especially the flights of multiplied metaphor and far-fetched metaphysical conceit – that typified the poetry of Shakespeare and Donne.[9] In Tolstoy it was more a case of the desire for ascetic self-denial with regard to all worldly pleasures (among them the pleasures of creative self-fulfilment through literature) coming up against the single most exuberant instance of just such unbuttoned creativity deployed in ways that he, like Shaw, found morally repugnant.

However, it is with Wittgenstein that the issues become more sharply focused and, I would suggest, more directly relevant to the question not only of Derrida's relationship to Shakespeare but also of how that relationship bears on the reception-history of Derrida's work at the hands of (some, not all) academic philosophers. For what Wittgenstein found so rebarbative about Shakespeare – especially (here in agreement with Johnson) the poet's deplorable lack of restraint in allowing language such a free rein against all the sanctions of social, communal or literary custom – is also what philosophers have often adduced as good enough reason to count Derrida an anti-philosopher, a latter-day sophist or (worse still) a literary critic with misplaced philosophical pretensions.[10] More precisely: what they often object to (perhaps because it challenges an ancient and still disputed line of demarcation) is Derrida's way of thinking in and through a language that is often deployed at full creative-exploratory stretch but also with the highest degree of conceptual and analytic rigour. That is to say, it is a mode of philosophising that shares something of the later Wittgenstein's famous aptitude for hitting on metaphors, similes and highly evocative turns of phrase in order to convey what would otherwise lack any adequate or sufficiently striking means of expression. Yet in Wittgenstein this goes along with the idea – witness his response to Shakespeare – that really such linguistic indulgences should have no place in philosophical work since the proper (indeed, the sole legitimate) purpose of such work is to talk us down from the giddy heights of metaphysico-linguistic delusion to a restored sense of how our various language games are normally, typically or properly played as components of some given communal practice or cultural 'form of life'.[11]

Thus one finds Wittgenstein on occasion lamenting his own proclivities in this regard – his proneness to substitute image or simile for the hard business of thinking constructively without falling back on such devices – and moreover, in a curious twist of redoubled self-criticism, confessing that he lacks the native genius to produce really strong, original, creative or (one is tempted to suggest) Shakespearean metaphors. Indeed there are passages where he goes so far toward qualifying his negative evaluation as to say that Shakespeare simply cannot be judged by normal literary-critical standards, that his plays are more like forces of nature than products of human contrivance, and that the only fit state of mind in which to appreciate their imaginative power is one that regards them as one might an overwhelming manifestation of nature's sublime (and potentially destructive) power. Indeed '[i]t may be that the essential thing with Shakespeare is his ease and authority and that you just have to accept him as he is if you are going to be able to admire him properly, in the way you accept nature, a piece of scenery for example, just as it is.'[12] And again:

> [h]is pieces give me the impression of enormous 'sketches' rather than paintings; as though they had been 'dashed off' by someone who can permit himself 'anything', so to speak. And I can understand how someone can admire that and call it 'supreme' art, but I don't like it. – So if anyone stands in front of these pieces speechless, I can understand him; but anyone who admires them as one admires, say, Beethoven, seems to me to misunderstand Shakespeare.[13]

Moreover, it is through comparisons of just this sort – clearly with their source in a certain, distinctively German-romantic conception of creative genius – that Wittgenstein tends to disparage or devalue his own (as he thinks it) essentially derivative and second-rate talent. What he is good at, so this gloomy self-assessment runs, is producing 'similes' that manage successfully to hit off some philosophic point or other. What he cannot create are the sorts of vital or visionary metaphor that extend beyond localised passages to entire works, and which bring about the kinds of revelatory or world-transformative experience that Wittgenstein famously gestured toward in the cryptic final passages of his early *Tractatus Logico-Philosophicus*.[14] It is a question of meanings or insights that may be 'shown' through some manner of oblique, suggestive or analogical expression but which cannot be 'said' – laid out in the form of articulate, coherent, logically concatenated statements or propositions – since their import intrinsically eludes or transcends any such means of conveyance.

II

So there is a tension, even a flat contradiction at the heart of Wittgenstein's philosophy and one that is brought home with particular force when he confronts the problem of Shakespearean language in relation to the claims of 'ordinary language' or the needs of practical-communicative discourse. For of course it was precisely in order to acknowledge those claims – to coax philosophy down from its delusions of metaphysical grandeur and put it back in touch with our everyday language games or cultural 'forms of life' – that Wittgenstein developed his later ideas about the open-ended multiplicity of ways in which our signifying practices made sense from one such context to another.

This development is most often portrayed as a drastic mid-career turning away from the austerely logical-atomist programme set out in the *Tractatus* with its numbered propositions and denial that statements could be meaningful unless they were either empirically verifiable or self-evidently valid (hence vacuous or tautologous) in virtue of their logical form. Thus the 'old' (roughly up to 1990) view, not without strong support from Wittgenstein's text, has him utterly repudiate the Tractarian concept of language as aspiring to a state of crystalline logical perfection and replace it with the communitarian view, i.e. that the standards of intelligibility are as many and various as the social practices or shared ways in life in which they play a role. For proponents of the 'new' Wittgenstein, conversely, there is no such radical mid-career break but rather – in the writings of his later period – a shift toward making more explicit what was always there to be gleaned from the *Tractatus* by those sympathetic readers, fit though few, who could grasp the purport of its last few cryptic remarks.[15] On this view, his sole purpose in composing what went before – the entire elaborate structure of numbered propositions ordered *more geometrico*, that is, in a quasi-mathematical or axiomatic-deductive mode – was to offer a kind of exemplary failure, an object lesson in the impossibility that any such logical-atomist approach could begin to make sense of language or the most important issues for human existence like those of ethics, aesthetics and religious belief.

At any rate both parties, old and new, are agreed that 'late' Wittgenstein was out to discredit any version of the logical-positivist project that he – along with Russell and members of the 1920s Vienna Circle – had thought of as a veritable new instauration or turning point in philosophic history. Where the revisionists demur from the orthodox account is merely in giving Wittgenstein greater credit for having shrewdly pre-empted the naive misreading of his work by those, like Russell, who first hailed it as a striking – if somewhat obscure – manifesto for their own set of doctrines. However, my main interest here is not so much in these often rather tedious wranglings among the Wittgensteinian faithful but rather in what they may have to reveal about Derrida's and Wittgenstein's respective (very different) relationships to Shakespeare. This connects in turn with the wider issue regarding philosophy's ambivalent and at times highly charged relationship to a certain idea of the poetic which finds its most prominent example in Shakespeare, or in a certain idea of

Shakespeare as the writer who exhibits these qualities in the highest possible degree.

So when Derrida's detractors (mostly speaking from a mainstream-analytic standpoint) describe him as a 'literary' thinker, one whose work belongs more to the province of literary criticism than philosophy, it is a safe bet that the characterisation is not meant as any kind of compliment. Still less should one take it to express the idea that Derrida's writing on philosophic themes has about it something of Shakespeare's capacity to raise the most complex and challenging philosophic issues through language of a likewise complex and intensely creative-exploratory kind. On the contrary, what these critics most often have in mind is the received 'analytic' image of Derrida as a latter-day sophist, a gadfly rhetorician or game-playing 'textualist' perverter of truth whose seeming ability to run rings around earnest or literal-minded opponents like John Searle is in fact just a sign of his refusal to engage the substantive philosophical issues. The same case was put by Jürgen Habermas when he accused Derrida of seeking to annul the genre-distinction between philosophy and literature, and thereby revoke the hard-won gains of an enlightenment discourse whose 'unfinished' character (or failure so far to realise its various emancipatory aims) was no good reason to renounce or betray the critical distinctions upon which its project had crucially depended.[16]

I have argued elsewhere that this line of attack, from whichever quarter, is demonstrably wide of the mark since it has to ignore what should strike any competent and attentive reader of Derrida who is not in the grip of a powerful foregone prejudice.[17] That is to say, his deconstructive readings of philosophers – or philosophically pertinent texts – from Plato and Aristotle to Rousseau, Kant, Marx, Nietzsche, Husserl, Heidegger, Freud, Saussure and J. L. Austin are none the less logically cogent, conceptually precise and analytically acute for their extreme sensitivity to matters of linguistic or rhetorical-stylistic nuance.[18] Of course there are salient distinctions to be drawn within Derrida's *oeuvre*, as between those texts that argue their way through a combination of close-focused rhetorical exegesis with rigorous (even if heterodox) conceptual or logico-semantic analysis and those that adopt what appears to be a more 'literary' mode of address. At the one extreme would be works like those on Plato, Rousseau and especially Husserl where, as always with Derrida, there is maximal attention to matters of linguistic detail – including the complex interplay between text and commentary – but where the reading remains tightly constrained by those 'classical' requirements of rigour, fidelity and truth to the author's (presumed) intent right up to the point at which it encounters an aporia, that is, an unresolvable conflict between two jointly and strictly entailed but also strictly incompatible chains of implication.[19] It is at this stage only – when the reading has deployed all those classical resources and shown how their application to the text cannot but produce such a moment of logico-semantic impasse – that there emerges a counter-logic (like those of *pharmakon* in Plato, 'supplement' in Rousseau or 'parergon' in Kant) which captures precisely what it is about certain problematical concepts or topics that induces such a symptomatic swerve from the standard principles of bivalence and excluded middle. Indeed there is a case for regarding these particular texts of Derrida as major contributions to current debate in the philosophy of non-classical (i.e. deviant, non-bivalent or paraconsistent as well as modal and tense) logic.

However, my point, more simply, is that opponents such as Searle and Habermas get Derrida badly wrong when they ignore this philosophically central dimension of his work and take it for granted that his penchant for 'wordplay' or ingenious verbal gymnastics – as no doubt it must appear from their own philosophical perspective – is sufficient to disqualify that work as a serious, constructive or good-faith contribution. Of course, as I have said, there are other texts of Derrida (among them, notoriously, his response to Searle on the topic of speech-act theory) which do tend more toward the kind of writing – allusive, metaphorical, rhetorically complex, thematically self-reflexive, 'performative' in every sense of the word – that his critics find especially hard to take and which often strikes them as a standing provocation.[20] Yet even here it should not escape notice that, despite this overtly ludic dimension, there are issues involved (such as whether or how one could possibly draw a categorical distinction between constative and performative orders of speech-act) which are no less philosophically pertinent for their being raised in such a subtle, oblique or shrewdly self-exemplifying mode. Of the many other instances in Derrida's work I would single out *Signsponge* (*Signéponge*) where he offers a highly inventive and idiosyncratic commentary on texts by the poet Francis Ponge along with some acute and far-reaching remarks about issues that have mostly preoccupied thinkers in the analytic line of descent, notably that of proper names and the debate between descriptivist and causal theories of reference.[21] So it is fair to conclude that his opponents have either not read the texts in question or read them with so fixed and determined a sense of what properly counts as philosophical discourse as scarcely to register their content.

This is where the comparison with Wittgenstein takes on an especially suggestive diagnostic force, not only as concerns what I have here described as Wittgenstein's ambivalent relationship to certain 'literary' aspects of his own work, but also as concerns that same ambivalence within the wider philosophical (at any rate mainstream US and British analytic) community. Not that this attitude is anything new, going back as it does to Plato's strictures on the poets – along with the sophists, rhetoricians and other such purveyors of a false (linguistically embellished) wisdom – despite all the evidence of his own strong attraction to a highly metaphorical and at times vividly poetic manner of expression. It tends to re-emerge with particular force at those historical junctures, like the seventeenth century, when philosophy is under considerable pressure to take sides in some high-profile dispute – like that between the 'old' scholastic tradition and the newly emergent natural-scientific disciplines – and is itself subject to deep-laid rifts of the kind that ranged 'continental' rationalists against home-grown British empiricist types. At such times philosophers are all the keener to establish their truth-telling credentials by asserting their absolute non-reliance on metaphor, simile, poetry, fiction or any mode of language that doesn't lay claim to the straightforward, literal conveyance of clear and distinct ideas.[22] Of course that virtue was differently construed on the one hand by rationalists who thought it a matter of direct, unimpeded or transparent access to a priori concepts and on the other hand by empiricists who thought it a matter of developing a language that would, so far as possible, conserve the vividness of sensory impressions and not yield to the obfuscating tendency of abstract or figural discourse. Hence the minor industry among deconstructionist literary critics devoted to revealing the various ways in which empiricists like Locke or idealists like Kant can be shown to tie themselves ever more deeply into knots of multiple metaphor or rhetorical displacement and substitution the more they attempt to purify their language of every last figural residue.[23]

If that issue has now resurfaced to vex the discourse of analytic philosophy then most likely this has to do with the current sense of crisis concerning philosophy's role and proper remit with respect to the various disciplines for which (until recently) it had often presumed to legislate. The crisis can be seen to have deepened ever since the arrival of logical positivism as a self-acknowledged under-labourer to the physical sciences – exactly the role that Locke assigned to it – and then its demise (or retreat to a posture of increasingly beleaguered rearguard defence) as a consequence of Quine's famous demolition job and various subsequent assaults.[24] Hence perhaps the extreme sensitivity among some philosophers with regard to any suggestion that their discipline might have something to gain in the way of sharpened self-critical awareness from the kind of close reading regularly practised by those, like Derrida, who combine that approach with a keenly analytic sense of its logical and conceptual as well as its rhetorical implications. Yet this leaves unanswered the obvious question as to why Wittgenstein's work has exerted such a powerful, indeed spellbinding, influence over so many thinkers in the broadly analytic tradition while Derrida's reception in that quarter has mostly been one of total indifference or downright hostility. An answer is perhaps to be sought in the fact that Derrida, unlike Wittgenstein, has been so far from denying, disowning or deploring the 'literary' aspects of his work as to place them very much up front in token of his principled resistance to a certain idea of what philoso-phy – serious, proper, responsible, professionally competent philoso-phy – ought to be. On the contrary, he has always set out to question any such confident beating of the bounds between philosophy and literature (or the kinds of language taken as appropriate to each of these domains) in so far as that dichotomy has often functioned as a means of restricting the creative-exploratory aspects of philosophical thought. However, he has also opposed it on account of its denying to literature the depth and acuity of critical engagement that might be attained through a reading informed by certain distinctively philo-sophic ways of thought.

This dual perspective is already clearly visible in his early Introduction to Husserl's essay on 'The Origin of Geometry', the text where Derrida undoubtedly comes closest to the interests and priorities of mainstream analytic philosophy, i.e. an approach that finds its paradigm instances in philosophy of mathematics, logic and language.[25] I have put the case elsewhere that this essay – like a good deal of Derrida's early work – can be shown to yield nothing in the way of conceptual rigour or precision to that 'other', supposedly remote but in fact closely related line of post-Kantian philosophical descent.[26] Thus it raises issues with regard to mathematical truth, objectivity, proof, knowledge, intuition, discovery and historical 'genesis' as opposed to atemporal or a priori 'structure' that are central to recent analytic debates, especially that between realist and anti-realist approaches to philosophy of the formal and natural sciences.[27] Of course Derrida broaches these issues from the very different standpoint of a thinker whose two most crucial and formative early influences were Husserlian transcendental phenomenology and the newly emergent structuralist 'revolution' across various disciplines.[28] However, he does so with the highest degree of conceptual-analytic rigour and also – though the fact has often escaped notice even among his better informed and more sympathetic commentators – with evident knowledge of the way these problems have been posed by analytically minded philosophers on both sides of that long-running (post-Fregean) dispute concerning realism as applied to mathematics and logic.

I shall not labour this particular point – having pushed it pretty hard elsewhere – except to remark on an odd and revealing passage in Derrida's Introduction to the 'Origin of Geometry' which has frequently been cited but not, I think, given the right kind or degree of exegetical weight. Here he talks about the choice – in his own case especially but also in the wider philosophical context – between, on the one hand, a language aimed toward the rationalist ideal of univocal sense and the attempt to eliminate such obfuscating features as metaphor, ambiguity or paronomasia and, on the other, a language that would not only find room for those same naturally occurring features but allow them to proliferate as far as possible toward the opposite ideal of a signifying practice freed from such irksome, artificial and anyway wholly unworkable constraints.[29] That Derrida invokes the example of Joyce in the latter connection should perhaps not be taken too much at face value, given the cult of *Finnegans Wake* among French avant-garde literary critics and theorists at the time. This was the poststructuralist idea – taken up programmatically by Barthes, Kristeva, Sollers and other members of the *Tel Quel* collective, with Derrida somewhat on the margins – that such a radically disruptive writing, one that unfixed the conventional or naturalised relation between signifier and signified, might itself be not only the symptom or harbinger but even the active bringer-on of revolutionary change.[30] However, just as he maintained a certain distance from that movement with regard to some of its more antic (and, as would later emerge, politically volatile) dispositions, so likewise Derrida can now be seen – right from the time of that early allusion to Joyce vis-à-vis Husserl – as having held out against any too direct or unqualified endorsement of the *Tel Quel* line. Thus his point is not so much to present the choice between rigorous, univocal sense and unrestrained Joycean 'dissemination' as a matter for some present, strictly binding and henceforth irrevocable act of commitment but rather as one that the philosopher always confronts – and must always resolve to best effect – whenever she writes.

III

This is why, as I have said, there are some texts of Derrida (such as the 'Envois' section of *La carte postale*, some lengthy stretches of his commentary on Hegel in *Glas* and a great many passages in his later writing) which do seem to come out strongly on the side of a 'literary' language that explores – indeed exploits – the maximum range of metaphorical, fictive or other such departures from what is normally taken (at least on analytic terms) to constitute the proper philosophical-linguistic norm.[31] Yet it remains the case – indisputably so for those who have read his work with anything like the requisite care – that Derrida has also produced many texts, starting out with that lengthy and meticulously argued essay on Husserl's philosophy of mathematics, that could be refused the title 'analytic' only on an understanding of the term which confined it to a merely parochial or honorific usage. Moreover, there are instances such as his writing on Austinian speech-act theory where one would (or should) hesitate to venture any such confident classification since the texts in question exhibit a high degree of linguistic inventiveness or conceptual creativity while none the less arguing their philosophic case with impressive vigour and force.[32]

Indeed that very 'phrase 'conceptual creativity' might stand here as a kind of shibboleth in so far as it offers what a good many continental philosophers – Derrida among them – would happily accept as an accurate characterisation of one major aspect of their work, while to many trained up on the norms and protocols of analytic discourse it will strike an oddly discordant, even vaguely oxymoronic note. It is here, I believe, that we can find the chief source of that deep-laid, almost reflex hostility that has so typified (at times so disfigured) the analytic reception of Derrida's work, as well as a reason for Wittgenstein's mistrust of metaphorical or 'literary' language, whether in his own or others' writing. Moreover, it provides a likely explanation for the fact that Wittgenstein's stock has continued to ride so much higher than Derrida's among analytic philosophers. Finally, it offers a suggestive clue not only to Wittgenstein's thoughts about Shakespeare with their mixture of well-nigh contemptuous dismissal and well-nigh mystical regard but also to that wider philosophical unease as concerns any writing that stretches the bounds of linguistic discipline, decorum or propriety beyond what is required by a decent regard for the needs of straightforward communicative discourse.

Those bounds have been policed in different ways and with different looming perils in view by rationalists, empiricists, logicists, positivists and other linguistic-reformist types as well as by those – like the ordinary-language philosophers and current neo-pragmatists – who would seek to bring about a complete reversal of roles and thereby turn the gamekeepers into poachers. What these all have in common is a strongly marked sense of the dangers attendant on any too drastic a departure from, or infraction of, the various linguistic-conceptual norms that are taken to inform the business of serious, good-faith, competent debate in a well-regulated philosophic or wider intellectual and cultural community. To repeat: Derrida is very far from rejecting those norms and is indeed more than capable of turning the tables to convincing effect on any hostile commentator – such as Searle – who thinks to catch him out in logical blunders or blind spots of presupposition.[33] However, he is just as far from accepting *either* the *echt*-analytic idea that linguistic creativity of, say, the Shakespearean-Joycean order has no place in philosophical debate *or* the Wittgensteinian approach that in principle allows all manner of language games their role as parts of some given, communally warranted form of life but which in practice draws the line pretty firmly at some such games and the life-forms involved. These latter include, above all, the sorts of expression that Wittgenstein regarded as ill-begotten products of the typically philosophic urge to use language in abstract, specialised, technical or otherwise deviant ways for which it is simply not suited – not having evolved or developed for such purposes – and through which it exerts a malign propensity for creating philosophical and other kinds of bewilderment. Yet they also include, less emphatically, those various figural or 'literary' modes that he seems to have regarded as all very well in their place – that is say, when bearing the generic markers 'poetry', 'fiction', or (at a stretch) 'religious, hence analogical' – but as liable to cause great harm elsewhere by encouraging language to 'go on holiday' or to 'idle' like an engine detached from its machine or a philosopher content with mere gratuitous word-spinning.[34]

Of course Shakespeare's plays come tagged with a whole range of such markers – tragic, comic, tragi-comic, poetic (or mixed verse-and-prose) drama and 'Renaissance' as a complex temporal descriptor with numerous cultural values attached – that must be supposed to have informed Wittgenstein's response as a highly cultivated reader with wide literary interests. Besides, there is long tradition of proprietary attitudes toward Shakespeare among German (or German-speaking) literary critics, philosophers and others who sometimes go so far as to state their preference for the Schlegel/Tieck translation over the English original, or again – with slightly less chutzpah – to claim that only German thinkers after Kant have possessed the kind of philosophic insight or profundity required to take full measure of Shakespeare's achievement.[35] My point is that Wittgenstein came to Shakespeare with a good deal of cultural baggage whose effect might well have been to predispose him in a certain admiring, reverential, even bardolatrous direction. Signs of this do occasionally show through in those quasi-mystical passages where Wittgenstein indulges an inherited taste for the rhetoric of sublimity and the idea of creative genius as more like a force of nature than a humanly cultivated gift or capacity. On balance, however, his exposure to this notion seems to have had just the opposite effect, that is, to have focused his attention (like Johnson's and Tolstoy's before him) on the moral aspect of Shakespearean drama as distinct from – or indeed as grounds for ignoring or condemning – its creative-linguistic qualities. It strikes me that Wittgenstein's moral sensibility was most keenly offended by the specific combination – one that Shakespearean drama exemplifies in the highest degree – of extreme verbal inventiveness with a tendency (as in *King Lear*) to push far beyond tolerable limits with the tragic assault on all accepted or normative ideas of just desert. Thus in Wittgenstein, as in Johnson, there is strong sense that the objection to Shakespeare's 'weakness' for multiplied metaphors, puns, ambiguities and other such forms of linguistic self-indulgence goes along with a stern disapproval of the dramatist's failure in this latter, i.e. moral, regard.

There are echoes of the same joint response in those critics of Derrida who seem to suppose that a highly developed, even preternatural capacity for verbal inventiveness is sure to be a mark of philosophical frivolity at best and at worst a malevolent drive to subvert all the norms of rational, good-faith, ethically responsible discourse. More than that: what seems to trigger this response in a particularly sharp, at times quite virulent form is the contra-Wittgensteinian idea – apt to be prompted by a close-reading of Shakespeare and Derrida alike – that language does most to advance and refine our powers of intellectual, moral and communicative grasp when it manifests a power to break with the currency of this or that language game or cultural form of life. That is to say, there is ultimately no distinguishing those aspects of verbal creativity that are most prominent when viewed in a 'literary' perspective from those other aspects – of subtlety, acuity, range and depth of analytic grasp – that tend to rate higher on the philosophic scale of significance or value. It seems to me that the chief result of Wittgenstein's influence on Anglophone philosophy of language over the past four decades has been to close many minds to this very possibility by reinforcing a strongly communitarian – and to this extent strongly conservative – idea of the scope and limits of linguistic and cultural intelligibility.[36] Thus it has tended to foreclose the idea of philosophy as a genuine adventure in thought, one that is able (like the best of Derrida's writing) to reconcile the need for conceptual clarity and logical rigour with a remarkable gift for the invention of new linguistic resources whereby (or wherein) to test and refine its analytic powers.

Indeed one could put the case that this has been the main problem with a good deal of work in that Anglophone tradition since the advent of 'ordinary language' philosophy – whether in its Wittgenstein-derived or its more homely Austinian guise – as an antidote to the perceived failures or excesses of purebred analytic thought. For, as Derrida shows to striking effect in his reading of *How to Do Things with Words*, there is a constant and strictly unresolvable tension between Austin's appeal to ordinary language as the final arbiter of what makes good or acceptable sense and his desire for a generalised theory of speech-acts that would sometimes usurp that role.[37] Then again there is Austin's singular willingness – one that potentially conflicts with each of those already potentially conflicting aims – sometimes to let speculation ride on the evidence of puns, jokes, anecdotes and supposedly 'deviant' modes of utterance that create large problems for any such (on the face of it) strongly normative project.[38] This is why Derrida's reading of Austin is more 'faithful' – more attentive to the spirit as well as the letter of Austin's text – than an account of speech-act theory, like Searle's, that pursues the high road of system and method while necessarily (given these ruling priorities) taking it for granted that those deviant samples are by very definition not such as could raise serious questions concerning the validity of that account. However, it achieves this fidelity not by abandoning the analytic virtues of conceptual precision, logical clarity and detailed engagement with the text in hand but – on the contrary – by applying those standards so far as the text allows and only then, at the point where it resists such treatment, seeking out alternative resources in the form of a deviant, paraconsistent, dialethic, non-bivalent or other such 'deviant' logic.[39]

Of course these are terms that belong very much to the analytic lexicon and which derive their specific sense and application precisely from their role within a certain discourse – philosophy of logic in the mainstream post-Fregean line of descent – where they mark both the limit of that discourse and the prospect that its motivating aims and priorities might yet be extended to encompass instances beyond its classical remit. That is to say, the 'analytic' label is decidedly elastic and capable of stretching around a whole range of developments (like those mentioned above along with other, e.g. modal, departures from the strict remit of the first-order quantified predicate and prop-ositional calculi) all of which – as Quine was wont to lament – resist any possible 'regimentation' in first-order extensionalist terms.[40] Still, it is not hard to show how those various kinds of analytically acknowledged departure from the classical norm find their analogues in Derrida's equally various (though likewise closely related) logics of 'supplementarity', 'différance', 'parergonality', 'iterability' and so forth.[41] Where his approach does diverge rather sharply from that of thinkers within the analytic tradition who have struck out in a new direction with regard to philosophy of logic is in Derrida's constant practice of raising such issues *in and through* language, that is, both the language of the texts he reads and the language of his own engagement with them. Hence the mode of intensely ana-lytic, close-focused and responsive textual exegesis that typifies so much of Derrida's work. Here one might cite his pursuit of the term 'supplement' through its numerous instances in Rousseau's writing, of 'différance' as it functions to complicate the logic of Husserl's meditations on language and time-consciousness, of the 'parergon' (or frame) as a likewise problematic topos in Kantian aesthetics, and of 'iterability' as that which marks the conceptual limit of Austinian speech-act theory.

One might also hazard the conjecture – borne out by many hostile responses to his work – that this particular way of doing philoso-phy goes very much against the grain of certain currently deep-laid philosophical (mainly analytic) habits of thought. What so irks these respondents is, I suggest, something very like the unusual combina-tion of qualities that struck such a dissonant chord with Dr Johnson in his reading of Shakespeare and the metaphysical poets, and which likewise stretched Wittgenstein's patience to the point of his declaring Shakespeare in some way a nonpareil genius but Shakespeare's admirers just a bunch of charlatans or fools. In short, it is the highly unusual (and at times highly disconcerting) combination of a singular power of linguistic creativity – what Johnson famously deplored in Donne as 'heterogeneous ideas linked violently together' – with a likewise singular power to tax the best efforts of conceptual and analytic thought. For Johnson, famously, the reading of *Lear* was painful almost beyond endurance, so that having read it a second time by way of editorial obligation he hoped very much that he would never be compelled to take it up again.[42] However, just as painful – though for different reasons – was the experience of reading (and, worse still, of having to edit) language that was so 'inextricably perplexed' or so tied up into knots of figural and logico-semantic complication as to render his task well-nigh unendurable.

Thus: '[n]ot that always where the language is intricate the thought is subtle, or the image always great where the line is bulky; the equality of words to things is very often neglected, and trivial sentiments and vulgar ideas disappoint the attention, to which they are recommended by sonorous epithets and swelling figures'.[43] Nevertheless, as with Locke and other empirically minded mistrusters of figural language, it is instructive to observe how Johnson finds himself embroiled in thickets of multiplied metaphor – in talk of 'fatal Cleopatras', of 'malignant powers' and 'luminous vapours' that lead the unwary traveller off his path – in the very act of denouncing Shakespeare's proclivities in that regard.[44] So likewise Wittgenstein repeatedly expresses a deep unease about what is likely to result when language metaphorically 'goes on holiday' even though there is nothing more characteristic of his thought – and nothing that has contributed more to its extraordinary impact and influence – than his remarkable capacity for striking out suggestive metaphors whose very suggestiveness has since given rise to endless debate around just the sorts of problem (or pseudo-problem) for which he believed those writings to have offered a cure.

IV

It is just forty years since Richard Rorty, in his preface to an influential anthology entitled *The Linguistic Turn*, put the case that philosophy of language had gone in two very different directions – the

analytic line descending from Frege-Russell and the 'ordinary language' line with its sources in Wittgenstein and/or Austin – and
that these were so far apart in their basic aims and priorities as to
offer no prospect of reconciliation.[45] Later on Rorty hailed Derrida
as one of those thinkers (along with the American pragmatists and
assorted other 'post-philosophical' types) who could best help us
out of such pointless dilemmas by teaching us to see that philosophy
was just a 'kind of writing' with no special claim to reason, truth,
logical rigour, conceptual precision and so forth. Rather it should
junk the whole range of concerns (especially the so-called 'problem
of knowledge) that had mostly defined its mainstream agenda from
Plato, via Descartes and Kant, to their present-day inheritors on
both sides of the supposed 'continental'/'analytic' gulf. Once shorn
of its pretensions to truth or other such grandiose claims philosophy
could then resume its role in the ongoing cultural conversation as
one more, strictly non-privileged supplier of ideas, images, inventive
narratives and inspirational metaphors we can live by. In which case,
Rorty advised, we had better just tactfully ignore all those aspects of
Derrida's early work – all the technical-sounding talk of *différance*,
supplementarity, logocentrism, the 'metaphysics of presence' and
so forth – which merely bore witness to his backsliding tendency
or unfortunate proneness to substitute his own deconstructionist
jargon for the older jargon (of truth, knowledge, a priori concepts,
sense-data, propositional content or whatever) that he rightly wanted
to jettison. For we should then be more receptive to those other,
primarily stylistic or 'literary' aspects which showed how something
called 'philosophy' might still be practised but without its erstwhile
delusions of epistemological grandeur and on a par with the kinds
of discourse – fiction and poetry among them – that could do a lot
better in making sense of our communal and individual lives.

Thus Rorty has the highest possible regard for one dimension of
Derrida's genius, as I have described it: that is to say, his well-nigh
Shakespearean capacity for striking out in new, unexpected and
revealing metaphorical directions and doing so, moreover, in ways
that demand a likewise creative or inventive stretch of mind on
the reader's part. Where he differs from Derrida – indeed, I would
contend, gets Derrida wrong as a matter of plain exegetical as well
as philosophic warrant – is in supposing that this metaphorical,
performative or 'literary' aspect of Derrida's writing is as far as one
can go (or should wish to go) in deriving its philosophical content or
relevance. Indeed, one may conjecture that it is largely on the basis of

their having read Rorty or perhaps picked up on the literary-critical reception of Derrida's work – rather than their having read Derrida beyond the most cursory or second-hand acquaintance – that detractors like Habermas or (more egregiously) Searle are able to launch their confident attacks on his supposed irrationalism, illogicality, misreading of source texts and so forth. What is crucially lacking from the Rortian view is any recognition of the other chief attribute that sets Derrida decisively apart from those among his literary-critical followers who celebrate deconstruction as a licence for unlimited textual-interpretative or hermeneutic 'freeplay'.[46] In short, it is the operation of a first-rate analytic mind whose mark is precisely the way that its pursuit of terms such as 'supplement', 'différance' and 'iterability' involves not only their semantic ambivalence in this or that localised context but also their logico-syntactic functioning over large stretches of text, whether as concerns an individual work (like Plato's *Phaedrus* or Austin's *How to Do Things with Words*) or ranging across an entire *oeuvre*, as in Derrida's reading of Rousseau. This dimension quite simply drops out of sight on any reading, like Rorty's, that plays up the creative, metaphorical or broadly 'literary' aspects of Derrida's writing while playing down – or rejecting outright – its equally remarkable powers of analytic or conceptual grasp.

Such a partial account is all the more questionable for the fact that Derrida went out of his way, in the essay 'White Mythology: Metaphor in the Text of Philosophy', to insist that deconstruction could not stop short at the point of declaring 'all concepts are metaphors', 'all philosophy a kind of literature', 'all truth-claims rhetorical', etc.[47] On the contrary: it had to present, articulate and justify that case in terms necessarily derived in large part from the various analytic and conceptual resources bequeathed by a two-millennia-long tradition of philosophic thought about metaphor. Indeed 'White Mythology' is a prime example of Derrida's ability – one that provokes an extraordinary degree of resistance among many analytic philosophers – to show how philosophy will always be played off the field at some point if it attempts to regulate, conceptualise or codify the workings of metaphor even though that attempt is not only built into the project of philosophy from its very inception but is also prerequisite to any understanding of the way that metaphor functions in other fields, among them (not least) the natural sciences. This he does, to repeat, through a mode of analytic commentary – encompassing texts from Aristotle, Cicero and the Renaissance rhetoricians to Bachelard, Canguilhem and other modern thinkers – which combines the most meticulous attentiveness to detail with a high degree of conceptual rigour and also (what sets it apart from most of those sources) an acutely self-reflexive awareness of the issues thrown up by its performative dimension, that is, by the richly metaphorical character of Derrida's prose. If 'White Mythology' is a veritable *tour de force* of such mixed-mode writing since, after all, it has to do thematically with just these features of its own textual constitution then it is none the less a representative sample of Derridean philosophy of language. Moreover, like his equally perceptive and (in the best sense) inventive essay on Austin, it suggests further reasons not only for Derrida's hostile reception at the hands of many Anglophone philosophers – whether of the *echt*-analytic or the ordinary-language persuasion – but also for the frequent description of his texts as distinctly 'Shakespearean' in character.[48]

What these reactions have in common despite issuing from sharply opposed evaluative standpoints is a keen sense of the way that such writing cuts across some of the most problematic and sensitive distinctions in present-day philosophy of language. What they are reacting to, in Derrida as in Shakespeare, is not – or not only – the stylistic brio, the extraordinary power of metaphoric suggestion or the way that its logico-semantic complexities exceed the furthest bounds of straightforward explication or plain-prose paraphrase. Rather it is a question of the conflict induced between a mindset responsive to those commonly acknowledged features of 'literary' (especially poetic) language and a mindset schooled in the primary 'philosophic' virtues of conceptual precision, logical rigour and – supposedly prerequisite to those – univocal or unambiguous sense. This goes some way toward explaining the signs of acute cognitive dissonance that have periodically surfaced in the annals of Shakespeare criticism from Johnson to Wittgenstein and have also been such a marked feature of the strong, sometimes febrile resistance to Derrida's work among analytic philosophers. Hence, I would suggest, the striking resemblance between their respective reception histories and the pattern of extreme antithetical response – of fiercely opposed valuations 'for' and 'against' – which seems to have its source in something other and more than a difference of attitude concerning issues of linguistic or stylistic propriety. So likewise, when Johnson registers his sense of unease with regard to Shakespeare, Donne and other representatives of the seventeenth-century 'conceited' style this doesn't have to do merely with localised instances of multiple meaning such as puns, ambiguities or other forms of semantic overdetermination.

It is also – and I think more crucially – concerned with the challenge so insistently posed by a language that presses these departures from the norm of straightforward, literal sense to the point where any adequate analysis will have to take account of the way they function in a larger context of logically co-implicated uses or occurrences.

Thus what Johnson perceives as a threat to the stable economy of usage and representation is not so much Shakespeare's endemic weakness for 'quibbles' – though he certainly considers that a fault – but more the kinds of intricate logico-syntactic complication that are often manifest in just such instances of localised wordplay but can also be seen to involve much deeper and longer-range conflicts of sense. This helps to explain Johnson's rueful account of his editorial work on Shakespeare as having frequently required such a strenuous effort of reconstruction as to make the business of textual scholarship an almost superhuman undertaking. 'Where any passage appeared inextricably perplexed', he writes, 'I have endeavoured to discover how it may be recalled to sense with least violence.'[49] Such a task indeed 'demands more than humanity possesses', so that 'he who exercises it with most praise has very frequent need of indulgence' and may reasonably join Johnson in protesting: '[l]et us be told no more of the dull duty of an editor'. What exacerbates the problem for Johnson is also what provokes the curious mixture of hostility and fascination among those of Derrida's analytically minded detractors who have at least made some attempt to engage with his work, rather than dismissing or denouncing it outright on the strength of second-hand (often grossly inaccurate) report.[50] Once again it is that truly remarkable power of creative-exploratory thinking in and through language whose demands upon the reader go well beyond anything that philosophers (or textual editors) are accustomed to confront in their normal line of work.

Moreover, as Johnson plaintively admits, this aspect of Shakespearean language tends to exert a seductive spell over those – the hapless textual editors – whose business it is to rectify errors of transmission, to select among variant or disputed readings and to strive with least 'violence' (his own term) to make rational sense of corrupt, confused or impossibly convoluted passages. On the one hand he comes out firmly against that free-for-all attitude of hermeneutic licence that had led some previous editors of Shakespeare into regions of self-indulgent creative 'emendation' far in excess of what their task required or indeed what their strictly subordinate role properly allowed. Such excesses must lead to an 'unhappy state' wherein 'pleasure is hid under danger' since they leave the editor hopelessly stranded in a fantasy land of unsupported conjecture where his obtrusive revisions become a kind of ersatz poetry or inferior substitute for the real Shakespearean thing. Even so, Johnson acknowledges, '[t]he allurements of emendation are scarcely resistible', since '[c]onjecture has all the joy and all the pride of invention, and he who has once started a happy change is too much delighted to consider what objections may rise against it.'[51] Thus the scholar's predicament is strangely akin to that of Shakespeare himself for whom, we recall, a pun or other such verbal excrescence

> is what luminous vapours are to the traveler; he follows it at all adventures, it is sure to lead him out of his way . . . It has some malignant power over his mind, and its fascinations are irresistible . . . A quibble was to him the fatal *Cleopatra* for which he lost the world, and was content to lose it.[52]

Where of course their situations differ is with respect to the far greater licence that poetry enjoys in comparison to textual scholarship or literary criticism, even according to Johnson and despite his strictures on Shakespeare in that regard. To be sure, he finds much to deprecate in Shakespeare and, more generally, in the poetry of a period – the early seventeenth century – that he sees as having led up to the English Civil War, for Johnson (like most of his contemporaries) a dreadful recollection and one which he seems to have associated with the kinds of intellectual and cultural disorder manifest in this sort of language. Still he cannot conceal his intense admiration for Shakespeare, especially in the face of classically minded French objectors such as Voltaire.

On occasions this produces a downright conflict between Johnson's sense of the dangers presented by unbridled figuration and his desire to celebrate Shakespeare as a native genius simply not subject to all those crampingly abstract classical rules. Thus 'he who has mazed his imagination in following the phantoms which other writers raise up before him, may here be cured of his delirious ecstasies by reading human sentiments in human language.'[53] The former, strongly negative assessment on grounds of linguistic impropriety or stylistic self-indulgence is one that finds any number of echoes in the hostile commentaries on Derrida – or, one might say, on a certain idea of what Derrida stands for – by analytic philosophers. The latter, just as strongly appreciative remark has no such direct resonance in terms of Derrida's reception history since, after all, his most fervent admirers would scarcely claim that his work has the chief merit of leading us back (as Johnson and Wittgenstein would wish) to a restored sense of being properly at home in the language and culture to which we belong. On the contrary: the likeliest effect of Derrida's writing – on receptive and antipathetic readers alike – is to bring about a sharpened sense of the ways in which language can sometimes throw into question all our self-assured ideas of propriety, intention, communicative purpose and cultural-linguistic 'at-homeness' generally. When he traces out those various deviant logics of 'supplementarity' in Rousseau, 'iterability' in Austin, 'parergonality' in Kant, *différance* in Husserl, the *pharmakon* in Plato and so forth, the result is to raise serious doubt as to whether – in Paul de Man's more dramatic phrasing – 'it is *a priori* certain that language is in any way human'.[54]

Although he shares this doubt at least up to a point and very often finds texts turning out to mean something other (and more) than the author could conceivably have had it in mind to convey, still it is safe to say that Derrida would never make the case in such starkly uncompromising terms. Thus he typically concedes that authorial intentions have a real though limited role to play as an 'indispensable guardrail', that is to say, as imposing some needful restraint on the range of plausible interpretations but not excluding those most likely unintended complexities of sense and logic that a deconstructive reading brings to light.[55] Still, this has the consequence – objectionable to some – that language must be thought of as belonging rather less to the sphere of purposeful and shared (since mutually accessible) meaning and more to a complex interplay of codes, structures, logical entailments and always defeasible expectations that cannot be equated *tout court* with even the most liberal or elastic conception of utterer's intent. Indeed, the whole project of deconstruction can be seen to require the possibility – the necessary possibility, as Derrida insists in one of his many excursions into the realm of modal logic – that intentions may indeed miscarry or be subject to changes of context so far beyond the subject's foreknowledge as to create large problems for any approach (whether in philosophy of language or ethics) premised on a straightforward intentionalist approach.[56]

V

It is not hard to see why this aspect of Derrida's work has tended to generate a hostile response among philosophers belonging to each of the two main categories that William James distinguished in his own time. On the one hand are those 'tough-minded' analytic types, like Searle, for whom his (to them) highly irregular procedures and even more heterodox conclusions can only be evidence that Derrida is either deliberately flouting the basic conditions for logical argument or failing to grasp those conditions. On the other are those 'tender-minded' thinkers whose chief desire is to conserve the intimate and, as they believe, the properly indissoluble tie between language and the various human contexts – social, interpersonal, above all intentional – that constitute the very element or condition of possibility for meaningful language. From both points of view – dividing as they do pretty much along the line that currently distinguishes hardcore analytic from this or that variety of 'ordinary language' philosophy – there is something about Derrida's writing that constitutes a standing provocation or downright affront. So I should not wish to press too hard on the comparison between Derrida's and Shakespeare's reception histories, partly because the two cases involve such grossly disparate time spans but also because there is no plausible equivalent, on Derrida's side, to the idea expressed by Johnson (along with many others) that Shakespeare, despite his verbal excesses, none the less stands out as a true representative of natural feelings naturally expressed. That is to say, his writings and the kinds of response they evoke (or provoke) are about as far as possible from the Wittgensteinian idea of philosophy as a form of linguistic therapy – a non-Freudian 'talking cure' – designed to grant readers a welcome release from the toils of obsessive philosophical enquiry or metaphysical 'bewitchment by language'.

All the same one might object that this therapeutic reading of late Wittgenstein is itself as far as possible from the actual effect of Wittgenstein's late writings on the many enquirers who have found themselves bewitched by the various problem topics – such as private language, rule-following, other minds, intentionality or the role of logic vis-à-vis the natural sciences – which have each now given rise to a vast amount of close textual exegesis and (very often) fiercely partisan debate.[57] Indeed there is a certain irony about the claim of some Wittgenstein-influenced philosophers that anyone who has read and truly absorbed the lesson of his thought will be wholly unimpressed by Derrida's arguments since they are the product of a sceptical mindset that purports to doubt what is simply self-evident as soon as one accepts the authority of communal warrant and is thereby absolved from raising such futile and misbegotten philosophic questions.[58] For there is, I would suggest, about as much plausibility in this claim as in the notion that some of Shakespeare's more challenging, intricate or downright baffling passages might – in Dr Johnson's emollient phrase – be 'recalled to sense' with minimal 'violence'. Thus to read Derrida via Wittgenstein as an exercise in the therapeutic powers of 'ordinary language' is in truth no more convincing than those famously inept eighteenth-century attempts to tame the excesses of Shakespearean language and dramatic content by various kinds of heavy-handed editorial intervention.

Here I should note that there do exist alternatives to this particular view of the Wittgenstein/Derrida relationship, one that sees the Wittgensteinian appeal to 'language games' and shared cultural 'forms of life' as having provided all the needful resources for drawing the sting of Derrida's (supposedly) ultra-sceptical approach. Thus some recent commentators, among them Henry Staten (drawing on the work of O. K. Bouwsma), put the case for a reading that stresses the adventurous, sceptically inclined, philosophically risky and – above all – linguistically self-reflexive quality of Wittgenstein's writing, or those aspects that bring it much closer to Derrida than to the kinds of 'therapeutic' reading promoted by mainstream exegetes.[59] For others it is not so much a question of showing Wittgenstein to have been a deconstructionist *avant la lettre* but rather of showing how his texts lie open to a deconstructive approach precisely in so far as they purport (or are purported by his orthodox disciples) to demonstrate the wrong-headedness or downright nonsensical nature of any such approach.[60] On this view the problems just won't go away for any amount of therapeutic coaxing or well-meant curative advice.

So the question is really, as Derrida remarks apropos Rousseau and the 'logic of supplementarity', that of deciding the scope and limits of any appeal to authorial intention, or – in this case – the extent of Wittgenstein's deliberative power in selecting just those expressive resources that will best, most effectively (or least mistakably) serve to convey his intentional gist. Thus on the one hand some regard for what the author had in mind – so far as one can hope to retrieve it – is a *sine qua non* of responsible commentary since '[w]ithout this recognition and this respect, critical production would risk developing in any direction at all and authorize itself to say almost anything.'[61] Yet on the other, as Derrida remarks, such recognition neither can nor should take the form of simply 'reproducing, by the effaced and respectful doubling of commentary, the conscious, voluntary, intentional relationship that the writer institutes in his exchanges with the history to which he belongs thanks to the element of language'.[62]

For this is to espouse both a notion of privileged epistemic access which Wittgenstein, for one, would be quick to denounce and a likewise highly questionable notion of 'respect' – of interpretative truth or fidelity – the effect of which would be to close off any active engagement on the reader's part with aspects of the text that might go against the received, canonical or orthodox intentionalist account. Rather it is a question of descrying and tracing through the text 'a certain relationship, unperceived by the writer, between what he commands and what he does not command of the patterns of the language that he uses'.[63]

In which case, so the Derridean will argue, there may be much that escapes the notice of those orthodox interpreters who claim to take Wittgenstein strictly at his word when advancing their view of his later work as purely an exercise in linguistic therapy, or a cure for that strange form of 'bewitchment by language' that has led philosophers so far off the path of communal (or common-sense) usage. What drops out completely on this account – or gets passed over in tactful silence – is the conjunction of a highly figurative style where the metaphors are crucially load-bearing in terms of argumentative content with a literal-minded habit of pursuing their implications to the point where these create large problems both for Wittgenstein and his fideist commentators. Thus, to take the most conspicuous example, the whole debate around rule-following can be seen to have become hung up on his use of certain strongly tendentious (not to say grossly misleading) metaphors which thereafter acquired a talismanic power over those who accepted them as setting the terms for debate.[64] Among them is the 'super-rigid rail' metaphor which asks us to treat the issue of correctness in mathematics, logic and the formal sciences as a choice between getting things right as a matter of communal warrant and getting things right as a matter of reasoning in accordance with objective, practice-transcendent rules that stretch out to encompass every possible application beyond the utmost limits of our present conceptual grasp. So if the latter notion lacks credibility then the former communitarian idea is, according to Wittgenstein, the best we can hope for and in any case all that we properly or practically need.

I have written elsewhere about the power over thought wielded by this super-rigid rail metaphor and others like it, a contagious power whose effect is most often to impose a crampingly narrow idea of the philosophical options available rather than the liberating sense of new possibilities that metaphor is commonly supposed to offer by those (whether literary critics or philosophers) who extol its creative virtues.[65] What is so odd about Wittgenstein's reception history – and symptomatic of the unresolved (maybe unresolvable) tensions within his work – is the way that certain figures of thought take over and dictate the subsequent course of his own and the orthodox commentators' thought. Indeed they exercise a force of suggestion very like those 'super-rigid' rails whose existence – or aptness as a metaphor for rule-following – he posits only to reject it outright, but which have figured centrally in recent debate as a foil for the Wittgenstein-approved (yet deeply problematical) conception of truth or correctness in such matters as entirely a matter of communal 'agreement in judgement'. That is to say, their metaphorical-suggestive power becomes an instance of that same linguistic 'bewitchment' – that tendency of language to set thought running along false or dead-end tracks – that Wittgenstein regarded as a chief source of philosophical error and confusion.

Here again one can see how Derrida and Wittgenstein both occupy a fiercely contested zone in terms of this 'ancient quarrel' (as Plato already described it) between philosophy and poetry, concept and metaphor, or reason and rhetoric. However, they occupy that zone in very different ways and with very different kinds of impact on the thinking of those who have been influenced by them. In Wittgenstein's case, it has led to a curious situation where some of the most intensive consequent debate often gives the distinct impression of having been pre-programmed by metaphors or idiosyncratic turns of thought in Wittgenstein's writing which have just the opposite of their intended (therapeutic or problem-solving) effect. If anything this tendency has been reinforced by his insistence, faithfully echoed in the orthodox camp, that philosophy should not be in the business of propounding doctrines, theories, hypotheses or (least of all) Russell-Frege style projects for correcting or reforming – even seeking to clarify – our everyday forms of communicative utterance. For very often the main result of this self-denying ordinance has been to block just the kind of keenly analytic self-awareness with regard to its own and other thinkers' linguistic practices that has typified alternative, more heterodox modes (hardly 'schools') of Wittgenstein commentary. Among the latter, as I have said, are hermeneutically adventurous readings that draw upon Derrida's work as a means of opening up Wittgenstein's text, so to speak, by performative example or else by way of deconstructing those various metaphors that can be shown to have exerted a powerful grip on his own thought, as likewise on that of his more fideist or literal-minded interpreters.

In Derrida's case, conversely, what we find is a remarkable, at times well-nigh Shakespearean degree of verbal creativity joined to a level of self-conscious linguistic as well as conceptual-analytic awareness that again has a markedly divisive effect on the commentators although not in quite the same way. On the one side are those – like his earliest admirers in the 'literary' camp, such as Geoffrey Hartman, not to mention 'post'-philosophers like Rorty – who gently deplore or just ignore what they see as Derrida's residual attachment to certain philosophical ways of thought and instead play up his extraordinary gifts as a stylist or imaginative writer.[66] On the other are those, like myself and Rodolphe Gasché, who make the case for his continued (however heterodox) engagement with distinctively philosophical issues.[67] However, it is fair to say that both parties, whatever their sharp and much-debated differences of view, would at any rate be able to reach broad agreement on two major claims. Thus they could each without loss of face assent to the thesis that Derrida's philosophical investigations are conducted in and through what Hartman once termed an 'answerable style', or a language that answers in the highest degree to the demands placed it by sustained reflection on the nature and scope of human linguistic creativity.[68] At the same time – and by no means incompatibly with this – it should be evident (anti-philosophical prejudice aside) that such reflection requires a degree of critical acumen that goes well beyond the kinds of free-associative verbal gymnastics that some of those early commentators took to be Derrida's greatest gift not only to literary criticism but also to philosophy and the human sciences in general. Few writers have managed to offer so distinctive and creative a slant on our everyday or specialised (e.g. philosophical) modes of talk while none the less maintaining an acute awareness – an acutely *analytical* awareness, in the non-proprietary sense of that term – of what is going on in the production and reception of just such utterly singular yet utterly commonplace linguistic events.

It is here that Derrida's texts invite comparison with Shakespeare despite belonging to a genre of discourse that cannot be reduced – *pace* admirers like Rorty and also those, like Habermas, who criticise Derrida on the same putative grounds – to yet another 'kind of writing' fully on a par with poetry, fiction, literary criticism or any other genre you care to name so long as it finds room for creativity of Derrida's kind.[69] Moreover it is here that one can best make a start in explaining why they have met with a degree of resistance, hostility and resolute misreading unequalled except in the case of those philosophers – Epicurus, Hume, Spinoza and Sartre among them – who have been exposed to such treatment largely on account of their heterodox religious or political views. In the context of present-day analytic (or 'post-analytic') philosophy there are still clear signs of that conflict – nowadays more of an uneasy truce – that Rorty wrote about in 1967 when assembling the various essays for his edited volume *The Linguistic Turn*.[70] It is a context in which there can be seen to exist certain strongly marked generic expectations, among them that any philosophical text belonging to that same (albeit very broad) tradition will owe allegiance to one or other of its two main sub-genres. That is to say, there should be some indication – explicit or otherwise – of its alignment either with that *echt*-analytic mode of thought descending from Russell and Frege which grants logic pride of place over natural ('ordinary') language or else with that other, Wittgenstein- or Austin-influenced mode that endorses the reverse, i.e. 'language-first', order of priority. When the signal is absent, as so often in Derrida's analytically acute yet hermeneutically ultra-responsive investigations, then there tends to develop just the kind of resistance for which psychoanalysts could no doubt produce any number of plausible explanations but which are better accounted for in terms of this clash between opposing philosophical viewpoints. For again it is among the most notable (and also most suggestively Shakespearean) aspects of Derrida's writing that he manages so often to combine an extraordinary power of metaphorical or figural expressiveness with an equally remarkable power of self-reflexive conceptual and critical analysis.

Indeed, one effect of reading his work upon any but the most diehard opponent must be to raise large questions concerning the very idea of 'ordinary' language given how many and varied are the ways in which language typically (not exceptionally) proves to outrun the utmost resources of any such normalising approach. Even then – as Derrida brings out to such striking (and for some, like Searle, such disquieting) effect – there is a further important distinction to be drawn between that approach in its orthodox Wittgensteinian or 'therapeutic' guise and Austin's keenly self-critical, at times ironically self-subverting sense of linguistic possibility. It seems to me that what has prevented many Anglophone philosophers from taking adequate stock of Derrida's work is also what might yet enable that work to exercise a highly beneficial effect on the impasse that Rorty was among the first to diagnose and which still leaves its mark on the various debates that occupy present-day philosophy of language. In brief, it is the capacity – shared by Austin and Derrida – to see some way around the communicative block that typically results when the analytic drive for logical rigour or conceptual precision comes up against the contrary emphasis (most often with its source in late Wittgenstein) on the sheer multiplicity of language games or cultural life-forms along with their equally diverse range of context-specific criteria.

VI

One version of the story, recounted on both sides but mostly by those of an analytic mind, prefers to tell it in terms of the rift between Anglophone and 'continental' (i.e. post-Kantian mainland European) philosophy. What this version manages to keep from view – whether or not by conscious design – is the extent to which late Wittgenstein, despite his recruitment as an honorary member of the former camp, in fact stands squarely and avowedly askew to every chief tenet of mainstream analytic thought. After all this was just the purport of his celebrated mid-career switch of priorities from logical analysis to a wise acceptance of the wisdom enshrined in ordinary language, thereby demoting logic (along with mathematics and philosophy of science) from any kind of privileged status vis-à-vis our everyday-communicative modes of linguistic exchange. However – as I have argued – the effect of Wittgenstein's therapeutic ministrations has been not so much to help philosophy get over its various needless (since self-inflicted) problems and dilemmas but rather to reinforce them by encouraging the view that analysis somehow excludes or debars an adequate respect for the subtleties, nuances and depths of implication conveyed by such everyday usage. Moreover, this idea of a basically antagonistic relation between language as deployed in its 'normal' kinds of expressive or communicative context and language as a proper subject or topic of conceptual analysis is one that runs deep in Wittgenstein's thinking and which emerges with particular force in his remarks about Shakespeare's deplorable lapses of style and taste.

Such negative responses have a long pre-history in Shakespeare criticism and – as the example of Johnson very pointedly shows – are by no means confined to rabid detractors or those (like Tolstoy and Shaw) with their own doctrinal or in some way self-interested axe to grind. Rather it seems to be a matter of resistance to that highly specific combination in Shakespeare – as likewise in Derrida's most complex and philosophically challenging texts – of performative inventiveness or creativity with a power and depth of analytical thought that often overtaxes the best efforts of plain-prose commentary. If there is one characteristic that Shakespeare possesses in the highest degree and that is brought out by his best, most perceptive and rewarding exegetes it is just this capacity to stretch and redefine what counts as an adequate (that is, a duly appreciative but also a sufficiently thought-out or analytically cogent) response. In this chapter I have focused mainly on critics, from Johnson to Wittgenstein, in whom the experience of reading Shakespeare and the effort to achieve that response have somehow been thwarted or thrown off track by an unresolved conflict between those apparently opposite and mutually exclusive poles. That is to say, the business of conceptual analysis has typically been seen as posing a threat to any mode of 'appreciative' response that would claim to value the poetry for what it is – or what it holds out to the sympathetic reader – quite apart from such alien since overly rationalist and hence *ipso facto* un-poetic (or anti-poetic) intrusions.

This pattern of response goes back to the earliest debates within Western literary criticism, such as Socrates' exchanges with the rhapsodes and other purveyors of (as he thought) a false and beguiling poetic pseudo-wisdom which collapsed into manifest incoherence at the least touch of rational or philosophic thought. Since then it has rumbled on at intervals, especially during the Renaissance and whenever the claims of poetry seemed set to encroach upon the philosophers' domain or vice versa. This 'ancient quarrel', as Plato already described it, acquired a yet more strident and defensive edge in the face of those modern developments – spectacularly heralded by William Empson's 1930 book *Seven Types of Ambiguity* – which made a virtue of hard-pressed verbal analysis and therefore tended to place highest value on the most (to them) rewardingly complex kinds of literary language.[71] Thus Empson went out of his way to anticipate the objections of 'appreciative' critics who – sure enough – lined up to denounce his tough-minded rationalist approach as at best a tedious distraction from the poetry and at worst a threat to the sources of any genuine, i.e. sensitive and deeply attuned, poetic response. Moreover, this concern to keep analysis (or a certain kind of analysis) safely apart from the business of literary criticism is evident not only among the apostles of pure, unaided intuition but also in other, more robustly unsentimental critics whenever issues of 'theory' loom into view. Thus it is often prominent in the work of those – like F. R. Leavis – who stress the importance of textual close-reading but who focus on the typically 'Shakespearean' aspects of poetic language (imagery, metaphor, sensuous 'enactment', the subtle heightening of dramatic tension through a complex interplay of speech-rhythm and metre) as distinct from the sorts of logico-semantic complication that so preoccupy a critic like Empson.[72]

The *locus classicus* here is Leavis's largely dismissive, even scornful response to René Wellek's well-meant request that he offer some explicit 'philosophical' account of the aims, priorities and modes of evaluative judgement that lay behind his various readings of poetry and the firm declarations of comparative worth that always issued from them. To which Leavis just as firmly replied by rejecting Wellek's invitation and denying *tout court* that 'philosophy' – or theory – could or should have anything whatever to do with the process of responding as intently as possible to the poem in hand and thereby arriving at a properly discriminate, critically (rather than theoretically) informed evaluation.[73] In short, this idea of a 'Shakespearean' use of language does triple duty as a compact statement of critical belief, a touchstone by which other poets may be judged or ranked, and – not least – a means of signalling his downright opposition to any idea that literary criticism might stand to benefit (i.e. to improve or refine that process) by some advance in its powers of theoretical grasp.

Along with it goes the kindred idea that too much analysis, especially when focused on the logical (or logico-semantic) structures of language, is sure to have a deleterious effect by diverting attention from those other, more authentically 'Shakespearean' attributes that call upon the reader's capacity to realise their vividly enacted sensuous, i.e. visual or tactile, character. Here, as so often, the term 'analytic' tends to hide a significant difference of views since in Leavis's case the analysis of language very markedly observes certain limits on its range or scope of application. They have to do with what he – like T. S. Eliot before him – considers the high-point or *echt-*Shakespearean moment in English poetic tradition where the perfect fusion of intellect and feeling or thought and emotion that typified the poetry of the early seventeenth century gave way to a subsequent 'dissociation of sensibility' and a constant pendulum-swing between periods of overly cerebral, emotionally undercharged versifying and periods of intense but intellectually vapid (e.g. romantic) self-indulgence.[74] This is not the place for an extended commentary on the gaps, elisions and distortions involved in the Eliot-Leavis historical purview and its highly selective account of that canonical or critically sanctioned line of descent.[75] More to the point is its way of encoding that anti-theoretical or anti-philosophic bias through a largely mythic but none the less effective historical and cultural narrative. This in turn derives much of its persuasive force – for those of a likewise sceptical mind concerning the claims of analysis – from its invocation of the various dualisms (as between thought and feeling or theory and experience) which are then taken to show just how far we have travelled from the kind of complex yet unimpeded response that Shakespeare both embodies in the highest degree and requires of the fit reader.

On the contrary, I would argue: the best modern critics of Shakespeare are those like Empson who have shown the most sensitive attunement to nuances of verbal implication while also – quite compatibly with this – providing some account of the linguistic structures (in Empson's case, the logico-semantic 'machinery') without which those subtleties would fail to register. Indeed, the main line of development in Empson's thought is precisely an advance from the brilliant though somewhat ad hoc and intuitive approach of *Seven Types of Ambiguity* to the kinds of philosophically informed (that is to say conceptually precise and logically articulated) reading that typify his essays on Shakespeare, Pope, Wordsworth, Jane Austen and other writers in *The Structure of Complex Words*.[76] Above all it is the chapters on Shakespeare – on the semantics of 'sense' in *Measure for Measure*, of 'dog' in *Timon of Athens* and (most impressively) of 'fool' in *King Lear* – that show Empson exploring this ground between the normative constraints of 'ordinary language' and the limits to which language may at times be forced under pressure of extreme expressive, dramatic or indeed 'ordinary' (everyday-practical) circumstance. I have put the case here that analytic philosophy – whether in the Frege-Russell or the late Wittgensteinian line of descent – has shown itself peculiarly prone to the sorts of dilemma that typically arise when these two dimensions are allowed to come apart, or so far apart that any attempt at mediation is apt to appear misguided or forlorn. Indeed one could claim without serious overstatement that its history has been slung between these rival conceptions (most strikingly embodied in Wittgenstein's mid-career change of mind) and, moreover, that it is through their kindred resistance to this drastically compartmentalised mode of thought that Shakespeare and Derrida have come to represent so potent or provocative a challenge.

Hence the striking resemblance between their two reception histories, at least in so far as they have both attracted criticism – or downright hostility – on account of their proneness (so the charge sheet runs) to let language run amok in figural excesses or metaphoric deviations from the normative standards of straightforward communicative discourse. In more positive terms, what they both have to offer is a striking example of the way that language can transgress those standards – as for instance through the kinds of 'deviant' performative that Derrida enacts as well as describes in his work on Austin – while none the less maintaining an acutely analytical awareness with regard to just such inherent possibilities of divergence from the everyday or commonplace expressive norm.

VII

That analytic philosophy has problems in this respect can perhaps best be seen by comparing two stages in Donald Davidson's thinking about the issue of 'radical interpretation'. This is basically the issue as to how, or whether, we can possibly achieve mutual understanding across large differences of cultural-linguistic or socio-historical context. The contrast in question is that between his erstwhile arguments for a truth-based logico-semantic approach to the problem with his later claim that we had much better junk the appeal to 'prior theories' of whatever kind since they operate at a level of abstraction so remote from the business of practical-communicative uptake as to offer no help whatsoever in answering the question.[77] Rather we should give up not only our attachment to those generalised theories of language but also (remarkably) the very idea that there exists any such thing as 'a language' if by that is meant the sort of notional entity talked about by structuralists, Chomskian grammarians, philosophers of language after Frege and Russell, and systematising linguists of various technical persuasion. Quite simply we figure out what other people mean through an ad hoc mixture of 'wit, luck and wisdom' joined to a knack for picking up contextual clues and cues and also, crucially, a readiness (on the Davidsonian 'principle of charity') to make large allowance for the sundry malapropisms, slips of the tongue, agrammaticalities, out-of-the-way idioms, associative quirks and so forth which infect far more of our everyday discourse than we might wish to think. Thus it is a sheer waste of time to devise abstract theories of grammatical competence or linguistic-communicative grasp since they will either be pitched at too a high a level of generality (and hence do nothing to explain what transpires in particular contexts of utterance) or else go so far toward scaling down their systematic claims that their 'field of application' will be 'vanishingly small', i.e. very often just the one-off exchange or item of discourse in question. For according to this ultra-pragmatist or 'minimalist-semantic' account there is no difference – or none that makes any difference in practical terms – between 'knowing a language' and 'knowing our way around in the world generally'. And again: '[w]hat two people need . . . is the ability to converge on passing theories from utterance to utterance', since '[t]heir starting points, however far back we want to take them, will usually be very different', in which case '[s]o also, then, will the strategies and stratagems that bring about convergence differ'.[78]

I have written elsewhere about the problems (to put it mildly) with Davidson's minimalist approach and its failure to provide anything like an adequate account of how language-users manage to communicate despite and across the various kinds of semantic, syntactic, conceptual, doctrinal, cultural or other such differences between them.[79] These problems are all the more striking for the fact that Davidson had earlier devoted so much attention to the business of explaining why conceptual-scheme talk – along with the Quinean idea of ontological relativity, the Kuhnian notion of 'incommensurable' paradigms, Whorfian cultural-linguistic relativism and other such contemporary academic fads – should best be regarded as merely the product of an over-concentration on the semantics of natural languages and an underestimation of the role played by certain logical constants or structural invariants.[80] Thus the remedy for all these philosophical afflictions is to switch focus from semantics – which of course will embody a great variety of culturally salient terms, features and distinctions – to the range of logico-syntactic properties (e.g. connectives, prepositions, pronouns, modal auxiliaries, devices for conjunction, disjunction, cross-reference, anaphora and the like) which must form a part of any socially or humanly adequate language since without them it would be unable to express the most basic thoughts and beliefs. However, nothing remains of all this in Davidson's theory to end all theories except a vestige of the Principle of Charity which he had once specified in strongly normative and philosophically substantive terms but which now serves merely as a pretext for ensuring that other people's meanings, intentions and beliefs come out right (that is, make adequate sense or possess a fair claim to rational warrant) by our own interpretative lights. In other words it is a somewhat patronising version of 'charity' that, in cases of communicative difficulty, leans so far toward discounting or ignoring the plain linguistic sense of what they say in order to impute some (to us) acceptable version of speaker's intent that it risks treating them rather in the way that high-minded (or high-handed) benefactors once treated the deserving poor.

Thus the upshot of Davidson's minimalist-semantic approach is pretty much to abandon any thought of providing what he had set out to achieve in his earlier work. There he had sought mainly to build a case against relativist talk of language games, discourses, paradigms or conceptual schemes, one that would show such talk to be incoherent and, moreover, make room for a truth-based, logico-semantic approach through what amounts to a form of transcendental deduction from the conditions of possibility for language and communication in general. All the more ironic, therefore, that this approach shows distinct signs of having been influenced (however far back or unwittingly) by his reading of Empson's *The Structure of Complex Words*.[81] In particular he seems to have retained the idea of how certain words can take on a force of 'compacted statement' by reason of their being not merely 'ambiguous' (as in Empson's earlier, rather all-purpose use of that term) but possessed of an internal semantic structure – an implied 'equation' or set of equations between its various component senses – which in turn gives a hold for ascriptions of authorial intent. What makes this possible is the way that language users can modify the gist of complex words so as to communicate heterodox meanings, ideas or even doctrines of an ethical, political or philosophic sort by implying a non-standard order of priority within these structures of logico-semantic entailment. Given that Davidson footnotes Empson's book in the course of his essay on metaphor it seems likely that Empson's cardinal distinction between 'head' and 'chief' senses – that which predominates in common usage at any given time and that which a speaker/writer 'pushes forward' as locally most germane to their purpose – may have had a role in Davidson's formulation of the prior theory/passing theory dualism.

However, some crucial elements have dropped out along the way including not only Empson's entire theoretical apparatus but also any attempt to explain how language might communicate beyond that ultra-pragmatist and (as Davidson is keen to stress) in large part extra-linguistic appeal to 'wit, luck and wisdom'. So likewise, in Davidson's theory of metaphor, what we are left with – and what has struck many readers as a massive evasion of the issue – is another theory-to-end-all-theories, that is to say, the idea that quite simply there is no such thing as 'metaphor' if by that we mean some special or distinctive use of language concerning which it might be possible (or useful) to have some correspondingly special or distinctive theoretical account.[82] Rather we should just take metaphorical language at its face (i.e. literal) value and imagine what the world would indeed be like if, for instance, the sea danced, or one's love was a red, red rose, or one saw eternity in a grain of sand, or could take up arms against a sea of troubles. That this fails to answer (or even to address) the philosophical issue about metaphor – how it is that certain 'deviant' uses of language can produce such a truly extraordinary range of striking, revelatory, at times disconcerting and often thought-provocative effects – is the verdict of those unconvinced by Davidson's brisk way with that issue, while others (mostly of a pragmatist or minimalist-semantic persuasion) regard it as offering a welcome release from all that misapplied philosophic effort. My own view, as should be clear by now, is that it doesn't and cannot come close to explaining how everyday talk – let alone Shakespearean and other such densely metaphoric or semantically complex language – manages to communicate despite (or precisely in virtue of) its frequent deviations from the everyday norm.

Of course it may be said that this is just Davidson's point: that there is no use for theories of grammatical, semantic or general linguistic 'competence' if these embody some range of assumed normative constraints which are sure to be constantly flouted in the business of actual (whether routine, practical-informative or poetic and creative) utterance. Thus his argument turns precisely on the claim that language – both in its 'ordinary' and its more extraordinary modes – is full of such slips, malapropisms, nonce-usages, metaphors, ambiguities and other such infractions of the communal norm, in which case we must as practised interpreters be tolerant of them to a high degree as well as very good at making allowance and implicitly correcting for perceived errors as the talk goes along. Whence – to repeat – Davidson's idea that 'prior theories' are pretty much useless when it comes to figuring out speaker's (as opposed to linguistic) meaning, that is, what people intend to get across rather than what they would be taken to mean according to some merely notional standard of correctness specified in structural or logico-semantic terms. However his appeal to 'passing theories' can scarcely fill the gap thus created since, on Davidson's own submission, they are not so much 'theories' in the normal, generalised or trans-contextual sense of that term but rather the kinds of adaptive strategy or one-off interpretative rules of thumb whose usefulness is apt to vary inversely with their scope or range of application.

If comparison with Empson – especially with Empson's writings on Shakespeare – brings out very sharply the inherent limitations of any such approach, then so does comparison with Derrida's practice of rhetorically alert and linguistically inventive but none the less analytically acute as well as philosophically informed close-reading. I stress this point because it has lately struck some commentators keen to build bridges between the 'two traditions' that Davidson's 'mini-malist-semantic' idea might latch neatly onto Derrida's proposal – in the context of speech-act theory – for a likewise minimalist concep-tion of performative 'iterability'.[83] The latter he conceives in largely negative terms as that which somehow carries across from one utterance to the next despite all the problems that arise with Austin's attempt to specify just what should count as an authentic (sincere or good-faith) performative uttered in the right (circumstantially apt or contextually warranted) conditions. So there would seem, on the face of it, good enough reason for drawing this analogy and, moreover, for proposing an *entente cordiale* between certain developments in 'post-analytic' philosophy for which Davidson's essay stands as a representative sample and that aspect of recent 'continental' thought which finds one of its most typical (albeit, to some, most sharply provocative) rehearsals in Derrida's deconstructive reading of Austin. However, this apparent convergence of the twain is really no such thing since Davidson's approach, if consistently applied, would leave no room for that subtle interplay of creative and analytic thought – or language in its performative and constative dimensions – which is such a marked feature of Derrida's work.

The same applies to Empson's literary criticism in so far as it explores depths and degrees of logico-semantic complexity that go beyond anything remotely describable in Davidsonian minimalist terms. To be sure, there is little enough in common between Empson and Derrida as regards just about every other aspect of their work. Nothing could be further from Derrida's intellectual temperament than Empson's outlook of sturdy common-sense rationalism, tending as it did to place a curb on his otherwise notably Derridean flair for brilliant, often (as some thought) far-fetched or over-ingenious but never less than exhilarating forays into the realm of speculative thought. However, what they do have in common – and what gives them both a fair claim to represent the 'Shakespearean' element that is firmly repressed in a good deal of present-day literary-critical as well as philosophic discourse – is this striking capacity to bring together aspects of language (the poetic-creative and the conceptual-analytic) that are often very firmly put asunder. Hence the extreme hostility sometimes evoked among analytic types by Derrida's readings of philosophical texts, especially texts from their own canonical tradition, and above all texts – like those of Austin – which allow him to demonstrate just how much is concealed from view by an orthodox approach that reads them in accordance with its own fixed preconceptions and which thus regularly fails to perceive the extraordinary nature of (so-called) ordinary language.

Hence also the irony that Wittgenstein's influence should have done so much to discourage the kinds of speculative thinking that might result from an over-willingness to let language 'go on holiday' and thereby risk losing touch with the wholesome restraints of 'ordinary', communal or non-philosophical usage. As I have said, this irony is all the more curious (and all the more curiously lost on his orthodox disciples and exegetes) for the fact that Wittgenstein was himself such a gifted inventor of metaphors, similes, stretched (even strained) analogies, fictive exempla, imaginary dialogues, zany thought experiments and other such markedly 'literary' means of oblique or indirect communication. He can thus be read – like Johnson on Shakespeare and various philosophers (Locke and Kant among them) on the topic of metaphor or figural language in general – as a victim of that same perverse compulsion that seems to push the detractors of such language into venturesome or downright extravagant flights of metaphorical fancy.[84] All the same, as Derrida is quick to point out in 'White Mythology', one has scarcely started to broach this topic if one jumps – like Rorty and a good few literary deconstructionists – to the conclusion that all concepts are metaphors, all philosophy just a 'kind of writing', all appeals to reason just a mode of rhetorical imposition, and so forth. Rather it is necessary to think these oppositions through with a degree of conceptual rigour and precision that cannot be achieved except by deploying the various descriptive, analytic and explanatory resources bequeathed by the philosophic discourse on metaphor from Aristotle to the present. What Derrida shows in various ways throughout his work is how philosophy can do just that – can fully respect those exacting standards of historically informed and logically disciplined argument – even while exploring the outermost bounds of linguistic-conceptual possibility. It is in this respect chiefly that his texts have presented such a pointed challenge – or standing provocation – to philosophers of various doctrinal persuasions, whether *echt*-analytic or Wittgensteinian, whose concern is more with beating those bounds than with reflecting creatively and critically upon them.

Notes

1. John Keats, *The Letters of John Keats: A Selection*, ed. Robert Gittings (Oxford: Oxford University Press, 1970), p. 43.
2. For a survey and critique of various hostile or uncomprehending responses to Derrida, see Christopher Norris, 'Of an apoplectic tone recently adopted in philosophy', in Norris, *Reclaiming Truth: Contribution to a Critique of Cultural Relativism* (London: Lawrence & Wishart, 1996), pp. 222–53; also Maurice Charney (ed.), *'Bad' Shakespeare: Revaluations of the Shakespeare Canon* (London and Toronto: Associated University Presses, 1988).
3. See especially the various references to Shakespeare in Ludwig Wittgenstein, *Culture and Value*, 2nd edn, ed. G. H. von Wright, trans. Peter Winch (Oxford: Blackwell, 1980); also Norris, 'Extraordinary language: why Wittgenstein didn't like Shakespeare', in *Fiction, Philosophy and Literary Theory: Will the Real Saul Kripke Please Stand Up?* (London: Continuum, 2007), pp. 159–211.
4. See especially Martha Nussbaum, *Love's Knowledge: Essays on Philosophy and Literature* (New York: Oxford University Press, 1990).
5. See, for instance, Stanley Cavell, *Disowning Knowledge in Seven Plays of Shakespeare*, 2nd edn (Cambridge: Cambridge University Press, 2003).
6. See note 2, above; also Derrida, 'Afterword: toward an ethic of conversation', in Gerald Graff (ed.), *Limited Inc* (Evanston: Northwestern University Press, 1989), pp. 111–54.
7. Wittgenstein, *Culture and Value*, op. cit., p. 48e.
8. See George Bernard Shaw, *Shaw on Shakespeare*, ed. Edwin Wilson (Harmondsworth: Penguin, 1968), and Leo Tolstoy, *What Is Art?*, trans. Almyer Maude (New York: Macmillan, 1960).
9. Samuel Johnson, 'Preface to the plays of William Shakespeare', in *Dr Johnson on Shakespeare*, ed. W. K. Wimsatt (Harmondsworth: Penguin, 1969); also Johnson, *The Lives of the Most Eminent English Poets: With Critical Observations on Their Works*, ed. Roger Lonsdale, 4 vols (Oxford: Oxford University Press, 2006).
10. See notes 2 and 6, above; also John Searle, 'Reiterating the differences', *Glyph*, Vol. 1 (Baltimore: Johns Hopkins University Press, 1975),

pp. 198–208, and Bernard Harrison, 'White mythology revisited: Derrida and his critics on reason and rhetoric', *Critical Inquiry*, 25: 3 (Spring 1999), pp. 505–34.

11. See especially Ludwig Wittgenstein, *Philosophical Investigations*, trans. G. E. M. Anscombe (Oxford: Blackwell, 1953), and *On Certainty*, ed. and trans. G. E. M. Anscombe and G. H. von Wright (Blackwell, 1969); also – for some highly illuminating commentary – Stanley Cavell, *Must We Mean What We Say?* (New York: Oxford University Press, 1969), and *Philosophical Passages: Wittgenstein, Emerson, Austin, Derrida* (Oxford: Blackwell, 1994).

12. Wittgenstein, *Culture and Value*, op. cit., p. 49e.

13. Ibid., p. 83e.

14. Wittgenstein, *Tractatus Logico-Philosophicus*, trans. D. F. Pears and B. F. McGuiness (London: Routledge & Kegan Paul, 1961).

15. See especially Alice Crary and Rupert Read (eds), *The New Wittgenstein* (London: Routledge, 2000); also James Conant, 'Putting two and two together: Kierkegaard, Wittgenstein and the point of view for their work as authors', in Timothy Tessin and Mario von der Ruhr (eds), *Philosophy and the Grammar of Religious Belief* (Basingstoke: Macmillan, 1995), pp. 248–331.

16. Jürgen Habermas, 'Excursus: on levelling the genre-distinction between philosophy and literature', in *The Philosophical Discourse of Modernity: Twelve Lectures*, trans. Frederick Lawrence (Cambridge: Polity Press, 1987), pp. 185–210; also Norris, 'Deconstruction, postmodernsm and philosophy: Habermas on Derrida', in *What's Wrong with Postmodernism* (Hemel Hempstead: Harvester Wheatsheaf, 1990), pp. 49–76.

17. See notes 2 and 16, above; also Norris, *Derrida* (London: Fontana, 1987); *Fiction, Philosophy and Literary Theory*, op. cit.

18. See, for instance, Derrida, *'Speech and Phenomena' and Other Essays on Husserl's Theory of Signs*, trans. David B. Allison (Evanston: Northwestern University Press, 1973); *Of Grammatology*, trans. Gayatri C. Spivak (Baltimore: Johns Hopkins University Press, 1974); *Writing and Difference*, trans. Alan Bass (London: Routledge & Kegan Paul, 1978); *Dissemination*, trans. Barbara Johnson (London: Athlone Press, 1981); *Margins of Philosophy*, trans. Alan Bass (Chicago: University of Chicago Press, 1982); 'Parergon', in *The Truth in Painting*, trans. Geoff Bennington and Ian McLeod (Chicago: University of Chicago Press, 1987), pp. 15–147.

19. See especially Christopher Norris, 'Derrida on Rousseau: deconstruction as philosophy of logic', in Norris and David Roden (eds), *Jacques Derrida*, 4 vols (London: Sage, 2003), Vol. 2, pp. 70–124; also Graham Priest, 'Derrida and self-reference', *Australasian Journal of Philosophy*, 72 (1994), pp. 103–11 and – from a somewhat different standpoint

– Samuel C. Wheeler, *Deconstruction as Analytic Philosophy* (Stanford: Stanford University Press, 2000).

20. See Jacques Derrida, 'Signature event context', *Glyph*, Vol. 1 (Baltimore: Johns Hopkins University Press, 1975), pp. 172–97; John Searle, 'Reiterating the differences', op. cit., and Derrida, 'Afterword: toward an ethic of conversation', op. cit.

21. Derrida, *Signéponge/Signsponge*, trans. Richard Rand (New York: Columbia University Press, 1989); also Norris, 'What's in a name? Derrida's *Signsponge*', in *Deconstruction and the Interests of Theory* (London: Pinter Publishers, 1988), pp. 227–35.

22. See especially Derrida, 'White mythology: metaphor in the text of philosophy', in *Margins of Philosophy*, op. cit., pp. 207–71; also Paul de Man, 'The epistemology of metaphor', in Sheldon Sacks (ed.), *On Metaphor* (Chicago: University of Chicago Press, 1979), pp. 11–28; Norris, *The Deconstructive Turn: Essays in the Rhetoric of Philosophy* (London: Methuen, 1983), and *The Contest of Faculties: Philosophy and Theory After Deconstruction* (London: Methuen, 1985).

23. See notes 10, 17 and 22, above.

24. See W. V. Quine, 'Two dogmas of empiricism', in *From a Logical Point of View*, 2nd edn (Cambridge, MA: Harvard University Press, 1961), pp. 20–46.

25. Derrida, *Edmund Husserl's 'The Origin of Geometry': An Introduction*, trans. John P. Leavey (Pittsburgh: Duquesne University Press, 1973); also *'Speech and Phenomena'*, op. cit., and – for some acute commentary on this aspect of his work – Marian Hobson, *Jacques Derrida: Opening Lines* (London: Routledge, 1998).

26. See notes 17 and 19, above.

27. See especially Norris, *Truth Matters: Realism, Anti-realism and Response-dependence* (Edinburgh: Edinburgh University Press, 2002); *Language, Logic and Epistemology: A Modal-realist Approach* (London: Palgrave, 2004); *Philosophy of Language and the Challenge to Scientific Realism* (London: Routledge, 2004).

28. See notes 18 and 25, above.

29. Derrida, *Edmund Husserl's 'The Origin of Geometry': An Introduction*, op. cit.

30. For further discussion, see Norris, 'Saussurean linguistics as model and metaphor: the structuralist "revolution" revisited', in *Fiction, Philosophy and Literary Theory*, op. cit., pp. 77–106; also John Mowitt, *Text: The Genealogy of an Anti-disciplinary Object* (Durham, NC: Duke University Press, 1992).

31. Derrida, *Glas*, trans. John P. Leavey and Richard Rand (Lincoln, NE: University of Nebraska Press, 1986), and *The Post Card: From Socrates to Freud and Beyond*, trans. Alan Bass (Chicago: University of Chicago Press, 1987).

32. See note 20, above; also Derrida, 'Limited Inc a b c', *Glyph*, Vol. 2 (Baltimore: Johns Hopkins University Press, 1977), pp. 75–176.

33. See notes 20 and 32, above.

34. Wittgenstein, *Philosophical Investigations*, op. cit.

35. For some interesting background information and commentary see Ken Larson, '"The classical German Shakespeare" as emblem of Germany as "Geistige Weltmacht": validating national power through cultural prefiguration', online at: http://aurora.wells.edu/~klarson/papers/mla91.htm; and 'Did Shakespeare really write in German? How the Bard became *ein Klassiker*', online at: http://aurora.wells.edu/~klarson/papers/facclub1.htm. See also Terence Hawkes, *Meaning by Shakespeare* (London: Routledge, 1992).

36. Norris, 'Extraordinary language', op. cit.; also 'The limits of *whose* language? Wittgenstein on logic, science and mathematics', in *Language, Logic and Epistemology*, op. cit., pp. 66–110, and 'Kripkenstein's monsters: anti-realism, scepticism, and the rule-following debate', in *On Truth and Meaning: Language, Logic and the Grounds of Belief* (London: Continuum, 2006), pp. 155–202.

37. Derrida, 'Signature event context', op. cit.

38. J. L. Austin, *How to Do Things with Words* (Oxford: Clarendon Press, 1962).

39. See note 19, above.

40. Quine, *From a Logical Point of View*, op. cit., and *Methods of Logic* (New York: Henry Holt, 1950).

41. See notes 18 and 19, above.

42. Johnson, 'Preface to Shakespeare', op. cit.

43. Ibid., pp. 67–8.

44. Ibid., p. 68.

45. Richard Rorty (ed.), *The Linguistic Turn: Recent Essays in Philosophical Method* (Chicago: University of Chicago Press, 1967).

46. See Richard Rorty, 'Philosophy as a kind of writing: an essay on Jacques Derrida', in *Consequences of Pragmatism* (Brighton: Harvester Press, 1982), pp. 89–109, and 'Is Derrida a transcendental philosopher?', in *Essays on Heidegger and Others* (Cambridge: Cambridge University Press, 1991), pp. 119–28; also Christopher Norris, 'Philosophy as *not* just a "kind of writing": Derrida and the claim of reason', in Reed Way Dasenbrock (ed.), *Re-Drawing the Lines* (Minneapolis: University of Minnesota Press, 1989), pp. 189–203, and Rorty, 'Two versions of "logocentrism": a reply to Norris', in ibid., pp. 204–16.

47. See notes 16, 17 and 22, above.

48. See especially Patricia Parker and Geoffrey Hartman (eds), *Shakespeare and the Question of Theory* (London: Methuen, 1985); also Hartman, *Criticism in the Wilderness: The Study of Literature Today* (New

Haven, CT: Yale University Press, 1980), and *Saving the Text: Literature, Derrida, Philosophy* (Baltimore: Johns Hopkins University Press, 1981).

49. Johnson, 'Preface to Shakespeare', op. cit., p. 93.
50. See, for instance, Simon Glendinning (ed.), *Arguing with Derrida* (Oxford: Blackwell, 2001); also Dasenbrock (ed.), *Redrawing the Lines*, op. cit.; Newton Garver and Seung-Chong Lee, *Derrida and Wittgenstein* (Philadelphia: Temple University Press, 1994); Norris and Roden (eds), *Jacques Derrida*, op. cit.; Wheeler, *Deconstruction as Analytic Philosophy*, op. cit.
51. Johnson, 'Preface to Shakespeare', op. cit., p. 96.
52. Ibid., p. 68.
53. Ibid., p. 61.
54. Paul de Man, 'The resistance to theory', in *The Resistance to Theory* (Manchester: Manchester University Press, 1986), pp. 3–20, at p. 17.
55. Derrida, *Of Grammatology*, op. cit., p. 158.
56. For an earlier (and more extreme) variety of anti-intentionalist doctrine, see Cleanth Brooks, *The Well Wrought Urn: Studies in the Structure of Poetry* (New York: Harcourt Brace, 1947), and W. K. Wimsatt, *The Verbal Icon: Studies in the Meaning of Poetry* (Lexington: University of Kentucky Press, 1954).
57. See notes 11, 15 and 36, above.
58. See, for instance, Cora Diamond, *The Realistic Spirit: Wittgenstein, Philosophy and the Mind* (Cambridge, MA: MIT Press, 1995).
59. Henry Staten, *Wittgenstein and Derrida* (Lincoln, NE: University of Nebraska Press, 1984); also O. K. Bouwsma, *Without Proof or Evidence: Essays of O. K. Bouwsma* (Lincoln, NE: University of Nebraska Press, 1984); Garver and Lee, *Derrida and Wittgenstein*, op. cit.
60. See, for instance, Norris, 'The insistence of the letter: textuality and metaphor in Wittgenstein's later writing', in *The Deconstructive Turn*, op. cit., pp. 34–58.
61. Derrida, *Of Grammatology*, op. cit., p. 158.
62. Ibid.
63. Ibid.
64. Ludwig Wittgenstein, *Philosophical Investigations*, op. cit., Sections 201–292 *passim*; also Saul Kripke, *Wittgenstein on Rules and Private Language* (Oxford: Blackwell, 1982); Alexander Miller and Crispin Wright (eds), *Rule-Following and Meaning* (Aldershot: Acumen, 2002); Norris, 'Kripkenstein's monsters', op. cit., pp. 155–202.
65. Norris, 'Kripkenstein's monsters', op. cit.
66. See notes 46 and 48, above.
67. See notes 17, 19 and 46, above; also Rodolphe Gasché. *The Tain of the Mirror: Derrida and the Philosophy of Reflection* (Cambridge, MA: Harvard University Press, 1986).

68. See note 48, above; also G. Douglas Atkins, *Geoffrey Hartman: Criticism as Answerable Style* (London: Routledge, 1990).

69. See notes 16 and 46, above.

70. Note 45, above.

71. William Empson, *Seven Types of Ambiguity*, 2nd edn (London: Chatto & Windus, 1953).

72. See especially F. R. Leavis, *The Living Principle: 'English' as a Discipline of Thought* (London: Chatto & Windus, 1975), and *Valuation in Criticism and Other Essays*, ed. G. Singh (Cambridge: Cambridge University Press, 1986).

73. Leavis, 'Literary criticism and philosophy: a reply', in *The Importance of Scrutiny*, ed. Eric Bentley (New York: New York University Press, 1964), pp. 30–40.

74. T. S. Eliot, 'Tradition and the individual talent', in *Selected Essays* (London: Faber, 1964), pp. 3–11.

75. On this topic, see various contributions to Norris and Richard Machin (eds), *Post-Structuralist Readings of English Poetry* (Cambridge: Cambridge University Press, 1987).

76. William Empson, *The Structure of Complex Words*, 2nd edn (London: Chatto & Windus, 1961).

77. For the 'early' Davidson position, see especially 'On the very idea of a conceptual scheme', in *Inquiries into Truth and Interpretation* (Oxford: Clarendon Press, 1984), pp. 183–98. For his later 'minimalist-semantic' approach, see Davidson, 'A nice derangement of epitaphs', in R. Grandy and R. Warner (eds), *Philosophical Grounds of Rationality: Intentions, Categories, Ends* (Oxford: Oxford University Press, 1986), pp. 157–74; also Ernest LePore (ed.), *Truth and Interpretation: Essays on the Philosophy of Donald Davidson* (Oxford: Blackwell, 1986).

78. Davidson, 'A nice derangement of epitaphs', op. cit., p. 169.

79. Norris, *Resources of Realism* and *Meaning, Truth and Interpretation*, op. cit.

80. Davidson, 'On the very idea of a conceptual scheme', op. cit.

81. See Norris, *Resources of Realism*, op. cit., for further argument to this effect.

82. See Davidson, 'What metaphors mean', in *Inquiries into Truth and Interpretation*, op. cit., pp. 245–64.

83. See, for instance, W. J. T. Mitchell (ed.), *Against Theory: Literary Theory and the New Pragmatism* (Chicago: University of Chicago Press, 1985); S. Pradhan, 'Minimalist semantics: Davidson and Derrida on meaning, use, and convention', *Diacritics*, 16 (Spring 1986), pp. 66–77; Wheeler, *Deconstruction as Analytic Philosophy*, op. cit.

84. See note 22, above.

Index